A Bio-bibliography of Langston Hughes

LANGSTON HUGHES

Photograph by Louis Draper

A Bio-bibliography of

LANGSTON HUGHES

1902 - 1967

by

DONALD C. DICKINSON

with a Preface by

ARNA BONTEMPS

**Second Edition
Revised**

ARCHON BOOKS

1972

The Shoe String Press, Inc.
995 Sherman Avenue
Hamden, Ct. 06514

ISBN 0–208–01269–9

Library of Congress Catalog Card Number: 70–181877

Printed in the United States of America

To Colleen and our six lovely daughters

Contents

Preface

Even a dependable memory sometimes plays tricks, and often enough I have had to call mine to task. This has never been true, I hasten to add, when the subject was the life and works of Langston Hughes. Even his adolescent poems were unforgettable. His personal history, as one picked it up from fragments in newspapers and magazines, had begun to read like a legend long before he finished college.

I seem to be the member of the Harlem literary group of the twenties elected to hold in trust a certain legacy of recollections, and the first of these is that he was our bellwether in that early dawn. The first poems by Langston that I read appeared in the *Crisis* in the summer of 1924. That magazine had been publishing articles, stories and poems by him for several years, but being away at a college that did not subscribe to such periodicals, immersed in the reading of the "Chief American Poets" and collections of British poetry of the Victorian era, I had missed the earlier Hughes works as well as most of the other American Negroana of the period. Lines like "We have tomorrow/ Bright before us/ Like a flame" and "I am waiting for my mother/ She is Death", as they appeared in those months, struck me with such surprise, seemed so quietly disturbing, they immediately convinced me I had been missing something important, something I needed.

But I was rushing away to New York as I made the discovery, and it was not 'till I arrived in Harlem that I was able to go to the Public Library and look up back issues of the *Crisis* and *Opportunity* and other periodicals hospitable to the work of Langston Hughes and his contemporaries of that period. I did not have to be told, as I browsed, that I had been short-changed in a significant area of my basic education. So many lights began flashing all around me, I could not fail to get the message. I eagerly set about trying to correct the omissions and perhaps repair some of the damage to dreams and aspirations that should have normally flourished in school and college days.

That winter I met Langston himself. He returned to Harlem from seafaring and sojourning, and the word was passed up and down the Avenues that the Poet was back. He had been seen. I heard it first from one of the librarians in the 135th Street Branch of the New York Public Library. Then I heard it in a rather strange way in the parsonage of the Salem Methodist Church on Seventh Avenue. I had gone there by appointment to meet another young poet whose foster father was the church minister, and it was the Rev. Cullen who opened the door to me. Without even pausing to speak to me, he spun around and shouted up the steps toward the second floor, "Countee! Countee! Come here! Langston Hughes is back."

In a sense I considered this my official welcome, under mistaken identity, into the Harlem literati. I promptly explained the situation and introduced myself, but these two friends of Langston remained cordial (albeit let down) and assured me that they could not tell one of us from the other by sight, so much did we look alike in those years. A night or two later Countee and I were both included in a small group invited to the apartment shared by Regina Anderson Andrews, the librarian, and Ethel Ray Nance, an editorial secretary in the office of either the *Crisis* or *Opportunity*, welcoming the real Langston Hughes home and listening to his reading of some of the poems he had written aboard the ships on which he worked and more recently in the kitchen of the Grand Duke night club in Paris.

One of the poems he read that night won the first *Opportunity* poetry prize soon thereafter and then became the title poem for *The Weary Blues*, his first book. A few weeks later Langston sent me from Washington, D.C., manuscript copies of these and other unpublished poems in which I had expressed interest. So it becomes an enormous satisfaction to one who has watched his bibliography grow over an arch of more than forty years to see it now compiled in manuscript form and awaiting publication.

It would be much too casual to merely observe that Hughes has been prolific. He has been a minstrel and a troubadour in the classic sense. He has had no other vocation, and he has lived by his writing since that winter evening we met in Harlem late in 1924 or early in 1925. Naturally, the lean years and the full years considered, this has required versatility. Hughes has worked competently in all the literary forms. As a man of letters he has done what needed to be done: poems, song lyrics, librettos; short stories, novels, sketches, articles; plays, pageants, revues; autobiographies, books for children, and adult nonfiction. But nothing he has written has been out of tune with his first poems. Almost any biographical piece about him could appropriately be called "The Negro Who Spoke of Rivers." And his repeated use of the word *soul* in the refrain of his first widely published poem represents the first extension of this word into its current connotations, indicating a kind of "Negro" quality in certain areas of American self-expression and culture.

Arna Bontemps

May 1967

Acknowledgments

The writer became interested in Langston Hughes in 1956 while working on the staff of the University of Kansas library. At that time Kansas started to collect all of Hughes's published works. As a boy, Hughes had lived in Lawrence, Kansas, and enjoyed the University activities "particularly the museum, and the morgue," as he recalled in a letter in 1957, "where I used to watch the students dissecting—to my juvenile interest and amazement." Hughes's active support of the collection prompted the writer to begin a bibliography. The work of compiling the bibliography was furthered in 1961 by a grant from the Association of College and Research Libraries which allowed the writer to spend several weeks in Hughes's home, in the Schomburg Collection in New York, and later in the James Weldon Johnson Collection at Yale University. Subsequently, an examination of Hughes's writing was approved by the University of Michigan Department of Library Science as a dissertation topic. The present work is an expansion of that thesis.

I am indebted to the Association of College and Research Libraries for the financial assistance which contributed to the preparation of the bibliographic portion of this study and to Dr. Raymond Kilgour and the other members of the committee for advice and guidance. Thanks are also due to Mr. William Koshland of Alfred A. Knopf, Inc., for permission to quote freely from correspondence sent to Hughes by members of that firm. My special thanks are reserved for Langston Hughes who has contributed not only many elusive factual details but also a genial and constant encouragement which has made this study a pleasant undertaking.

part one

BIOGRAPHY

Introduction

Editors, anthologists, and the general public find Langston Hughes one of the most eloquent spokesmen for the American Negro. His published works through 1965 include nine volumes of poetry, eight of short stories and sketches, two novels, seven children's books, a quantity of plays, essays, translations, and a two-volume autobiography. Hughes's books have been published by large commercial houses, educational institutions, and private presses, while his poems and stories have appeared separately in magazines that range in point of view from *The Woman's Home Companion* to *The New Masses*. Foreign publishers have also demonstrated a lively interest in his work by providing translations into a dozen languages. This record, impressive enough on the surface, assumes a special importance because Hughes often writes on controversial, racial themes. His own career illustrates the problems faced by the Negro artist who wishes to portray his people with realism.

In order to assess Hughes's accomplishments as a writer it is important to consider the changing role of the Negro in American life. Early in the twentieth century Negroes in the North, aided by white friends, began a determined drive toward social and economic equality. This was a goal far beyond anything advocated in the past. Booker T. Washington, for example, had only wanted to extend the old plantation system in order to make the Negro a docile and satisfactory working man. The movement for an enlarged concept of equality prompted a group of young writers to reject the old patterns and create a new Negro literature. Hughes's career is closely connected with this group's assertion of literary independence which was a part of a more general racial awakening sometimes referred to as the Harlem Renaissance or the New Negro Movement. In the past Negro writers had found it impossible to attract an audience unless they used stereotyped characters or ignored race completely. Paul Lawrence Dunbar, in novels and verse, chose the first course, William Braithwaite, in his anthologies and critical writing, the second. Hughes and his friends decided to write the story of the Negro without pretense or apology. Their stories, poems, and essays mark a turn from the old self-consciousness and self-denial to a proud new realism. Because of the quality of their work, and the general interest in all facets of Negro life in the 1920's, editors eagerly accepted the manuscripts of the new realists.

Like most members of the New Negro group Hughes began to publish in *The Crisis* and *Opportunity*, the journals of the National Association for the Advancement of Colored People, and the National Urban League. From this base he branched out to place his writing with magazines and book companies that catered to the white reading public. Far from forsaking Negro journals, however, Hughes continued to publish in *The Crisis, Ebony, The Negro Digest,* and *Phylon.* One of his greatest assets is an ability to please large elements of both the white and Negro audience.

The chronological approach to Hughes's work shows many fluctuations in style and attitude. Between 1920 and 1930 he produced a large quantity of poetry, formed some of his important friendships, and set the direction for much of his future writing. This is perhaps the most important period in Hughes's writing career. In the 1930's he virtually abandoned poetry to concentrate on fiction and drama. More recently, while he has produced both poetry and prose, there is an emphasis on editorial work, writing for the theatre, and translation. He has experimented with many forms but his central purpose has remained constant—to interpret the living American Negro. Hughes's writing is, in a sense, a social document reflecting the various nuances of race relationships since 1920. Happily, it is a document written with both humor and artistry.

Evaluation of Hughes's work is hampered by lack of critical commentary in standard sources on recent American literature.[1] To locate commentary of any kind one must go to studies of Negro achievement written by Negro authors.[2] Aside from a dissertation

[1] No discussion of Hughes can be found in such basic works as: Robert Spiller, *et al., The Literary History of the United States* (New York: Macmillan, 1948); Arthur Quinn, *The Literature of the American People* (New York: Appleton, Century Crofts, 1951); Alfred Kazin, *On Native Grounds* (New York: Reynal and Hitchcock, 1942).

[2] Hughes is mentioned in such works as: Margaret Butcher, *The Negro in American Culture* (New York: Alfred A. Knopf, 1956); Richard Bardolph, *The Negro Vanguard* (New York: Random House, 1959); Saunders Redding, *To Make a Poet Black* (Chapel Hill: University of North Carolina Press, 1939).

on the short stories and several brief articles in *Phylon*[3] no scholarly studies are available in English.[4] In 1932 Ludwig Lewisohn commented that he must leave the evaluation of "the piercing Negro folk-notes of Langston Hughes" to the "definition of the future."[5] Apparently, critics are not yet ready to make that definition.

While critics have ignored Hughes, anthologists and editors have always favored his writing. Beginning in the 1920's his work has appeared in many important selections of prose and poetry. Hughes's writing has received popular acceptance if not extensive critical acclaim.

This study includes the entire compass of Hughes's published work through 1965. Although this broad scope prohibits close attention to details of the author's poetry, fiction, or drama, it does provide a better understanding of his total literary contribution. The biographical and bibliographical portions of this study are intended to complement one another in the hope that taken together they may provide material for further research on the writing of Langston Hughes.

[3] James Emanuel, "The Short Stories of Langston Hughes," Unpublished Ph.D. dissertation. Columbia University, 1962; Arthur Davis, "The Harlem of Langston Hughes's Poetry," *Phylon*, XIII (Winter, 1952); Arthur Davis, "Jessie B. Semple: Negro American," *Phylon*, XV (Spring, 1954); Arthur Davis, "The Tragic Mulatto Theme in Six Works of Langston Hughes," *Phylon*, XVI (Winter, 1955).

[4] Two studies of Hughes's poetry are available in French—Jean Wagner, *Les Poètes Nègres des Etats-Unis* (Paris: Librairie Istra, 1963); Raymond Quinot, *Langston Hughes* (Bruxelles: Editions CELF, 1964).

[5] Ludwig Lewisohn, *Expression in America* (New York: Harper, 1932), p. 583.

Chronology of Important Events

in the Life of Langston Hughes*

1902   James Langston Hughes born February 1, in Joplin, Missouri, to Carrie Langston Hughes and James Nathaniel Hughes.

1902–1914   Lived in Mexico, Missouri, and Kansas for short periods with his mother and father, then, after they separated, with his grandmother in Lawrence, Kansas.

1914   Moved from Lawrence to join his mother and step-father in Lincoln, Illinois.

1916   Elected class poet for grammar school graduation at Lincoln. Moved from Lincoln to Cleveland, Ohio.

1920   Chosen editor of Central High School Yearbook, Cleveland. Graduated from Central High School. Spent the year after graduation in Mexico with his father.

1921   Published juvenile poetry in *The Brownie's Book*. "A Negro Speaks of Rivers" published in *The Crisis*. Entered Columbia University in New York.

1922   Left Columbia to take assorted jobs in New York area.

1923   Employed as cook's helper on tramp steamer to Africa and Europe.

1924   Employed as cook in Paris night club. Returned from Europe to live with his mother in Washington, D.C.

1925   Won first prize for poetry in *Opportunity* contest. Won second prize for essay and third prize for poetry in *The Crisis* contest. Met Carl Van Vechten who introduced his poetry to Alfred Knopf.

1926   Entered Lincoln University in Pennsylvania. *Weary Blues* published. *Fire* published. Won first prize in Witter Bynner Undergraduate Poetry Contest.

*Including publication dates for some of his best known books.

6

1927	*Fine Clothes to the Jew* published.
1929	Graduated from Lincoln University.
1930	*Not Without Laughter* published. Won Harmon award for literature. Traveled to Haiti.
1931	Conducted poetry reading tour in the South and West.
1932	Traveled to Russia.
1933	Returned to California from Russia by way of Japan. Spent year writing at Carmel by the Sea.
1934	*Ways of White Folks* published.
1935	Received Guggenheim Fellowship.
1937	Traveled to Spain as correspondent for *Baltimore Afro-American.*
1940	*The Big Sea* published.
1941	Received Rosenwald Fellowship.
1942	*Shakespeare in Harlem* published.
1943	Granted Hon. Litt. D. from Lincoln University.
1946	Elected to membership in National Institute of Arts and Letters.
1947	*Fields of Wonder* published.
1947–1948	Appointed Visiting Professor of Creative Writing at Atlanta University.
1949–1950	Appointed Poet in Residence at the Laboratory School, University of Chicago.
1950	*Simple Speaks His Mind* published.
1951	*Montage on a Dream Deferred* published.
1952	*Laughing to Keep From Crying* published. *First Book of Negroes* published.
1953	Received Ainsfeld-Wolfe Award (Best book of year on race relations). *Simple Takes a Wife* published.
1954	*Famous American Negroes* published.
1955	*Sweet Flypaper of Life* published.
1956	*I Wonder As I Wander* published.
1958	*Tambourines to Glory* published.

1959   *Selected Poems* published.

1960   Received Spingarn Medal.
          African Treasury published.

1961   *Ask Your Mama* published.

1962   *Fight for Freedom* published.

1963   *Five Plays* published.

1964   Granted Hon. Litt. D. from Western Reserve.

1965   *Simple's Uncle Sam* published.

1967   *Black Magic: A Pictorial History of the Negro in American
          Entertainment* published.

1967   *May 22, Langston Hughes died.*

1969   *Black Magic* published.
          Don't You Turn Back published.

1970   *The Poetry of the Negro 1746–1970* published.

chapter one

Early Years 1902—1925

> I've been a singer
> All the way from Africa to Georgia
> I carried my sorrow songs.
> I made ragtime.
>   "Negro."

Langston Hughes wrote his first poem at the age of thirteen when the pupils in the Lincoln, Illinois, grammar school elected him class poet. Because he was a Negro the other children thought he would have the natural rhythm to write a graduation poem. Their choice was a good one. Hughes produced sixteen verses in praise of the teachers and class of Lincoln, and when he stood up and read the poem on graduation night, he says, "everybody applauded loudly. That was the way I began to write poetry."[1]

Hughes spent a lonely boyhood after his mother and father separated, living his first twelve years with grandparents and friends of the family in Lawrence, Kansas. For one short period he stayed with his mother in Topeka, and it was there that he discovered books. The Topeka Public Library was a pleasant oasis in which he could forget his troubles:

> The silence inside the library, the big chairs, and long tables, and the fact that the library was always there and didn't seem to have a mortgage on it, or any sort of insecurity about it— all of that made me love it. And right then, even before I was six, books began to happen to me, so that after a while, there came a time when I believed in books more than in people— which, of course, was wrong.[2]

It was also in Topeka that Hughes made his first discoveries about race. As the only Negro attending a white school he was occasionally exposed to beatings from the other students and insults

[1]Langston Hughes, *The Big Sea* (New York: Alfred A. Knopf, 1940), p. 24.
[2]*Ibid.*, p. 26.

9

from one of the teachers. Most of the teachers were pleasant, however, and some of the children always took his part in the fights.
These early experiences, Hughes says, taught him to trust in the
goodness of most people. This faith in humanity is reflected in
Hughes's writing, and it is particularly evident in his treatment of
Negro-white relationships. It seems certain, he says in an early poem
entitled "I Too," that Americans will eventually accept the Negro
not only for his strength but also for his beauty. The poem ends:

> Tomorrow,
> I'll be at the table
> When company comes.
> Nobody'll dare
> Say to me,
> "Eat in the kitchen,"
> Then.
> Besides,
> They'll see how beautiful I am
> And be ashamed—
>
> I, too, am America.[3]

After graduating from the school in Lincoln, Hughes moved
with his mother and step-father to Cleveland, Ohio. The city opened
a new world to the young man raised in the small towns of Kansas
and Illinois. Here he saw southern Negroes for the first time and, in
Central High School, he met the children of newly arrived immi-
grants from Russia, Poland, and Germany. These young people,
many of them Jewish, introduced Hughes to Guy de Maupassant,
Friedrich Nietzsche, *The Liberator*, and *The Socialist Call*. He read
de Maupassant in French and recalled later "I think it was de
Maupassant who made me really want to be a writer and write
stories about Negroes, so true that people in far-away lands would
read them—even after I was dead."[4]

In school he enjoyed the poems his teachers read from the work
of Carl Sandburg, Vachel Lindsay, and Edgar Lee Masters. When
he first tried to write poetry it was in the free verse style of Sandburg or in a dialect like Paul Lawrence Dunbar's. In these early

[3]Langston Hughes, *Selected Poems of Langston Hughes* (New York: Alfred A.
Knopf, 1959), p. 275.
[4]Hughes, *The Big Sea*, p. 34.

literary efforts Hughes shows the strength that was to mark his
more mature verse. The poems deal with subjects close at hand, the
language is direct, and the images are colorful and well conceived.
In a high school poem influenced by Sandburg he wrote about the
grinding out of steel and the grinding out of men's lives:

> The mills
> That grind and grind,
> That grind out steel
> And grind away the lives
> Of men—
> In the sunset their stacks
> Are great black silhouettes
> Against the sky.
> In the dawn
> They belch red fire.
> The mills—
> Grinding new steel,
> Old men.[5]

In another poem he paid flowery tribute to Sandburg, whom he
called his guiding star:

> Carl Sandburg's poems
> Fall on the white pages of his books
> Like blood-clots of song
> From the wounds of humanity.
> I know a lover of life sings
> When Carl Sandburg sings.
> I know a lover of all the living
> Sings then.[6]

The Central High School literary magazine, *The Belfry Owl,*
printed some of Hughes's poems; others were sent to magazines in
New York. Printed rejection slips came back with monotonous
regularity. Hughes only remembers one such notice with any pleasure
and that one because it carried a handwritten word of encouragement from Floyd Dell, editor of *The Liberator.*

The summers following his junior and senior years in Central
High School Hughes spent with his father in Mexico. The experience
was trying for both father and son. A domineering man, the elder

[5]*Ibid.*, p. 29.
[6]*Ibid.*

Hughes's favorite expression to young Langston was, "Hurry up!" Hughes hurried when his father was watching but secluded himself with reading and writing whenever he could.

The Brownie's Book, a magazine sponsored by the National Association for the Advancement of Colored People (NAACP), gave Hughes his first publishing opportunity.[7] Early in 1921 two poems, "Winter Sweetness" and "Fairies," and a prose description of Mexican games appeared in the juvenile. Hughes's first published poems in *The Brownie's Book* are brief, rhymed compositions of little substance. "Winter Sweetness," describes a candy house:

> The little house is sugar,
> Its roof with snow is piled,
> And from its tiny window,
> Peeps a maple-sugar child.[8]

The poems published in *The Brownie's Book* reflect Hughes's youthful search for a proper medium and a shrewd assessment of the magazine's editorial standards. He was soon to abandon this fragile lyricism for the more forthright, free verse patterns of Sandburg and Lindsay.

Subsequent issues of *The Brownie's Book* carried five more poems, three stories, and a one-act play. The poems describe the beauties of nature while the stories deal with various aspects of the Mexican countryside. Only one story, "Those Who Have No Turkey," departs from the Mexican scene to develop what came to be one of Hughes's favorite themes, the tragedy of poverty in a land of plenty. The story describes how a country girl innocently invites a poor boy and his family to share Thanksgiving dinner with her rich, city relatives. The poor folks get a meal but very little hospitality from the astonished city people. Only the little girl thinks it unjust that there should be those who have no turkey. In this story, and in later poems dealing with the same theme, any identification of the characters as black and white is incidental to the more general concern with justice. Although Hughes is chiefly known for his writing on racial themes, he is capable of producing memorable characterization quite apart from race.

[7]*The Brownie's Book* was published monthly from January 1920 to December 1921.

[8]Langston Hughes, *The Brownie's Book*, II (January, 1921), p. 27.

The financial collapse of *The Brownie's Book* in December, 1921, had little effect on Hughes's career. Six months after his first poem appeared in the juvenile organ of NAACP, he placed "The Negro Speaks of Rivers" in its official journal, *The Crisis*. This was accomplished with the encouragement of Jessie Fauset, literary editor for both magazines. During the next four years Hughes's poems appeared often and exclusively in *The Crisis*.

The Crisis was a publishing phenomenon. Nine years after its origin, in 1910, copies were being distributed monthly to 100,000 readers. While some of this interest can be attributed to the increase in Negro literacy, the major factor behind the success of *The Crisis* was the determination and editorial leadership of W. E. B. Du Bois. In deference to his scholarship and writing ability he has properly been called, "The Elder Statesman of The Race."[9]

When NAACP was founded in 1909 it was apparent to Du Bois, the Director of Publicity and Research, that some kind of journal was needed to further the cause of the Negro. In 1915, looking back on the founding of *The Crisis*, he commented:

> When the Director entered his office, September 1, 1910, he was faced with a baffling difficulty. . . . He sought publicity for a cause which was markedly unpopular with the white periodical press. He faced a colored press which did not know or understand the objects or ideas of the Association and which could not afford to give it much publicity. What should be done? The Director of Publicity determined it must have an organ.[10]

In the first issue Du Bois said the object of the publication would be "to set forth the facts and arguments which show the danger of race prejudice, particularly as manifested today toward the colored people."[11] He further described the threefold policy the magazine would follow. It would: (1) record in newspaper style movements related to the Negro in America; (2) review literature and opinion; (3) publish short articles. By 1915 Du Bois felt that the magazine had been successful in reporting news and opinion but that "its space, however, for two great departments of serious essays and literature

[9] Edwin Embree, *13 Against the Odds* (New York: Viking, 1944), p. 153.
[10] W. E. B. Du Bois, "The Crisis and the NAACP," *The Crisis*, XI (November, 1915), p. 26.
[11] W. E. B. Du Bois, "The Crisis," *The Crisis*, I (November, 1910), p. 10.

has been hitherto straitly, almost dishearteningly, curtailed."[12] Ten years later he reemphasized the importance of the literary arts by praising a group of rising young writers, Jean Toomer, Claude McKay, Countee Cullen, and Langston Hughes.[13]

Hughes's first poems to appear in *The Crisis* were completely different from those he had published in *The Brownie's Book*. He discarded the delicately phrased nature lyrics and turned to free verse statements on the joys and sorrows of the Negro. He eloquently expressed a deep admiration for the race in one of his best early poems, "The Negro Speaks of Rivers."

> I've known rivers:
> I've known rivers ancient as the world and older
>   than the flow of human blood in human veins.
> My soul has grown deep like the rivers.
> I bathed in the Euphrates when dawns were young.
> I built my hut near the Congo, and it lulled me to sleep.
> I looked upon the Nile and raised the pyramids above it.
> I heard the singing of the Mississippi when Abe
>   Lincoln went down to New Orleans, and I've seen its
>   muddy bosom turn all golden in the sunset.
>
> I've known rivers:
> Ancient, dusky rivers.
>
> My soul has grown deep like the rivers.[14]

This poem is an epic tribute to the Negro race, rich in expression and moving in its message. As Jean Wagner has commented, this poem "proclamait l'existence d'une unité mystique entre les Nègres de tous les pays et de tous les temps."[15] Here again Sandburg's influence is strongly felt although Hughes's poem has a beauty and distinction all its own.[16] In "The Negro Speaks of Rivers" Hughes emphasized the dignity and sensitivity of the Negro, a theme he was to use throughout his career.

After the appearance of "The Negro Speaks of Rivers", *The*

[12]W. E. B. Du Bois, "The Future," *The Crisis*, XI (November, 1915), p. 28.

[13]W. E. B. Du Bois, "The Younger Literary Movement," *The Crisis*, XXVII (February, 1924), pp. 161–163.

[14]Hughes, *Selected Poems*, p. 4.

[15]Jean Wagner, *Poètes Nègres des Etats-Unis* (Paris: Istra, 1963), p. 432.

[16]An examination of Sandburg's "Old Timers" shows the closeness with which Hughes followed the style of the older poet.

Crisis published in succeeding months a stream of provocative and vital poems including "Negro," "Mother to Son," "The South," "Beggar Boy," and "My People." In these poems, still favored by anthologists, Hughes tells us how the Negro feels and what he wants. In "Negro," for example, Hughes voices joy in his blackness and then describes four roles played by the Negro throughout history:

> I am a Negro:
>   Black as the night is black,
>   Black like the depths of my Africa.
>
> I've been a slave:
>   Caesar told me to keep his door-steps clean.
>   I brushed the boots of Washington.
>
> I've been a worker:
>   Under my hand the pyramids arose.
>   I made mortar for the Woolworth Building.
>
> I've been a singer:
>   All the way from Africa to Georgia
>   I carried my sorrow songs.
>   I made ragtime.
>
> I've been a victim:
>   The Belgians cut off my hands in the Congo.
>   They lynch me still in Mississippi.
>
> I am a Negro:
>   Black as the night is black,
>   Black like the depths of my Africa.[17]

In this poem and in "The Negro Speaks of Rivers" the "I" of the speaker refers not only to Hughes but to the whole Negro race. It is the same "I" Hughes admired in Walt Whitman's poems and transferred to his own Negro verse. Hughes has written that, "Whitman is the greatest of American poets. . . . One of the greatest 'I' poets of all time."[18] Hughes's poems, like those of Whitman, stress the worth of the individual.

A theme of many of Hughes's early poems is pride: pride in

[17]Hughes, *Selected Poems*, p. 8.

[18]Langston Hughes, "Ceaseless Rings of Walt Whitman," Introduction to *I Hear the People Singing, Selected Poems of Walt Whitman* (New York: International Publishers, 1946), p. 7.

color, pride in an African heritage, and pride, as he puts it, in "My
People."

> The night is beautiful,
> So the faces of my people.
>
> The stars are beautiful,
> So the eyes of my people.
>
> Beautiful also, is the sun.
> Beautiful, also, are the souls of my people.[19]

A more personal form of this pride is illustrated in the moving
"Mother to Son."

> Well, son, I'll tell you:
> Life for me ain't been no crystal stair.
> It's had tacks in it,
> And splinters
> And boards torn up,
> And places with no carpet on the floor—
> Bare.
> But all the time
> I'se been a-climbin' on,
> And reachin' landin's,
> And turnin' corners,
> And sometimes goin' in the dark
> Where there ain't been no light—
> So boy, don't you turn back.
> Don't you set down on the steps
> 'Cause you finds it's kinder hard.
> Don't you fall now—
> For I'se still goin' honey,
> I'se still climbin',
> And life for me ain't been no crystal stair.[20].

This poem and "Song for a Negro Wash-Woman" have been justly
praised as "unsurpassed genre pictures of Negro women," who like
most of Hughes's people "never whine, never complain. They are
stoic, ironic, often pessimistic, but never self-deluded."[21]

[19]Hughes, *Selected Poems*, p. 13.
[20]*Ibid*, p. 187.
[21]Margaret Butcher, *The Negro in American Culture* (New York: Alfred A.
Knopf, 1956), p. 132.

Of all the poems published at this time "The South" is the
most outspoken. The opening lines read:

> The lazy, laughing South
> With blood on its mouth.
> The sunny-faced South,
>   Beast strong,
>   Idiot-brained.[22]

It was the South that turned the Negro towards the North. The poem
concludes:

> So now I seek the North—
> The cold-faced North,
> For she, they say,
> Is a kinder mistress,
> And in her house my children
> May escape the spell of the South.[23]

In this poem Hughes demonstrates a form of protest which he
employed frequently in the next few years. Poems like "Song for a
Dark Girl," "Bound No'th Blues," "Daybreak in Alabama," and
"Mulatto" all cry out against the southern system of exploitation
and abuse.

In the fall of 1922 Hughes enrolled at Columbia University in
New York, not so much for the scholastic program as for the opportunity to see Harlem. It is hardly surprising, with this goal, that
college seemed a waste of time. Hughes made few friends at Columbia, he was unsuccessful as a reporter for the paper, and eventually
he failed most of his classes. The city, on the other hand, offered
many exciting diversions to the impressionable young man from the
Middle West. Hughes describes New York with great enthusiasm:

> I went to shows, read books, attended lectures at the Rand
> School under Ludwig Lewisohn and Heywood Broun, missed an
> important exam in the spring to go to Bert Williams's funeral,
> sat up in the gallery night after night at Shuffle Along. . . ."[24]

During the school year Hughes met various members of the
editorial staff of *The Crisis.* On one occasion he was invited to lunch
with Jessie Fauset:

[22]Hughes, *Selected Poems*, p. 173.
[23]*Ibid.*
[24]Hughes, *The Big Sea*, p. 85.

I was thrilled when she told me that readers of *The Crisis* had written in to say they liked my poems. I was interested, too, to hear that she was also writing poems and planning a novel.[25]

When the school year ended, and no more money was available from his father, Hughes started to work at odd jobs around New York. He delivered flowers, worked on a truck-farm, and finally became a sailor. The work was hard on shipboard but often there was time to play and sights to see in romantic African ports like Dakar and Lagos. Following the African trip Hughes worked as a mess-boy on a European line, but after several rough crossings he gave up the seafaring life to become a cook in a Paris night club. When the club closed Hughes worked his way back to the United States by way of Italy and Spain.

By the time he was twenty-two Hughes had seen a good share of the Western world, had held a variety of jobs, and had met many lively and unusual people. The poems he published at this time were frequently a reflection on his travels. "Young Sailor," for example, must be taken as an autobiographical comment on shipboard life:

> He carries
> His own strength
> And his own laughter,
> His own today
> And his own hereafter—
> This strong young sailor
> Of the wide seas.
>
> What is money for?
> To spend, he says.
> And wine?
> To drink.
> And women?
> To love.
> And today?
> For joy,
> And the green sea
> For strength,
> And the brown land
> For laughter.
>
> And nothing hereafter.[26]

[25]*Ibid.*, p. 94.
[26]Hughes, *Selected Poems*, p. 73.

This period in Hughes's life was relatively free from care since racial injustice was easy to forget in Europe. Back in the United States, however, the same old problems plagued the Negro. Hughes found Washington, D.C., where he lived with his mother from 1924 to 1925, particularly frustrating. The colored people with any means, according to Hughes, were inclined to petty snobbery, while many whites exercised blatant social and economic discrimination. Hughes worked first in a laundry, then as an assistant to Dr. Carter Woodson at the Association for the Study of Negro Life and History, and later as a bus boy in the Wardman Park Hotel.

The Washington years were unhappy years; as a result, Hughes produced a great deal of poetry. The connection between low spirits and literary production is important in Hughes's career. Commenting on his life in Mexico and New York he says, "I felt bad for the next three or four years, to tell the truth, and those were the years when I wrote most of my poetry. (For my best poems were all written when I felt the worst. When I was happy, I didn't write anything.)"[27] Later, in Washington, the same cause and effect produced the same result. During that time he states, "I didn't like my job, and I didn't know what was going to happen to me, and I was cold and half-hungry, so I wrote a great many poems. I began to write poems in the manner of the Negro blues and the spirituals."[28]

On Seventh Street, in Washington's Negro district, Hughes heard the same kind of rhythms he had enjoyed in Cleveland and in Harlem —the blues and shouts of the ordinary folks, their church songs, and their jazz. Seventh Street people accepted a man for what he was and as Hughes observed, they worked hard all the week but on Saturday they liked to sing the blues, eat watermelon, and shoot some pool. Hughes remembered the music from his boyhood in Kansas; the blues that seemed to laugh and cry in the same breath:

> I'm goin' down to de railroad, baby,
> Lay ma head on de track.
> I'm goin' down to de railroad, babe,
> Lay ma head on de track—
> But if I see de train a-comin',
> I'm gonna jerk it back.[29]

[27]Hughes, *The Big Sea*, p. 54.
[28]*Ibid.*, p. 205.
[29]*Ibid.*, p. 209.

After leaving Columbia Hughes had attempted to write a poem in the style of the blues, but the conclusion wouldn't work out.

> Every so often I would take it out of the suitcase and do something about the ending. I could not achieve an ending I liked, although I worked and worked on it—something that seldom happens to any of my poems.[30]

Perhaps because of his own unhappiness and perhaps because of the infectious rhythms he heard on Seventh Street, Hughes completed "The Weary Blues" in Washington in 1924. The following Spring it won first prize for poetry in *Opportunity's* literary contest.

Hughes has referred to "The Weary Blues" as his lucky poem because it was instrumental in launching his literary career. Written in the cadence of the blues, this poem tells the story of a Harlem musician who plays the piano all night and then goes home to sleep. The first verse is an alliterative invocation in the style of Lindsay's "The Congo."

> Droning a drowsy syncopated tune,
> Rocking back and forth to a mellow croon,
>   I heard a Negro play.
> Down on Lenox Avenue the other night
> By the pale dull pallor of an old gas light
>   He did a lazy sway . . .
>   He did a lazy sway . . .

Then, in the middle of the poem, the musician interjects a traditional verse of the blues:

> "I got the Weary Blues.
> And I can't be satisfied.
> Got the Weary Blues
> And can't be satisfied—
> I ain't happy no mo'
> And I wish that I had died."

Finally, the poem closes on a note of quiet resignation:

> The stars went out and so did the moon.
> The singer stopped playing and went to bed
> While the Weary Blues echoed through his head.
> He slept like a rock or a man that's dead.[31]

[30]*Ibid.*, p. 92.
[31]Hughes, *Selected Poems*, pp. 33–34.

"The Weary Blues" is melodious in its rhythms and completely delightful in its picture of the tired cabaret musician. In blues, such as
this, Hughes found a perfect medium for his verse. They spoke the
language of the common man with precisely the right mixture of
happiness and grief. According to C. S. Johnson, "In them [the
blues] is a curious story of disillusionment without a saving philosophy and yet without defeat. . . . Stark, full human passions crowd
themselves into an uncomplex expression, so simple in their power
that they startle."[32] The form of the blues, as Sterling Brown points
out, is fairly strict: "a leading line, repeated (sometimes with slight
variations), and generally a rhyming third line. Sometimes the first
line does not rhyme. The form is simple, but well adapted to express
the laments of folk Negroes over hard luck, 'careless' or unrequitted
love, broken family life, or general dissatisfaction with a cold and
trouble-filled world."[33]

   In "The Weary Blues," and other poems of this period, Hughes
shows a strength in the use of the language that makes the work of
earlier Negro writers like Paul Lawrence Dunbar seem sentimental
and trivial. Although Hughes says Dunbar influenced his poetry the
language of "The Weary Blues" is more like that of James Weldon
Johnson's *God's Trombones*. Dialect is used sparingly in complete
agreement with Johnson's view "that there are phases of Negro life
in the United States which cannot be treated in the dialect either
adequately or artistically."[34] Nowhere in Hughes's work can one find
artificial mouthings like those in Dunbar's "When De' Co'n Pone's
Hot." Hughes was one of the first Negro writers to answer Johnson's
call for a "form that will express the racial spirit by symbols from
within rather than by symbols from without, such as the mere muti-
lation of English spelling and pronunciation."[35] As Johnson points
out in the Preface to his anthology:

   Several of the poets of the younger group, notably Langston

[32]Charles S. Johnson, "Jazz, Poetry and Blues," *The Carolina Magazine*, (May,
1928), p. 17.
[33]Sterling Brown (ed.), *The Negro Caravan* (New York: Dryden Press, 1941),
pp. 426–427.
[34]James Weldon Johnson (ed.), *The Book of American Negro Poetry* (2nd.
ed.; New York: Harcourt Brace, 1931), p. 41.
[35]*Ibid.*, p. 41.

Hughes and Sterling Brown, do use a dialect; but it is not the dialect of the comic minstrel tradition or of the sentimental plantation tradition; it is the common, racy, living, authentic speech of the Negro in certain phases of real life.[36]

Winning *Opportunity's* poetry prize with "The Weary Blues" taught Hughes that his richest sources lay in the folk music of the Negro, and his most effective technique depended on the realistic portrayal of the common man. This discovery of source and technique was vital to Hughes's development. In effect it led him to become one of the leading literary spokesmen for the American Negro.

While *The Crisis* deserves the credit for publishing the bulk of Hughes's early poetry, it was his affiliation with *Opportunity* that brought him to national attention. Twelve years after the formation of the National Urban League, in 1909, the directors sponsored the first issue of the journal *Opportunity*, with Charles S. Johnson as editor. As the author of several important sociological studies on the Negro in the North, and as the editor of a League bulletin, Johnson seemed the perfect man to direct the new journal. Besides encouraging authors of sociological articles Johnson made a special effort to provide space for literary pieces of all kinds. During the first year of publication, along with articles on housing, job opportunities, and labor unions, *Opportunity* printed poetry by Countee Cullen, Angelina Grimke, and Georgia Johnson. In 1924, Johnson prompted Mrs. Henry Leach, a wealthy supporter of the Urban League, to provide $500 for a series of awards in five areas: short story, drama, essay, poetry, and personal experience. The competition was given special significance when famous literary figures agreed to act as judges. In the poetry division, Clement Wood, Witter Bynner, James Weldon Johnson, and John Farrar selected Hughes's "Weary Blues" as first prize winner, also listing his "America" as co-winner of third prize, and placing "Jester" and "Song for a Dark Virgin" in the honorable mention category. At the award banquet in New York James Weldon Johnson read "The Weary Blues" to the audience and presented Hughes with the first prize of forty dollars.

Hughes's success in the *Opportunity* contest led directly to a publishing contract. After the award banquet, author and critic Carl

[36]*Ibid.*, p. 4.

Van Vechten offered congratulations and asked to see more of Hughes's poems. The events that followed are carefully recorded in Hughes's autobiography, *The Big Sea*. He says, "When I got back to Washington, I promptly sent Mr. Van Vechten my poems. He wrote saying that he liked them, and asked my permission to submit my manuscript to his publishers, Alfred A. Knopf."[37] It was not long after this that Hughes received a warm letter from Blanche Knopf accepting the poems for publication. In this initial letter to Hughes Mrs. Knopf wrote:

> Mr. Van Vechten has sent us your manuscript and we like it very much. It is very delightful verse and I am glad to tell you that we want to publish it. I am enclosing a contract that I should like you to sign and return so that I may send you a copy for your own files.[38]

It was also at Van Vechten's suggestion that Hughes decided to call his first book *The Weary Blues*.[39]

Hughes could hardly have selected a better champion than Van Vechten, patron of Negro arts and friend of influential New Yorkers. Van Vechten had written both music and drama criticism for New York newspapers before Schirmer published his first book, *Music After the Great War*, in 1915. Following this all his books were published by the young firm of Alfred A. Knopf. Van Vechten soon became a close friend of the owners, Blanche and Alfred Knopf, advising them on manuscripts and authors. Alfred Knopf recalls, "we saw him frequently and he was from the beginning actively interested in all our publishing activities, making innumerable editorial suggestions on many of which we acted."[40] In the case of Negro authors Van Vechten was a specialist, for, as Knopf states, "we relied entirely

---

[37]Hughes, *The Big Sea*, p. 216.

[38]Letter from Blanche Knopf to Langston Hughes dated May 18, 1925. Yale University Library.

[39]The copy of *The Weary Blues* in the Rare Book Room of the New York Public Library carries the inscription, "For Carl Van Vechten who made this book possible—said call it "The Weary Blues" and so it was so called,—these poems of Harlem and elsewhere, Sincerely Langston Hughes New York January 31, 1926."

[40]Alfred A. Knopf, "Reminiscences of Hergesheimer, Van Vechten and Mencken," *Yale University Library Gazette*, XXIV (April, 1950), p. 151.

on Van Vechten's judgment in the case of James Weldon Johnson, Nella Larson, Chester Himes, and Langston Hughes."[41]

Besides providing an introduction to the Knopfs, Van Vechten brought Hughes to the attention of Frank Crowninshield of *Vanity Fair*.[42] This sophisticated journal printed several poems as did *The New Republic* and *The Bookman*, "sending checks that were small, but encouraging."[43] With Van Vechten's help Hughes rose from a relatively unknown contributor to Negro journals to become a commercially successful author. In an appreciative analysis of his relationship with Van Vechten, Hughes has stated:

> What Carl Van Vechten did for me was to submit my first book of poems to Alfred A. Knopf, . . . caused me to meet many editors and writers who were friendly and helpful to me, . . . cheered me on in the writing of my first short stories, and otherwise aided in making life for me more profitable and entertaining.[44].

The help provided by Van Vechten in the Spring of 1925 was far more important to the advance of Hughes's career than the widely publicized "discovery" by Vachel Lindsay in December of that year.[45] Although the meeting with Lindsay must have been an exciting ex-

---

[41]*Ibid.*, p. 156.

[42]In a letter to the writer dated October 28, 1962 Mr. Van Vechten states, "I interested Knopf in publishing Langston Hughes, Taylor Gordon, and Nella Imes. They would have published Countee Cullen, but he preferred to go to Harper's. I also persuaded Knopf to publish Chester Himes, The Walls of Jerico, by a Young doctor whose name I can't remember and to republish James Weldon Johnson's The Autobiography of an Ex-Colored Man. I had influence on Harold Ginsberg of the Viking Press. I persuaded Frank Crowninshield of Vanity Fair to publish two pages of poems by Langston Hughes and Countee Cullen and I wrote several articles for Vanity Fair on Colored subjects."

[43]Hughes, *The Big Sea*, p. 217.

[44]*Ibid.*, p. 272.

[45]In *The Big Sea*, pp. 212–214 Hughes describes an incident that occurred in Washington one evening when Vachel Lindsay dined at the Wardman Park Hotel. Hughes placed several poems beside the plate of the famous poet and quickly returned to his duties as a bus boy. Lindsay read the poems that night to his audience in the Little Theatre of the hotel and claimed to have discovered a Negro bus boy poet. The newspapers, attracted by the novelty of the story, gave Hughes wide attention. In reporting this incident Hughes gives the text of a note left by Lindsay which read in part, "Do not let any lionizers stampede you. Hide and write and study and think. I know what factions do.

perience, Hughes was neither unknown nor unpublished when it took place. Van Vechten was the chief architect of Hughes's early success.

In the same month that *Opportunity* offered its literary awards Mrs. Amy Spingarn, wife of the literary critic, Joel Spingarn, announced a similar event in *The Crisis.*

> My husband and I have long had a deep interest and faith in the contribution of the American Negro to American art and literature. It is with the hope of assisting The Crisis that I should like to offer through The Crisis a series of prizes for literary and possibly also artistic contributions. I am enclosing my check for three hundred dollars (300) for this purpose.[46]

Prizes were furnished for poetry, short story, essay, illustration, and drama. Hughes took second prize in the essay category with "Fascination of Cities," and in the poetry division he received third prize for a group of poems including "Cross," "Summer Night," "Minstrel Man," and "To a Negro Jazz Band in a Parisian Cabaret."[47]

In "The Fascination of Cities" Hughes describes his delight in the sounds, smells, and sights of the great urban centers of Europe and America. The rhythm vividly conveys the atmosphere of city life. "Minstrel Man" and "Cross" are the best of the poems. "Minstrel Man" is a refreshing challenge to the overdone image of the laughing, carefree Negro. Do not be fooled, Hughes says:

> Because my mouth
> Is wide with laughter
> And my throat
> Is deep with song,
>
> You do not think
> I suffer after
> I have held my pain
> So long.

Beware of them. I know what flatterers do. Beware of them. I know what lionizers do. Beware of them. Good wishes to you indeed, Nicholas Vachel Lindsay."

[46]Amy Spingarn, "Amy Spingarn Prizes," *The Crisis,* XXX (September, 1924), p. 199.

[47]The essay was entered under the pseudonym Raif Dickerson, the poems under the names Ralph Anson and Jerry Biera.

> Because my mouth
> Is wide with laughter
> You do not hear
> My inner cry.
> Because my feet
> Are gay with dancing
> You do not know
> I die.[48]

Hughes frequently emphasized the presence of tragedy behind the Negroes' smiling mask. "Minstrel Man" is one of his most successful presentations of this theme. The provocative "Cross" deals with the tragic mulatto theme:

> My old Man's a white old man
> And my old mother's black,
> If ever I cursed my white old man
> I take my curses back.
>
> If ever I cursed my black old mother
> And wished she were in hell,
> I'm sorry for that evil wish
> And now I wish her well.

Although the narrator can forgive both his mother and father, his own fate fills him with despair. The poem ends:

> My old man died in a fine big house.
> My ma died in a shack.
> I wonder where I'm gonna die,
> Being neither white nor black?[49]

As Alfred Kreymborg has accurately observed, "Hughes has given a poignant voice to the tragedy of mixed blood, and has done so in the terse lines of sharp lyrics."[50] Kreymborg goes on to suggest that the poem "contains the implications of a full-length novel or play."[51] Hughes himself saw these possibilities and used the theme in his play "Mulatto" and in the short story "Father and Son."[52]

[48]Langston Hughes, *The Crisis*, XXXI (December, 1925), pp. 66–67.

[49]Hughes, *Selected Poems*, p. 158.

[50]Alfred Kreymborg, *Our Singing Strength* (New York: Coward-McCann, 1929), p. 578.

[51]*Ibid.*, p. 578.

[52]Arthur Davis has written a full and excellent discussion of all of these works in his article "The Tragic Mulatto Theme in Six Works of Langston Hughes," *Phylon*, XVI (Winter, 1955), pp. 195–204.

With poems such as "Cross" and "Minstrel Man" Hughes placed himself directly in the stream of the so-called New Poetry Movement of the 1920's. Harriet Monroe, founder of *Poetry*, the principal organ of the movement, seems to describe Hughes's writing as she lays down her definition of the New Poetry:

> The new poetry strives for a concrete and immediate realization of life; it would discard the theory, the abstraction, the remoteness, found in the classics not of the first order. It is less vague, less verbose, less eloquent than most poetry of the Victorian period . . . It has set before itself an ideal of absolute simplicity and sincerity—an ideal which implies an individual, unstereotyped rhythm.[53]

Hughes's description of the common man who also happened to be a Negro was just as appropriate to the New Poetry Movement as Sandburg's refrains about Chicago. It was fortunate for Hughes that his talent should emerge at the precise time when direct, colloquial verse had considerable literary respectability.

While Negro authors like Hughes were achieving their first publishing successes, the race as a whole was coming to national attention for a variety of reasons. During the first two decades of the century two million Negroes migrated to the North in search of better jobs. As long as the Negro remained in the South, it was easy for northerners to forget his problems, but by 1920 it was obvious that the future of the Negro was a national concern. World War I also expanded old racial boundary lines and encouraged Negroes to demand a larger share of the benefits of democracy. As Du Bois stated in *The Crisis*, "Make way for Democracy! We saved it in France and by the Great Jehovah we will save it in the United States or know the reason why."[54]

The new spirit of militancy was furthered by NAACP and the National Urban League. These organizations, with their central offices in New York, became focal points for those interested in greater opportunities for Negroes. From the beginning a large number of literary people joined these organizations and in their writings supported the colored man's fight for freedom. Sherwood Anderson's

[53]Harriet Monroe and Alice Henderson (eds.), *The New Poetry* (2nd. ed.; New York: Macmillan, 1923), pp. xxxv–xxxvi.

[54]W. E. B. Du Bois, "Returning Soldiers," *The Crisis*, XVII (May, 1919), p. 14.

Dark Laughter, Eugene O'Neill's *Emperor Jones*, and DuBose Heyward's *Porgy* all brought attention to the black man's problems and also to his unique gifts. In the theatre, night clubs, and popular magazines, the Negro was featured as never before. Hughes tersely characterizes the 1920's as "Manhattan's black Renaissance."[55]

The publication of the "Harlem" issue of *Survey Graphic* in May, 1925, is a prime example of the growing interest in the Negro. As the editor pointed out in the introduction to the issue:

> The Survey is seeking, . . . to follow the subtle traces of race growth and interaction through the shifting outline of social organization and by the flickering light of individual achievement. . . . If the Survey reads the signs aright, such a dramatic flowering of a new race spirit is taking place close at home— among American Negroes, and the stage of that episode is Harlem.[56]

Under the guidance of Alain Locke, professor of philosophy at Howard University, a variety of articles, poems, essays, and reviews were assembled in an attempt to present a definitive picture of Negro life in New York. Locke's particular interest in the younger writers is indicated by his selection of lengthy contributions from Countee Cullen, Claude McKay, Jean Toomer, Rudolph Fisher, and Hughes. In his article, "Youth Speaks," Locke praised the achievements of this group saying:

> They have all swung above the horizon in the last three years, and we can say without disparagement of the past that in that short space of time they have gained collectively from publishers, editors, critics and the general public more recognition than has ever before come to Negro creative artists in an entire working lifetime.[57]

It was at Locke's invitation that Hughes submitted poems for the "Harlem" issue of *Survey Graphic*. This friendship and support was instrumental in furthering Hughes's literary career.

Several of Hughes's poems in the *Survey Graphic* explored the beauty and simplicity of Africa. In these poems the restraints of modern civilization are contrasted with the freedom and unspoiled

[55]Hughes, *The Big Sea*, p. 223.
[56]"The Gist of It," *Survey Graphic*, VI (March, 1925), p. 627.
[57]Alain Locke, "Youth Speaks," *Survey Graphic*, VI (March, 1925), p. 659.

charm of primitive society. In "Song," for example, the poet advises
a new spirit of abandon:

> Lovely, dark, and lonely one
> Bare your bosom to the sun
> Do not be afraid of light
> You are a child of night.[58]

A similar longing for freedom is expressed in "Dream Variation."

> To fling my arms wide
> To some place in the sun,
> To whirl and to dance
> Till the bright day is done.
> Then rest at cool evening
> Beneath a tall tree
> While night comes gently
> Black like me.[59]

Again, in "Our Land," the poet speaks of his deep love for the
homeland, Africa:

> We should have a land of sun,
> Of gorgeous sun,
> And a land of fragrant water
> Where the twilight is a soft bandana handkerchief
> Of rose and gold,
> And not this land
> Where life is cold.
>
> We should have a land of trees
> Of tall thick trees,
> Bowed down with chattering parrots
> Brilliant as the day,
> And not this land where birds are grey.
>
> Ah, we should have a land of joy,
> Of love and joy and wine and song,
> And not this land where joy is wrong.[60]

Africa is romantically pictured as a beautiful land of joy and freedom, far removed from the snares and deceits of civilization. The
tall trees, the silver moon, and the gorgeous sun symbolize a

[58]Langston Hughes, *Survey Graphic*, VI (March 1, 1925), p. 663.
[59]*Ibid.*
[60]*Ibid.*, p. 678.

warmer, happier way of life. The poet longs to be free of the white man's world. In "Lament for Dark Peoples," Hughes compares the condition of the Negro to that of circus animals:

> Now they've caged me
> In the circus of civilization.
> Now I herd with the many—
> Caged in the circus of civilization.[61]

This infatuation with primitivism was a definite part of the intellectual climate of the 1920's.[62] Andre Gide introduced African art to appreciative audiences in Europe, jazz music gained disciples all over the world, and in the United States, Marcus Garvey stirred hundreds of thousands with his vision of a Negro colony in Africa. Negro authors seeking values distinctly their own responded to this stimulus and concentrated on a romantic treatment of Africa and the slave era.

In Hughes's case, this infatuation with primitivism was short lived. He wrote poems about Africa in response to a mood of the 1920's rather than from any deep personal convictions. In 1930 Hughes renounced the whole body of primitivism:

> I did not feel the rhythms of the primitive surging through me, and so I could not live and write as though I did. I was only an American Negro—who loved the surface of Africa and the rhythms of Africa—but I was not Africa.[63]

Other poems in *The Survey Graphic* expressed Hughes's optimistic belief in the ability of democracy to solve the Negro's problems. In "I Too" the Negro laughs and eats well when he is told to go to the kitchen because he knows that tomorrow he will be accepted at the table in the front room. The same theme is expressed in "Poem," Hughes's battle hymn for his race:

> We have tomorrow
> Bright before us
> Like a flame

[61]Langston Hughes, *The Weary Blues* (New York: Alfred A. Knopf, 1926), p. 100.

[62]Frederick Hoffman has a good analysis of this phenomenon in his book *The Twenties* (New York: Collier Books, 1962), pp. 306–308.

[63]Hughes, *The Big Sea*, p. 325.

> Yesterday, a night-gone thing
> a sun-down name
>
> And dawn today
> Broad arch above the world we came,
> We march.[64]

By the time *The Survey Graphic* appeared, Hughes's interests in Harlem had intensified. Although he is better known for these Harlem blues, his earliest work is not without distinction. To the stylistic patterns of Sandburg, Masters, and Whitman he added his own insight and sensitivity. More importantly, perhaps, he added the music of the Negro. Hughes's early poetry transmits the dreams of the average Negro with a superb warmth and sympathy. White readers enjoyed the colorful style and the intimate revelation of the Negro life, while Negroes saw themselves in the poems as a race with a proud history and promising future.

By the end of 1925 Hughes was launched on a successful literary career. This had been accomplished partly through his own hard work and partly through the efforts of his friends. As he acknowledges, Jessie Fauset, Charles Johnson, and Alain Locke were responsible for the discovery and encouragement of most of the young Negro writers in the 1920's. "Kind and critical—but not too critical for the young—they nursed us along until our books were born."[65] Additional help came from literary figures like Van Vechten and philanthropists like the unnamed New York lady who provided funds for Hughes's forthcoming education at Lincoln University.

Hughes had developed a facility for writing between 1921–1925, that encouraged support and enthusiasm. His poems in *The Crisis* showed a promise that was rapidly fulfilled in a succession of dramatic, colorful verses on a wide variety of topics. From the first, race motivated Hughes's best work. He used its subtle overtones to give his writing strength. In five years of writing and travel, Hughes had laid a sound foundation for future success.

[64]Langston Hughes, *Survey Graphic*, VI (March, 1925), p. 663.
[65]Hughes, *The Big Sea*, p. 218.

chapter two

The Harlem Renaissance 1926—1930

> Goin' down the road, Lawd,
> Goin' down the road.
> Down the road, Lawd,
> Way, way down the road.
> Got to find somebody
> To help me carry this load.
>
> Road's in front o' me,
> Nothin' to do but walk.
> Road's in front o' me,
> Walk . . . an' walk . . . an' walk.
> I'd like to meet a good friend
> To come along an' talk.
> > "Bound No'th Blues."

Between 1926–1930 Hughes's literary activities were intimately connected with the social-cultural phenomenon known as the Harlem Renaissance or the New Negro Movement. Alain Locke characterized the major goal of the movement as follows:

> . . . the Negro today wishes to be known for what he is, even in his faults and shortcomings, and scorns a craven and precarious survival at the price of seeming to be what he is not.[1]

This philosophy, implying that a man be judged on his capabilties rather than his color, was, of course, nothing new. Since the beginning of the nineteenth century representatives of both races had condemned unfair restrictions of Negro rights. It was not until 1910, however, with the foundation of NAACP, that these groups achieved any effective focus. Through NAACP, and particularly in the pages

---

[1]Alain Locke, "Enter the New Negro," *Survey Graphic*, VI (March, 1925), p. 632.

of *The Crisis*, the New Negro spoke out against the harsh realities of the caste system in a democratic society.

If they wished, New Negro writers could have traced a line of protest literature back to 1789 when the first anti-slavery pamphlet appeared. For those less historically minded it was sufficient to cite Du Bois's "A Litany at Atlanta" as a forerunner and model. Written in 1909, in response to a bloody race riot, "A Litany at Atlanta" pours out the accumulated wrath of the Negro people:

> Doth not this justice of hell stink in Thy
> nostrils, O God? How long shall the mounting
> flood of innocent blood roar in Thine ears and
> pound in our hearts for vengeance? Pile the
> pale frenzy of blood-crazed brutes who do such
> deeds high on Thine altar, Jehovah Jireh, and
> burn it in hell forever and forever!
> Forgive us, good Lord; we know not what
> we say![2]

With Du Bois's appeal ringing in their ears the New Negro writers overturned the old doctrine of assimilation and emphasized instead distinctly Negro topics—the African heritage, the slave era, and Harlem. Also, for the first time, Negro folk material appeared without the crutches of apology or imitation. As Locke said:

> Our poets have now stopped speaking for the Negro—they speak as Negroes. Where formerly they spoke to others and tried to interpret, they now speak to their own and try to express. They have stopped posing, being nearer to the attainment of poise.[3]

One of the early New Negro writers, Claude McKay, set the tone of revolt with his famous sonnet, "If We Must Die." This poem, also prompted by a race riot, begins with the challenge:

> If we must die, let it not be like hogs
> Hunted and penned in an inglorious spot,

And it concludes with the courageous promise:

---

[2]W. E. B. Du Bois, "A Litany at Atlanta," *The Poetry of the Negro 1746–1949*, ed. Langston Hughes and Arna Bontemps (Garden City: Doubleday, 1951), pp. 19–20.

[3]Alain Locke, "Youth Speaks," *Survey Graphic*, VI (March, 1925), p. 659.

> Like men we'll face the murderous, cowardly
> pack,
> Pressed to the wall, dying, but fighting
> back.[4]

Hughes adopted this creed as his own. In a manifesto for the realistic portrayal of the American Negro he said:

> We younger Negro artists who create now intend to express our individual dark-skinned selves without fear or shame. If white people are pleased, we are glad. If they are not, it doesn't matter. We know we are beautiful. And ugly too. . . . We build our temples for tomorrow, strong as we know how, and we stand on top of the mountain, free within ourselves.[5]

As in any movement of revolt the leaders enjoyed a considerable amount of camaraderie. They gathered most often in Harlem, but occasionally they could be induced to attend parties given by white friends downtown. This was particularly true if there was a possibility of meeting a big publisher or a theatrical producer. Since public interest in the Negro was at a peak, agents and theatre owners were as eager to meet Negroes as Negroes were to meet them. Cullen remarked:

> Never before has such an acute interest existed in the Negro as a possible artist. Literary, musical and theatrical doors are opening for him at the touch of the knob.[6]

"It was a period," as Hughes reports, "when every season there was at least one hit play on Broadway acted by a Negro cast. And when Negro authors were being published with much greater frequency and much more publicity than ever before or since in history."[7] Major publishers not only sponsored individual Negro authors, but for the first time produced anthologies of Negro writing.[8]

[4]Claude McKay, "If We Must Die," *The Poetry of the Negro 1746–1949*, ed. Hughes and Bontemps, p. 333.

[5]Langston Hughes, "The Negro Artist and the Racial Mountain," *The Nation*, CXXII (June 23, 1926), p. 694.

[6]Countee Cullen, "The Negro Sings His Soul," *Survey Graphic*, VII (September, 1925), p. 583.

[7]Hughes, *The Big Sea*, p. 228.

[8]Five important anthologies issued in the twenties are; 1. James Weldon Johnson's *The Book Of American Negro Poetry*. New York: Harcourt, 1922. 2. Robert Kerlin's *Negro Poets and Their Poems*. Washington: Associated

No one expressed the flamboyant Harlem cabaret life better than Hughes and no one equaled him in setting down the spirit and challenge of the New Negro generation. He is, as Saunders Redding points out, "the most prolific and the most representative of the New Negroes."[9] It was therefore singularly appropriate when, in January, 1926, at the height of interest in the New Negro, Knopf published Hughes's first book, *The Weary Blues*. In the introduction Van Vechten described Hughes's wanderings and promised that he would create an important place for himself in the world of letters, a place at least equal to that held by Paul Lawrence Dunbar or James Weldon Johnson. The poems were arranged in groups to reflect Hughes's personal views on Mexico, Africa, Harlem, and the sea. As a whole the book may be taken as a kind of verse chronicle of Hughes's experiences and impressions up to that time. Physically, *The Weary Blues* was carefully printed according to the high standard Alfred Knopf set for all of his books. A colorful dust jacket by Miguel Covarrubias enhanced the book's general exterior appearance.

Because of the interest in everything relating to the Negro, and the appreciative introduction by Van Vechten, *The Weary Blues* received more than the usual attention given a first book of poems. DuBose Heyward said, "Always intensely subjective, passionate, and keenly sensitive to beauty and possessed of an unfaltering musical sense, Langston Hughes has given us a 'first book' that marks the opening of a career well worth watching."[10] The reviewer in the *New York Times* echoed this sentiment saying, "If he can go on as he has begun, America bids fair to have a poet worthy of far more than passing mention."[11] In the *Times Literary Supplement*, how-

---

Press, 1923. 3. N. I. White and W. C. Jackson's *An Anthology of Verse by American Negroes*. Chapel Hill: University of North Carolina, 1924. 4. Countee Cullen's *Caroling Dusk*. New York: Harper, 1927. 5. V. F. Calverton's *Anthology of American Negro Literature*. New York: Modern Library, 1929.

[9]Saunders Redding, *To Make a Poet Black* (Chapel Hill: University of North Carolina Press, 1939), p. 115.

[10]DuBose Heyward, Review of *The Weary Blues*, by Langston Hughes, *New York Herald Tribune Books* (August 1, 1926), p. 4.

[11]Review of *The Weary Blues*, by Langston Hughes, *New York Times*, (March 21, 1926), p. 6.

ever, the poems were classed as superficial, flamboyant, and sentimental.[12]

A balanced look at *The Weary Blues* suggests that the comments
of both the British reviewer and Heyward were exaggerated. The
book was neither a complete success nor an unqualified failure. The
collection is worthy of serious analysis in any case, as it provides an
enlightening view of Hughes's literary objectives and foreshadows
much of his later work. Here in these early poems are reflected the
author's love of life, his appreciation for the rhythms of Negro
music, and his enjoyment of Harlem and its people.

In many of the poems in *The Weary Blues* the reader obtains a
real sense of participation in the heady cabaret life which was an
important part of Harlem in the 1920's. In the poem "Negro
Dancers," for example, Hughes manages to distill all the carnival
gaiety of that time with the overtones of sadness and despair which
were often the lot of the Negro.

> Me an' ma baby's
> Got two mo' ways,
> Two mo' ways to do de buck!
>   Da, da,
>   Da, da, da!
> Two mo' ways to do de buck!
>
> Soft light on the tables,
> Music gay,
> Brown-skin steppers
> In a cabaret.
>
> White folks, laugh!
> White folks, pray!
>
> Me an' ma baby's
> Got two mo' ways,
> Two mo' ways to do de buck![13]

This was a Harlem desperately seeking pleasure as an antidote for
the blues. There is no real joy here, only a pathetic grasping for
transitory delights. The last lines of "The Weary Blues" convey the

[12]Review of *The Weary Blues*, by Langston Hughes, *The Times Literary
Supplement* (July 29, 1926), p. 515.

[13]Langston Hughes, *The Crisis*, XXVIII (March, 1925), p. 221.

same sense of frustration. The cabaret closes and the tired musician drags himself home to bed.

The Weary Blues, like most of Hughes's writing, is a vivid index to contemporary Harlem life. David Daiches, in a discerning comment on Hughes's literary objectives, emphasized this very point. Daiches said, "Langston Hughes's poetry is what, in terms of the art of the motion picture, would be called documentary. His concern is to document the moods and problems of the American Negro."[14] It is clear from one of Hughes's own statements that he agrees with this analysis. In answer to a question about the relationship between his writing and being a Negro he said, ". . . the major aims of my work have been to interpret and comment upon Negro life, and its relations to the problems of Democracy, . . ."[15] The poems in *The Weary Blues* contain a great many penetrating comments on Harlem in the 1920's, including both its surface gaiety and its deeper sorrow. From the first, Hughes produced realistic interpretations of the Negro, especially as he lived in the urban North.

The entire first section of *The Weary Blues* is devoted to a description of the sweet and sour aspects of Harlem cabaret life. Poems like "To Midnight Nan at Leroy's," "Young Singer," "The Cat and the Saxaphone," "Nude Young Dancer," and "Jazzonia" all concentrate on the same theme. In "Jazzonia" Hughes offers one of the truly colorful descriptions of the period:

> Oh, silver tree!
> Oh, shining rivers of the soul!
>
> In a Harlem cabaret
> Six long-headed jazzers play.
> A dancing girl whose eyes are bold
> Lifts high a dress of silken gold.
>
> Oh, singing tree!
> Oh, shining rivers of the soul!
>
> Were Eva's eyes
> In the first garden
> Just a bit too bold?

[14]David Daiches, Review of *One Way Ticket*, by Langston Hughes, *New York Herald Tribune Book Review* (January 9, 1949), p. 4.

[15]Langston Hughes, "Some Practical Observations: A Colloquy," *Phylon*, XI (Winter, 1950), p. 307.

>Was Cleopatra gorgeous
>In a gown of gold?
>
>Oh, shining tree!
>Oh, silver rivers of the soul!
>
>In a whirling cabaret
>Six long-headed jazzers play.[16]

As Arthur Davis comments, "The Harlem of *The Weary Blues* became therefore for him 'Jazzonia,' a new world of escape and release, an exciting never-never land in which 'sleek black boys' blew their hearts out on silver trumpets in a 'whirling cabaret.' "[17] This style, although melodious and pleasing to the ear, was not the kind to attract praise from the serious poetry reader. Hughes's cabaret poems remain, however, one of the best expressions of an important era in Negro social history.

Another section of poems in *The Weary Blues* dealt with the sea and Africa. Like the cabaret poems these too were drawn from Hughes's impressions and reactions to his travels. These verses sing a lusty song of love and sunshine. "Natcha" could have been a girl in any of a dozen ports of call:

>Natcha, offering love.
>For ten shillings offering love.
>Offering: a night with me honey.
>A long, sweet night with me.
>   Come, drink palm wine.
>   Come, drink kisses.
>A long, dream night with me.[18]

Although the poems in this group are lively and colorful they lack the individuality of Hughes's Negro verse. The sentiments are expressed in a free verse style typical of the New Poetry Movement, but they have little to distinguish them from the work of any other follower of Sandburg or Lindsay. Africa, like the cabaret, was but a stopping place for Hughes's inquisitive mind. As indicated in the previous chapter, he soon rejected the 'slow beating of the tom-tom' and the 'land of fragrant water' for more practical matters at home.

[16]Langston Hughes, *The Crisis*, XXVI (August, 1923), p. 162.

[17]Arthur Davis, "The Harlem of Langston Hughes' Poetry," *Phylon*, XIII (Winter, 1952), p. 277.

[18]Hughes, *Selected Poems*, p. 72.

The best poems in *The Weary Blues* group themselves around the themes of pride and protest. They state simply and precisely the reasons why the Negro is what he is and how he fits into the American way of life. The poems of pride, such as "The Negro Speaks of Rivers," "My People," "I, Too," and "Mother to Son," are as moving today as when they were first written. They remind us that for all its unpleasantness there is no shame in being a Negro in America. On the other hand, there is every reason for pride in the dignity and laughter of the Negro people.

Hughes brought a fresh point of view to racial writing. He described his people with love and enthusiasm, but avoided the trite, over-assertive style of the propagandist. He could say simply:

> I am a Negro:
>   Black as the night is black,
>   Black like the depths of my Africa.[19]

or:

> I've known rivers:
>   Ancient, dusky rivers.
>   My soul has grown deep like the rivers.[20]

And he could write warmly human portraits like "Aunt Sue's Stories," and "Mother to Son." It is easy to feel sympathy for the hard-working mother in "Mother to Son" who says, for the mothers of the world, "Life for me ain't been no crystal stair."[21] Again, the characterization of Aunt Sue is charming and homespun in the manner of James Whitcomb Riley:

> Aunt Sue has a head full of stories.
> Aunt Sue has a whole heart full of stories.
> Summer nights on the front porch
> Aunt Sue cuddles a brown-faced child to her bosom
> And tells him stories.[22]

Hughes's poems of pride have lasting quality because they are natural, sensitive interpretations of the Negro. As Locke discerningly put it, "Hughes brings to his portrayal of his folk not the ragged provincialism of a minstrel but the descriptive detachment of a

[19]Hughes, *Selected Poems*, p. 8.
[20]*Ibid.*, p. 4.
[21]*Ibid.*, p. 187.
[22]*Ibid.*, p. 6.

Vachel Lindsay and a Sandburg and promises the democratic sweep
and universality of a Whitman."[23]

The poems of protest, somewhat less numerous than the poems
of pride, also offer a fresh approach to race. In "Cross," "Minstrel
Man," "The South," and "As I Grew Older" Hughes attacks the
evils of the American Jim Crow system. "Cross" develops the mulatto
theme, "Minstrel Man" lampoons the laughing darky image, and
"As I Grew Older" describes the crippling effect of second-class
citizenship on the black man. Hughes devoted considerable attention
to all of these themes in subsequent works, with particular emphasis
on the latter. "As I Grew Older" offers a germ statement about one
of his basic beliefs. The poem opens:

> It was a long time ago.
> I have almost forgotten my dream.
> But it was there then,
> In front of me,
> Bright like a sun—
> My dream.
> And the wall rose,
> Rose slowly,
> Slowly,
> Between me and my dream.
> Rose slowly, slowly,
> Dimming,
> Hiding,
> The light of my dream.
> Rose until it touched the sky—
> The wall.
>
> Shadow.
> I am black.[24]

Hughes asks in a later poem:

> What happens to a dream deferred?
>
> Does it dry up
> like a raisin in the sun?
> Or fester like a sore—
> And then run?[25]

[23]Alain Locke, "Introduction," *Four Negro Poets* (New York: Simon and
Schuster, 1927), p. 6.
[24]Hughes, *Selected Poems*, p. 11.
[25]Langston Hughes, "Harlem," *Selected Poems*, p. 268.

This is a difficult and troublesome question, one which Hughes feels must be given careful attention. It is a question he asks his readers in many of his best poems and stories.

In the 1920's Hughes's poems made two major points; first, the Negro was a proud and sensitive member of society, and second, he resented the stereotypes, hate, and misunderstanding commonly directed at him by the whites. The poems are sparse and direct, written with a message that still commands attention. It is likely that these poems will remain unique statements on the Negro in America.

Sales of *The Weary Blues* pleased the Knopfs, as indicated by a letter sent to Hughes shortly before the third printing. Blanche Knopf wrote:

> I have noted your corrections for another printing and I hope we'll be making one. We have sold a little under twelve hundred which I think is pretty good, don't you?[26]

A second printing was released in February, 1926, and a third in October of the same year.

In short, *The Weary Blues* was a satisfying book from both the critical and commercial point of view. It furnished the sound beginning Hughes needed to build a literary career. The first printing coincided with Hughes's entry into Lincoln University.

During his first year at Lincoln Hughes had the distinction of winning another literary award—the Witter Bynner Undergraduate Poetry Prize.[27] The award winning "A House in Taos," Hughes concedes, "was a strange poem for me to be writing in a period when I was writing mostly blues and spirituals."[28] Hughes had never seen the New Mexico desert, but in his verse he tried to imagine

[26]Letter from Blanche Knopf to Langston Hughes of April 29, 1926. Yale University Library.

[27]In a letter to the writer dated March 29, 1963, Mr. Bynner states, "the prize was awarded by the Poetry Society of America's Undergraduate Contest through the magazine *Palms*, I having been associated with both the Society and the magazine: president of the former in 1920–22 and on the staff of *Palms* for several years at that period. I provided the amount of the prize, $150, every year for a decade and was assisted in judging the entries by two other poets each year. In Langston's year the judges were Rose O'Neill, Vachel Lindsay, and myself."

[28]Hughes, *The Big Sea*, p. 261.

what it looked like and what the Indians would think of the exotic
New York artists who came there. In the second stanza he describes
a house built by one of these city-bred people:

> That there should be a barren garden
> About this house in Taos
> Is not so strange,

then, he provides a description of the people themselves:

> But that there should be three barren hearts
> In this house in Taos—
> Who carries ugly things to show the sun?[29]

The poem contrasts the simplicity of nature with the complex life
and exotic dwellings of man. Hughes put aside his usual style of
writing to produce an effective satire on one of the curious segments
of cabaret society in the 1920's.

Hughes spent the summer following his first year at Lincoln in
New York with Wallace Thurman, another member of the New
Negro group. These two, along with Zora Hurston, Aaron Douglas,
Bruce Nugent, and several others devoted that summer to a labor
of love, the creation of an inflammatory little magazine called *Fire.*
The function of the new journal, as explained by Hughes, was two-
fold; first, it would provide an otherwise unavailable outlet for the
work of the editors, and secondly, "it would burn up a lot of the
old, dead conventional Negro-white ideas of the past, *épater le
bourgeois* into a realization of the existence of the younger Negro
writers and artists."[30]

The publication of *Fire* symbolized the spirit of revolt inherent
in the New Negro movement and also pointed up the dissatisfaction
younger writers had begun to feel toward *The Crisis* and *Opportunity.* The sponsors of these two magazines, who had nurtured
many of the New Negro writers, now found their offspring mature
and full of bizarre styles and radical ideas. To the conservative older
writers like Walter White, Jessie Fauset, and Du Bois, the stark
realism of the younger school was intolerable. The goal of the
conservative group was to educate whites to the existence of a
respectable Negro element, an element that could be trusted and

[29]*Ibid.,* p. 260.
[30]*Ibid.,* p. 235.

even admired. Novels like Fauset's *Chinaberry Tree*, Du Bois's *Dark Princess*, and White's *Fire in the Flint* reveal a world in which the Negro characters are well educated and endowed with all the middle class virtues. In their determination to make Negroes appear intelligent and worthy members of society the older authors often neglected to develop characterization or plot. Consequently, their books must be classed as propaganda rather than literature. Hughes, on the other hand, chose to write about any phase of society that seemed to offer a basis for literature of beauty. As Webster Smalley observed: "He prefers to write about those of his race who live constantly on the edge of financial disaster, who are used to living precariously, occasionally falling over the edge and crawling back up, and who have no time to be pretentious."[31]

While the conservative writers peopled their poems and stories with doctors, social workers, and dancers, Hughes and his friends wrote about prostitutes, laborers, and drunks. Hughes described the source of his inspiration with charm and candor:

> The people who have their nip of gin on Saturday nights and are not too important to themselves or the community, . . . they do not particularly care whether they are like white folks or anybody else. Their joy runs bang! into ecstasy. Their religion soars to a shout. Work maybe a little today, rest a little tomorrow. Play awhile. Sing awhile. O, let's dance![32]

He then proceeds to suggest that this is the proper working milieu for the Negro writer:

> Certainly there is, for the American Negro artist who can escape the restrictions the more advanced among his own group would put upon him, a great field of unused material ready for his art. Without going outside his race, and even among the better classes with their 'white' culture and conscious American manners, but still Negro enough to be different, there is sufficient matter to furnish a black artist with a lifetime of creative work.[33]

[31]Webster Smalley, "Introduction," *Five Plays by Langston Hughes* (Bloomington: University of Indiana Press, 1963), p. vii.
[32]Langston Hughes, "The Negro Artist and the Racial Mountain," *The Nation*, CXXII (June 23, 1926), p. 693.
[33]*Ibid.*

The contributions in the first and only issue of *Fire* were precisely in line with this declaration for racial writing. Hughes's "Elevator Boy," for example, demonstrated none of the virtues Du Bois thought Negro "heroes" should project. The poem ends:

> Two new suits an'
> A woman to sleep with.
> Maybe no luck for a long time.
> Only the elevators
> Goin' up an' down,
> Up an' down,
> Or somebody elses' shoes
> To shine,
> Or greasy pots in a dirty kitchen.
> I been runnin' this
> Elevator too long.
> Guess I'll quit now.[34]

This poem contains the essence of Hughes's most successful work, for it transcribes, with a sure touch, the hopes and fears of the ordinary Negro. In recognition of this, Louis Untermeyer has said: "His portraits of Negro workmen . . . are more memorable than those produced by any of his compatriots."[35] This was the kind of writing, however, that made enemies on both sides of the racial fence, as Hughes had discovered:

> The Negro artist works against an undertow of sharp criticism and misunderstanding from his own group and unintentional bribes from the whites. 'O, be respectable, write about nice people, show how good we are,' say the Negroes. 'Be stereotyped, don't go too far, don't shatter our illusions about you, don't amuse us too seriously. We will pay you,' say the whites.[36]

The rejection of *Fire* was a painful disappointment to the contributors. Negro critics castigated the magazine and the white critics ignored it.[37] Hughes recalls that Rean Graves, writing for the

[34]Hughes, *Selected Poems*, p. 195.

[35]Louis Untermeyer, *Modern American Poetry, Modern British Poetry* (New York: Harcourt Brace, 1936), p. 611.

[36]Langston Hughes, "The Negro Artist and the Racial Mountain," *The Nation*, CXXII (June 23, 1926), p. 693.

[37]The only exception to this, *The Bookman* of November 1926, referred to *Fire* as "particularly encouraging at a time when the Negro shows ominous signs of settling down to become a good American." p. 258.

Baltimore Afro-American, began his review by saying "I have just tossed the first issue of *Fire* into the fire."[38] Even with Thurman peddling the journal from door to door, printing costs could not be met. For years the contributors paid part of their meagre incomes to settle the debt. Ironically, a basement fire destroyed most of the unsold copies of *Fire* thereby making Volume I, Number 1, the only number issued, a valuable and rare piece of Americana.

Hughes's college years were necessarily lean in quantity of production, although new publishing avenues were opening constantly. Shortly after he entered college, poems were accepted by *The New Republic, The Saturday Review of Literature,* and *The New Masses.* Almost without exception these poems dealt with racial subjects. "Brass Spittoons," for example, is one of Hughes's most eloquent expositions of the world of the uneducated Negro:

> Clean the spittoons, boy.
>   Detroit,
>   Chicago,
>   Atlantic City,
>   Palm Beach.
> Clean the spittoons.
> The steam in hotel kitchens,
> And the smoke in hotel lobbies,
> And the slime in hotel spittoons:
> Part of my life.
>   Hey, boy!
>   A nickel,
>   A dime,
>   A dollar,
> Two dollars a day.
>   Hey, boy!
>   A nickel,
>   A dime,
>   A dollar,
>   Two dollars
> Buys shoes for the baby.
> House rent to pay.
> Gin on Saturday,
> Church on Sunday.
>   My God!
> Babies and gin and church

[38]Hughes, *The Big Sea,* p. 237.

and women and Sunday
all mixed up with dimes and
dollars and clean spittoons
and house rent to pay.
Hey, boy!
A bright bowl of brass is beautiful to the Lord.
Bright polished brass like the cymbals
Of King David's dancers,
Like the wine cups of Solomon.
Hey, boy!
A clean spittoon on the altar of the Lord,
A clean bright spittoon all newly polished—
At least I can offer that.
Com'mere, boy![39]

Hughes has identified "Brass Spittoons" as "one of the poems I like best."[40] In the last nine lines he raises the poem above the ordinary with a surprising shift of emphasis. Although the hero is engaged in the lowest kind of menial labor he is not wholly beaten. The poem carries a message of hope to all those who work out their days for pitifully small reward.

The rhythms of the blues which appear in the poetry of this period are so distinct that it is easy to imagine one of the great colored singers shouting them out to the accompaniment of a rickety piano. "Midwinter Blues" could certainly be enjoyed in this vein. In this poem Hughes shows how a certain stoic humor plays a part in the blues. The poem begins:

In the middle of the Winter
Snow all over the ground.
In the middle of the Winter,
Snow all over the ground—
'Twas the night befo' Christmas
My good man turned me down.

Don't know's I'd mind his goin'
But he left me when the coal was low.
Don't know's I'd mind his goin'
But he left when the coal was low.
Now, if a man loves a woman
That ain't no time to go.[41]

[39]*Ibid.*, pp. 264–265.
[40]*Ibid.*, p. 264.
[41]Hughes, *Selected Poems*, p. 151.

The rhythm of the blues was predominant late in 1926 when Hughes
had his work published for the first time in *Poetry*. One of the
poems, "Po' Boy Blues," is a particularly effective mixture of sorrow
and irony:

> I fell in love with
> A gal I thought was kind.
> Fell in love with
> A gal I thought was kind.
> She made me lose ma money
> An' almost lose ma mind.

Then, in the last verse, we hear the lament of the poor, working man
driven to the edge of exhaustion and despair:

> Weary, weary,
> Weary early in de morn.
> Weary, weary,
> Early, early in de morn
> I's so weary
> I wish I'd never been born.[42]

Hughes had taken his own advice, from "The Negro Artist and the
Racial Mountain," and created a moving verse based on authentic
Negro folk rhythms.

 Fine Clothes to the Jew, published midway through Hughes's
college career, concentrated on Negro folk music. As Charles S.
Johnson observed, the poems in *Fine Clothes to the Jew* were a
departure from those in *The Weary Blues* since the new book "marked
a final, frank turning to the folk life of the Negro, striving to catch
and give back to the world the strange music of the unlettered Negro
—his 'Blues.' "[43] When the book appeared, however, it was berated
as disloyal to the race. Negro critics felt that the poems presented
the wrong image of the Negro. How could the race hope to make
any progress, they argued, when whites could read about prostitutes
like "Ruby Brown"? The poem ends.

> Now the streets down by the river
> Know more about this pretty Ruby Brown,

[42]Langston Hughes, *Poetry*, XXIX (November, 1926), p. 89.
[43]Charles S. Johnson, "The Negro Renaissance and its Significance," *The New
Negro Thirty Years Afterward*, ed. Rayford Logan, Eugene Holmes, and G.
Franklin Edwards (Washington: Howard University Press, 1955), p. 83.

And the sinister shuttered houses of the bottoms
Hold a yellow girl
Seeking an answer to her questions.
The good church folk do not mention
Her name any more.

But the white men,
Habitues of the high shuttered houses,
Pay more money to her now
Than they ever did before,
When she worked in their kitchens.[44]

In the *Pittsburgh Courier*, a headline proclaimed "Langston Hughes Book of Poems Trash," *The New York Amsterdam News* commented "Langston Hughes—the Sewer Dweller."[45] Benjamin Brawley claimed it would have been better if the book had never been written since it concentrated on "the abandon and vulgarity of its age."[46] Hughes recalls that Eustace Gay wrote in the *Philadelphia Tribune*:

> It does not matter to me whether every poem in the book is true to life. Why should it be paraded before the American public by a Negro author as being typical or representative of the Negro? Bad enough to have white authors holding up our imperfections to public gaze. Our aim ought to be to present to the general public, already misinformed both by well meaning and malicious writers, our higher aims and aspirations, and our better selves.[47]

Hughes agreed that this kind of writing was useful, but objected to the philosophy that all Negro writers must follow the same pattern. Hughes felt he should write about what he knew best. As he said, "I knew only the people I had grown up with, and they weren't people whose shoes were always shined, who had been to Harvard, or who had heard of Bach."[48]

Allison Davis, writing in *The Crisis*, claimed the defects he saw in *Fine Clothes to the Jew* could be charged directly to Van Vechten. These weaknesses included false primitivism and over-emphasis on sordid and trivial detail. Davis stated that Van Vechten had "mis-

---

[44]Hughes, *Selected Poems*, p. 166.
[45]Hughes, *The Big Sea*, p. 266.
[46]Benjamin Brawley, *The Negro Genius* (New York: Dodd, Mead, 1937), p. 248.
[47]Hughes, *The Big Sea*, p. 267.
[48]*Ibid.*, p. 268.

directed a genuine poet, who gave promise of a power and technique exceptional in any poetry,"[49] and thereby cut off what promised to be a distinguished literary career. Hughes answered these charges with characteristic vigor, saying that most of the poems in *Fine Clothes to the Jew* had been written in Washington before he met Van Vechten and further that they "were not about him, not requested by him, not misdirected by him, some of them not liked by him."[50] The poems were his own, he continued, and were not molded to the taste of any person or group. Against the general criticism of his poetry he concludes, "I have never pretended to be keeping a literary grazing pasture with food to suit all breeds of cattle."[51]

White reviewers generally praised the book for its honesty and beauty. Babette Deutsch wrote, "The dialect pieces fairly sing themselves when read aloud and show craftsmanship of a high order."[52] In *Poetry* Julia Peterkin commented: "Tragic cries and questions, prayers and hallelujahs are turned into poetry with an art and skill that makes them available for the enjoyment and experience of all human beings, regardless of color or race."[53] The reviewer in the *Independent* said, "Mr. Hughes is best in his 'Blues.' It is hard to praise too highly one who expresses a race's emotions—and a moment in its life. Mr. Hughes has done both."[54]

Since most of the poems in *Fine Clothes to the Jew* are based on Negro folk music the book assumed a unity lacking in *The Weary Blues*. The book is less a study of Hughes and more a study of the Negro. Because of their form, however, these poems are somewhat more restricted in nature than the best work in *The Weary Blues*. There are no verses here as memorable as "The Negro Speaks of Rivers," "Mother to Son," or "Cross." Redding has commented that

[49]Allison Davis, "Our Negro Intellectuals," *The Crisis*, XXXV (August, 1928), p. 269.

[50]Langston Hughes, Letter to the Editor, *The Crisis*, XXVIII (September, 1928), p. 302.

[51]*Ibid.*

[52]Babette Deutsch, Review of *Fine Clothes to the Jew*, by Langston Hughes, *Bookman*, LXV (April, 1927), p. 221.

[53]Julia Peterkin, Review of *Fine Clothes to the Jew*, by Langston Hughes, *Poetry*, XXVI (October, 1927), p. 45.

[54]Review of *Fine Clothes to the Jew*, by Langston Hughes, *Independent*, CXVIII (April 9, 1927), p. 396.

none of these poems rise above the level of feeling. Hughes, he says, "feels in them but he does not think."[55]

If there is a lack of depth in these blues poems, as Redding suggests, no one can deny the strength of feeling they project. Redding offers a thoughtful and precise analysis of Hughes's ability in this line:

> There is this difference between racial thought and feeling; what the professors, the ministers, the physicians, the social workers think, the domestics, the porters, the dock hands, the factory girls, and the streetwalkers feel—feel in a great tide that pours over into song and shout, prayer and cursing, laughter and tears. More than any other writer of his race, Langston Hughes has been swept with this tide of feeling.[56]

Often the Negroes in *Fine Clothes to the Jew* feel discouraged. A "Porter" laments:

> I must say
> Yes, sir,
> To you all the time.
> Yes, sir!
> Yes, sir!
>
> All my days
> Climbing up a great big mountain
> Of yes, sirs![57]

and a "Young Gal" cries:

> When love is gone what
> Can a young gal do?
> When love is gone, O,
> What can a young gal do?
> Keep on a-lovin' me, daddy,
> Cause I don't want to be blue.[58]

In "Po' Boy Blues" the poet touches on a despondency that must have affected many:

> When I was home de
> Sunshine seemed like gold.

[55]Redding, *To Make a Poet Black*, p. 116.
[56]*Ibid.*, p. 115.
[57]Hughes, *Selected Poems*, p. 169.
[58]*Ibid.*, p. 148.

> When I was home de
> Sunshine seemed like gold.
> Since I come up North de
> Whole damn world's turned cold.[59]

It was this same longing for a distant home that prompted Hughes to write one of his most eloquent verses:

> De railroad bridge's
> A sad song in de air.
> De railroad bridge's
> A sad song in de air.
> Ever' time de trains pass
> I wants to go somewhere.[60]

Alain Locke discerningly identified the charm of this kind of poetry. He wrote, "The folk-lyrics of Langston Hughes have spontaneous moods and rhythms, and carry irresistible conviction. They are our really most successful efforts up to this date to recapture the folk-soul."[61] It seems somewhat unnecessary to question the depth of poems like these which speak so surely on the level of emotion.

In order to banish the blues the Negro frequently turned to the church. In *Fine Clothes to the Jew* Hughes provides many samples of gospel rhythm. The sinner shouts out his grief in "Fire."

> Fire,
> Fire, Lord!
> Fire gonna burn my soul!
>
> I ain't been good,
> I ain't been clean—
> I been stinkin', low-down, mean.[62]

and asks for pardon in "Feet O' Jesus."

> At the feet o' Jesus,
> Sorrow like a sea.
> Lordy, let yo' mercy
> Come driftin' down on me.

[59]Langston Hughes, *Poetry*, XXIX (November, 1926), p. 89.

[60]Langston Hughes, "Homesick Blues," *Fine Clothes to the Jew* (New York: Alfred A. Knopf, 1927), p. 24.

[61]Alain Locke, "The Negro in American Culture" *Anthology of American Negro Literature* ed. V. F. Calverton (New York: Modern Library, 1929), p. 255.

[62]Hughes, *Selected Poems*, p. 20.

> At the feet o' Jesus
> At yo' feet I stand.
> O, ma little Jesus,
> Please reach out yo' hand.[63]

Sometimes, however, there is grief too deep for prayer:

> Way down South in Dixie
>   (Break the heart of me)
>
> They hung my black young lover
>   To a cross roads tree.
>
> Way down South in Dixie
>   (Bruised body high in air)
> I asked the white Lord Jesus
>   What was the use of prayer.[64]

These poems, as Charles S. Johnson has commented, are the "finest expression of the New Negro poetry."[65] Through them we are able to understand what life means to the cabaret singer, the porter, and the men and women who inhabit the fields of the South and the ghetto streets of the North. In Hughes's lines we get "the warm sweat and breath of their lives, their shallow joys, the echoing emptiness."[66] In a latter day appraisal of the Harlem Renaissance Johnson continued his high praise of Hughes, claiming that "No Negro writer so completely symbolizes the new emancipation of the Negro mind. His was a poetry of gorgeous colors, of restless brooding, of melancholy, of disillusionment."[67] Excepting perhaps James Weldon Johnson, Hughes has no equal in rendering the folk rhythms of the Negro into poetry.

A completely different facet of Hughes's talent appears in a series of five short stories published in *The Messenger* and *Harlem*, two magazines edited in the twenties by Wallace Thurman. Founded in 1917 by A. Philip Randolph and Chandler Owen to further the cause of socialism, *The Messenger* had developed uncertain political leanings by the mid-twenties. According to Hughes, The *Messenger*

[63]*Ibid.*, p. 17.

[64]Langston Hughes, "Song for a Dark Girl," *Selected Poems*, p. 172.

[65]Charles S. Johnson, "Jazz, Poetry and Blues," *Carolina Magazine* (May, 1928), p. 18.

[66]*Ibid.*

[67]Charles S. Johnson, *The New Negro Thirty Years Afterward*, p. 83.

printed whatever paid the best. He says, "*The Messenger* bought my first stories. They paid me ten dollars a story. Wallace Thurman wrote me that the stories were very bad stories, but better than any others they could find, so he published them."[68]

Hughes's stories, like some of his early poems, stress primitive themes. The results, however, are not the same, for Hughes fails to handle the short story form with the sensitivity found in his poems. "Luani of the Jungle," for example, is a rather naive contrast of black strength and white weakness. The story begins as a black princess and her white husband arrive in Africa. A short time after the couple settle in Luani's jungle village the husband sees his wife walking naked in the moonlight with a muscular African prince. The miserable man creeps back into his tent unable to do anything but grind his teeth. Several times he tries to leave Africa and Luani, but he never gets beyond the seaport bar-rooms. The obvious message of this kind of writing could only have appealed to the most uncritical readers. Happily, it was not the pattern Hughes chose to follow in his next prose work.

During his last two years at Lincoln Hughes devoted all of his free time to writing *Not Without Laughter*, a novel about a Negro family in Kansas. The setting and characters are partially based on the life he knew as a boy. Concerning the genesis of the novel Hughes says:

> I created around myself what seemed to me a family more typical of Negro life in Kansas than my own had been. I gave myself aunts I didn't have, modeled after other children's aunts whom I had known. But I put in a real cyclone that had blown my grandmother's front porch away. And I added dances and songs I remembered.[69]

The story describes a boy named Sandy, his hard-working mother, Annjee, and his wandering, romantic father, Jimboy. Besides the immediate family, Hughes introduces Sandy's grandmother, Aunt Hager, and his two aunts, Harriett and Tempy. The characters each have a part to play in contrasting the life of freedom and laughter with the life of serious intent. Sandy enjoys the high spirits of his father and Harriett, but he also loves his mother and his

[68]Hughes, *The Big Sea*, p. 234.
[69]*Ibid.*, p. 304.

grandmother. Sandy's dilemma is foreshadowed early in the book:

> "Uh huh! Bound straight fo' de devil, that's what they is,"
> Hager returned calmly to her place beside the pump. "You
> and Harriett both—singin' an' dancin' this stuff befo' these
> chillens here." She pointed to Sandy and Willie-Mae, who sat
> on the ground with their backs against the chicken-box.
> "It's a shame."
> "I likes it," said Willie-Mae.
> "Me too," the little boy agreed.[70]

This conflict is never resolved. Sandy, who should have controlled
the direction of the story, remains a rather colorless figure. *Not
Without Laughter* might have been a more satisfying work if the
action had centered on Aunt Hager or Harriett. They are both heroic
and believable figures, while Sandy seems caught between two worlds
without understanding either. Although Hugh Gloster comments
favorably on the novel he concedes that "Hughes would have done
well to treat Sandy at greater length as James T. Farrell handled
'Studs' Lonigan."[71] At the end of the novel Sandy plans to return to
school and make something of himself; surely a victory for the
conservatism of his grandmother rather than the forces of laughter.
As Robert Bone says:

> The novel and its main character simply part company. Instead
> of supporting the defense of laughter theme, Sandy emerges as
> a symbol of racial advancement, which is hardly a laughing
> matter.[72]

Aside from this flaw in development the novel conveys a superb
picture of Negro life. Oscar Cargill rates *Not Without Laughter*
along with Carl Van Vechten's *Nigger Heaven* and Gertrude Stein's
Melanctha as one of "the best fictional treatments of the Negro in
American letters."[73] Considering the powerful works written by
Richard Wright and Ralph Ellison since Cargill's evaluation, it may

[70]Langston Hughes, *Not Without Laughter* (New York: Alfred A. Knopf,
1930), pp. 52–53.

[71]Hugh Gloster, *Negro Voices in American Fiction* (Chapel Hill: University of
North Carolina Press, 1948), p. 187.

[72]Robert Bone, *The Negro Novel in America* (New Haven: Yale University
Press, 1958), p. 77.

[73]Oscar Cargill, *Intellectual America* (New York: Macmillan, 1941), p. 511.

be easier to agree with Bone's assessment that the novel proves "Hughes more than any other author knows and loves the Negro masses."[74] The details of home, school, and church all attest to this love and understanding.

The characters in *Not Without Laughter* are credible individuals through whom the reader may perceive how the Negro lives and thinks. The book quietly underlines the fact that Negro life is neither sordid, spectacular or in most ways different from the life of any other people. A brief interchange between Annjee and Jimboy, for example, has a delightfully natural ring:

> "I wish you'd come in and eat the ham I brought you," she said as she picked up her chair and started towards the house. "And you Sandy! Get up from under that tree and go to bed." She spoke roughly to the little fellow, whom the songs had set a-dreaming. Then to her husband: "Jimboy, I wish you'd come in." . . . "You don't like my old songs do you, baby? You don't want to hear me sing 'em," he said, laughing. "Well, that's all right. I like you, anyhow, and I like your ham, and I like your kisses, and I like everything you bring me."[75]

This writing, sparse and authentic transmits valid human relationships with no intent to sermonize. Allen Angoff has remarked that *Not Without Laughter* is a victory for the artist and "shows more interest in life than in propaganda."[76] With its emphasis on the average man *Not Without Laughter* is similar to Hughes's best early poetry and a forerunner of his most successful later work such as the stories of Jesse B. Semple.

In *The Big Sea* Hughes describes the difficulties he faced in writing the novel. It was important, he felt, for the Negro to understand the saving power of laughter even if it was only laughing to keep from crying. The book, as he says, was not up to his expectations:

> Listen, Aunt Hager! Listen, Harriett!
> Listen, Annjee! Listen, Jimboy! Hey,
> Benbow!

[74]Bone, *The Negro Novel in America*, p. 75.

[75]Hughes, *Not Without Laughter*, p. 60.

[76]Allen Angoff, *American Writing Today* (New York: New York University Press, 1957), p. 101.

> I wanted to make you as wonderful as
> you really are—but it takes a lot of
> skill in words. And I don't know how.[77]

The reviews followed the line previously established in evaluating Hughes's poetry. White reviewers liked it; Negro critics damned it. Mary Ross commented that since the book was "written with understanding, tolerance and beauty, it lays special claim to the attention of those who love life and its mirroring in fiction."[78] In *The Crisis*, after listing "Books We Must Read," the editors included *Not Without Laughter* in a section called "Books One May Read." The brief note included there called the book a study of "black peasantry of the Middle-West."[79] Unfavorable notices such as this apparently had little effect on the public, for sales quickly outdistanced those of Hughes's books of poetry.[80] In spite of its unfriendly reception in the Negro press the novel became Hughes's first commercial success. Appearing in eight foreign languages it is also his most widely translated work.

Although some of the sections are slow paced, *Not Without Laughter* is a pleasing novel. Hughes handled race material in the well balanced manner advocated by Bone:

> A high protest content is not likely to produce good fiction; a studious avoidance of Negro life is scarcely more promising; the treatment of race material, though not necessarily race conflict, is by all odds the likeliest alternative.[81]

In brief, *Not Without Laughter* is an understanding and objective portrait of Negro life in America.

During the time Hughes worked on his novel "a distinguished and quite elderly white lady"[82] subsidized his writing. The change in Hughes's life was startling:

[77]Hughes, *The Big Sea*, pp. 305–306.

[78]Mary Ross, Review of *Not Without Laughter*, by Langston Hughes, *New York Herald Tribune* (July 27, 1930), p. 5.

[79]Review of *Not Without Laughter*, by Langston Hughes, *The Crisis*, XXX (September, 1930), p. 321.

[80]A letter from Bernard Smith of Alfred A. Knopf to Langston Hughes, dated February 15, 1938, reports, "The sales of your books are as follows: Not Without Laughter 6113, Weary Blues 4356, Fine Clothes to the Jew 2067.

[81]Bone, *The Negro Novel in America*, p. 225.

[82]Hughes, *The Big Sea*, p. 312.

I found myself with an assured income from someone who loved and believed in me, an apartment in a suburban village for my work, my brother in school in New England and no longer a financial difficulty to my mother, myself with boxes of fine bond paper for writing, a filing case, a typist to copy my work, and wonderful new suits of dinner clothes from Fifth Avenue shops, . . .[83]

In the midst of this luxury, however, Hughes says, "New York began to be not so pleasant that winter."[84] His own good fortune contrasted sharply with the lot of many people stricken by the depression. Just at this time, while thousands roamed the streets hungry and jobless, the luxurious Waldorf Astoria Hotel opened its doors. In "Advertisement for the Waldorf Astoria" Hughes paid ironic tribute to the opulence now available to the few. The poem began:

> Look! See what Vanity Fair says about
>   the new Waldorf Astoria:
> "All the luxuries of a private home. . . ."
> Now, won't that be charming when the last
>   flop-house has turned you down this
>   winter?[85]

It is not surprising that Hughes's patron disliked the poem. Negro artists, she believed, had an obligation to transmit their primitive heritage to modern readers through song, poetry, and painting. From her point of view "Advertisement for the Waldorf Astoria" was not in the primitive tradition and was therefore not an appropriate form of expression for an American Negro writer. As a result of this difference Hughes asked to be released from any further writing obligations to the lady. The relationship was broken and at the same time Hughes renounced primitivism forever. For the next decade the spirit that motivated "Advertisement for the Waldorf" dominated all of Hughes's writing. The poem was crucial in releasing him from the encumbrance of his patron and also in setting the tone for his ensuing work.

In the spring and summer of 1930 Hughes completed his education, published *Not Without Laughter*, and broke relations with

[83]*Ibid.*, pp. 316–317.
[84]*Ibid.*, p. 319.
[85]*Ibid.*, p. 321.

his sponsor. For the first time he was independent and able to write as he pleased. While he had been completing his education, however, the climate for Negro writing had changed drastically. The boundless enthusiasm which greeted all Negro writing in the twenties suddenly found other channels. Hughes describes the turn of events as follows:

> Sophisticated New Yorkers turned to Noel Coward. Colored actors began to go hungry, publishers politely rejected new manuscripts, and patrons found other uses for their money.[86]

The Negro Renaissance had run its course. For a young Negro writer it was time to make a careful judgment about the future. If it was true, as Hughes reports, that "the big editors did not know my name, or gave no sign of knowing it,"[87] a decision to continue as a professional writer seems rather · bold. Perhaps winning the Harmon gold medal for literature and the accompanying four hundred dollar prize in 1930 strengthened his faith. In any event, he says, "I'd finally and definitely made up my mind to continue being a writer— and to become a professional writer, making my living from writing."[88]

. In the twenties Hughes wrote within two main streams of literary endeavor. With his everyday themes and free verse style he placed himself in step with the New Poetry Movement; with his proud and realistic racial portrayals he figured prominently in the Negro Renaissance. On this base he built an enviable reputation so that, as he says, "Shortly poetry became bread; prose, shelter and raiment. Words turned into songs, plays, scenarios, articles, and stories."[89] By fishing diligently in all corners of what he called "the big sea" of literature Hughes was becoming, by 1930, a recognized and commercially successful author.

[86]*Ibid.*, p. 334.
[87]*Ibid.*, p. 335.
[88]*Ibid.*
[89]Hughes, *The Big Sea*, p. 335.

chapter three

The Prose and Poetry of Protest 1931—1940

"Just because they pay you, they always think they
own you. No white man's gonna own me. I laugh with
'em and they think I like 'em. Hell, I'm from Arkansas
where the crackers lynch niggers in the streets. How could
I like 'em?"

Pauline in "A Good Job Gone."

Between 1921–1930, Hughes devoted his major writing efforts to
poetry, and on the basis of his success definitely decided to pursue
a literary career. In the 1930's, he turned to two new mediums of
expression, prose and drama. His best published work of this decade
is contained in a series of provocative short stories and in a volume
of autobiography.

Hughes was one of many writers who concentrated on treatment of economic problems in the decade of the 1930's. With the
collapse of the economy, realities of everyday life seemed more
crucial than the romantic and amusing personal themes that had
dominated the 1920's. It was not a happy time for the Negro writer.
To a large extent he had been a fad of the 1920's like bobbed hair
and Mah-jongg, but now that it was no longer profitable to feature
Negro songs and stories, publishing opportunities were rare. Hughes
begins his second volume of autobiography with a candid appraisal
of the situation:

The magazines used very few stories with Negro themes, since
Negro themes were considered exotic, in a class with Chinese or
East Indian features. Editorial offices then never hired Negro
writers to read manuscripts or employed them to work on their
staffs.[1]

And, looking back on the Harlem Renaissance, he philosophized:

[1]Langston Hughes, *I Wonder as I Wander* (New York: Rinehart, 1956), p. 4.

I was there. I had a swell time while it lasted. But I thought it wouldn't last long. . . . For how could a large and enthusiastic number of people be crazy about Negroes forever?[2]

While some Negro authors like Claude McKay and Arna Bontemps turned for support to the Federal Writers Project, Hughes took his poetry on the road. With the encouragement of Mary McLeod Bethune, President of Bethune-Cookman College, Hughes began a series of poetry readings in the educational centers of the South and West. To support this project Knopf issued a special dollar edition of *The Weary Blues* and the Golden Stair Press in New York produced an inexpensive pamphlet of poetry called *The Negro Mother*. The standard lecture fee of one hundred dollars was frequently waived for a meal, a room, and a chance to sell the books.

In Chapel Hill, North Carolina, Hughes's writing produced a major civic disturbance. After learning that he had been invited to lecture at the University, the editors of *Contempo*, a campus magazine, requested a sample of his work. Hughes sent an article and a poem that dealt with the Scottsboro Case, a highly charged affair in which a group of Negro boys were accused of attacking two white girls. After the citizens of Chapel Hill read Hughes's satirical piece they rose in a protest that nearly caused the University to cancel the lecture. Hughes gave his talk, but afterward one of the divisions that had promised to support him refused to pay its share of the fee.[3]

As a result of this adventure Hughes gained considerable stature in the southern Negro community, particularly when it became known that he had eaten lunch with the editors of *Contempo* in one of Chapel Hill's finest restaurants.

The speaking tour closed in California in the winter of 1932 shortly after Hughes met Noel Sullivan, a wealthy patron of the arts. Sullivan entertained Hughes for a short time until the poet received an offer to join a company planning to make a film in Russia. For the next year and a half Hughes traveled extensively; first with the

[2]Hughes, *The Big Sea*, p. 228.

[3]Hughes describes this and several other embarrassing incidents which his writing has provoked in the article "My Adventures as a Social Poet," *Phylon*, VIII (September, 1947), pp. 205–212. Probably the most publicized of these events occurred in 1942 when the followers of the evangelist Aimee Semple McPherson broke up a literary luncheon in Pasadena, California, where Hughes was to read his poetry.

film company and later, when that abortive venture failed, as a free lance writer.[4]

The same year that Hughes began his trip to Russia he completed two publishing projects for young readers—a book of poetry, and a travel book about Haiti. The Knopf firm handled the publication of *The Dream Keeper* with typical care and sensitivity. One of the editors wrote Hughes:

> You know that we are bringing out these poems as definitely for older boys and girls, from twelve years up, and so the little "Play that Might Be True," THE GOLD PIECE, which appeared in the BROWNIES' BOOK first, is too young to be included in this collection. We would rather include a few more of your poems from THE WEARY BLUES and FINE CLOTHES TO THE JEW. . . . In the DREAM KEEPER group, would you mind omitting MARCH MOON? Somehow I don't feel that it is in quite the same vein as the others, and as there is WINTER MOON it would be difficult for the artist to do an illustration for each of them so close together.[5]

In all major decisions regarding production of the book the publisher maintained complete control. When a difference of opinion arose on the proper illustrator, Mrs. Knopf settled the issue at once:

> I like Prentiss Taylor's style very much. . . . We have however, made arrangements with a Miss Sewell to illustrate your book and we have had samples of her work and find them absolutely right, and I am sure you will be pleased.[6]

Hughes said he was pleased in a letter of February 8, and offered to supply any help Miss Sewell might need to complete her drawings.

The product of this editorial effort was a book of pleasant poems for children selected from *The Weary Blues* and *Fine Clothes to the Jew*. William Rose Benét said that although he was unable to rank Hughes as a first class poet on the basis of *The Dream Keeper* he was a "melodist who touches with sensitiveness the stops on his

---

[4]A complete description of this period in Hughes's life is supplied in *I Wonder as I Wander* (New York: Rinehart, 1956).

[5]Letter from Helen Hayes to Langston Hughes dated January 11, 1932. Yale University Library.

[6]Letter from Blanche Knopf to Langston Hughes dated February 1, 1932, Yale University Library.

black flute."[7] Brawley revealed his personal enthusiasm for conservative, non-racial writing when he evaluated the children's verses in *The Dream Keeper* as "among the best things Hughes had done."[8] The reviewer in the *New York Times* merely remarked that the book should be "a welcome addition to the shelves of school and public libraries."[9]

In his second book for young people Hughes associated himself with an author-friend, Arna Bontemps. The two young poets turned their talents, surprisingly enough, to the creation of a story about children in Haiti. *Popo and Fifina*, as Bontemps explains, was a joint writing effort based on Hughes's impressions from a vacation trip:

> I suggested to Langston the children's book about Haiti. He had not until then considered the idea of writing a juvenile, but he assured me that all the material was at my disposal if I wanted to work with it. We talked it out, prepared an outline and showed it to Virginia Kirkus, then the Juvenile Editor at Harper's, and to Louise Seaman, who was in charge of the Department at Macmillan. Kirkus couldn't see it, but Seaman picked it up immediately. In the next few weeks Langston continued to feed me material, and I continued to write. He got so interested that he began doing some of the writing himself. I remember in particular that he wrote the whole chapter about "Drums in the Night."[10]

Popo and Fifina is a simple story describing the everyday events in the lives of a brother and sister. It is a quietly developed tale incorporating vivid descriptions of Haiti with perceptive insights about children. The authors seemed particularly adept at presenting the children's sadness at leaving their old home and their excitement at entering a new environment. As the *New York Times* reviewer noted, "it might be well if all travel stories were written by poets."[11]

[7]William Rose Benét, Review of *The Dream Keeper*, by Langston Hughes, *Saturday Review of Literature*, IX (November 12, 1932), p. 241.

[8]Brawley, *The Negro Genius*, p. 250.

[9]A. T. Eaton, Review of *The Dream Keeper*, by Langston Hughes, *New York Times* (July 17, 1932), p. 13.

[10]Letter to author from Arna Bontemps dated April 4, 1963.

[11]A. T. Eaton, Review of *Popo and Fifina*, by Langston Hughes and Arna Bontemps, *New York Times* (October 23, 1932), p. 13.

The book went through seven reprintings and sold well until 1960, when Macmillan finally let it go out of print. Bontemps himself identified the book's lasting interest:

> For a whole generation, we might say, it was about the only book on Haiti American youngsters could find in the children's departments of their libraries.[12]

In the 1920's Hughes wrote mainly poetry. In the 1930's he wrote mainly prose. His entire output of collected adult poetry in the 1930's is found in three brief pamphlets, *Dear Lovely Death, Scottsboro Limited,* and *A New Song.* The first of these, published in 1931, was a hand-printed edition prepared by Hughes's friends, Joel and Amy Spingarn. The hand-set type and handmade paper furnished an unusual format for Hughes's lyrics. It is no disparagement to Hughes to say that, in this case, the format dominated the poetry, although that too is striking. The first poem, "Drum," is a melodious chant on death:

> Bear in mind
> That death is a drum
> Beating forever
> Till the last worms come
> To answer its call,
> Till the last stars fall,
> Until the last atom
> Is no atom at all,
> Until time is lost
> And there is no air
> And space itself
> Is nothing nowhere,
> Death is a drum,
> A signal drum,
> Calling life
> To come!
> Come!
> Come![13]

Like "Drum," the rest of the poetry in *Dear Lovely Death* is dour and moody, quite apart from Hughes's usual carefree style. Because

[12]Letter to author from Arna Bontemps dated April 4, 1963.
[13]Hughes, *Selected Poems*, p. 87.

of this, the poems seem experiments rather than a transcription of deeply felt emotion.

Scottsboro Limited, issued in 1932, was more in the critical mood of the 1930's. It contained a one-act play and four poems that centered on the seizure and trial of the so-called Scottsboro boys. Some of the facts in the case are difficult to evaluate but it seems plain that Alabama justice had abridged the constitutional rights of the boys in matters of proper arrest and fair trial. The same sentiment that supported Sacco and Vanzetti ten years before gathered behind the jailed Scottsboro boys. Kay Boyle, Muriel Rukeyser and others wrote impassioned verse on the travesty of Alabama justice. Hughes's pamphlet questioned the whole system of southern law, the handling of the boys, and the morality of the girls. One poem, "Justice," is in the best tradition of the protest literature of the 1930's:

> Justice is a blind goddess
> To this we blacks are wise
> Her bandage hides two festering sores
> That once perhaps were eyes.[14]

As an adjunct to the wide publicity given to the Scottsboro Case in the Soviet Union, Hughes's pamphlet was translated and printed in large quantity. This was precisely the kind of literature the Communist Party encouraged.

In 1938 The International Worker's Order published a collection of seventeen protest poems entitled *A New Song*. In the introduction Michael Gold, editor of *New Masses*, explained that *A New Song* would be the first of a number of pamphlets produced to enrich the workers' awareness of life through literature. Because of his knowledge of Negro deprivation, Hughes was introduced as an author who could speak for the underprivileged of all races.

Perhaps the finest poem in the collection, the dramatic "Let America Be America Again," contrasts the American dream of equality with the unfortunate position that was reality for many Americans. Hughes wrote:

[14]Langston Hughes, *Scottsboro Limited* (New York: Golden Stair Press, 1931), p. 1.

> Who said the free? Not me!
> Surely not me. The millions on relief today?
> The millions shot down when we strike?
> The millions who have nothing for our pay?
> For all the dreams we've dreamed
> And all the songs we've sung
> And all the hopes we've held
> And all the flags we've hung,
> The millions who have nothing for our pay—
> Except the dream that's almost dead today.[15]

Finally, with all its mistakes and injustice America, Hughes says, is good. The spirit of "Let America Be America Again" is basically optimistic:

> O, yes,
> I say it plain,
> America never was America to me,
> And yet I swear this oath—
> America will be![16]

Unlike many authors of his day Hughes saw the weaknesses of democracy without despair. As John Parker observed, "his healthy view of tomorrows yet to be is an outgrowth of his faith in the essential goodness of the human heart and hence the ultimate flowering of the democratic way of life in America."[17] Like Whitman, Hughes places his faith in the people:

> We, the people, must redeem
> The land, the mines, the plants, the rivers,
> The mountains and the endless plain—
> All, all the stretch of these great green states—
> And make America again.[18]

The poem emphasizes one of Hughes's favorite themes, that the strength and hope of democracy resides in the common man.

"Let America Be America Again" is also significant in illustrating Hughes's widening concern for all mankind. Earlier his verse

[15]Langston Hughes, *A New Song* (New York: International Worker's Order, 1938), p. 10.

[16]*Ibid.*, p. 11.

[17]John Parker, "Tomorrow in the Writing of Langston Hughes," *College English*, X (May, 1949), p. 441.

[18]Hughes, *A New Song*, p. 11.

spoke only of the Negro, but now it encompassed unfortunates of all races:

> I am the poor white, fooled and pushed apart
> I am the Negro bearing slavery's scars.
> I am the red man driven from the land
> I am the immigrant clutching the hope I seek
> And finding only the same old stupid plan.
> Of dog eat dog, of mighty crush the weak.[19]

Hughes recognizes in his poem that multitudes share the social and economic burdens of the Negro. He sorrows for them in the same way he sorrows for members of his own race. Like Whitman he could say:

> In all people I see myself, none more
> and not one a barley-corn less.[20]

"Let America Be America Again" is a powerful poem in the Whitman tradition speaking for the humble folk of all creeds and colors.

Other poems in *A New Song* restate salient points from "Let America Be America Again," apparently the theme poem of the collection. The people, Hughes says in "Union," must band together:

> Not me alone
> I know now—
> But all the whole oppressed
> Poor world,
> White and black
> Must put their hands with mine
> To shake the pillars of those temples
> Wherein the false gods dwell
> And worn out altars stand
> Too well defended,
> And the rule of greed's upheld
> That must be ended.[21]

In "Open Letter to the South," Hughes suggests the ultimate in camaraderie; friendship between white and black workers in the South:

[19]*Ibid.*, p. 9.
[20]Walt Whitman, "Song of Myself," *Walt Whitman Representative Selections*, ed. Floyd Stovall (New York: American Book, 1934), p. 21.
[21]Hughes, *A New Song*, p. 31.

> We did not know that we were brothers
> Now we know!
> Out of that brotherhood
> Let power grow![22]

From this union of black and white will come "A New Song."

> Revolt! Arise!
> The Black
> And White World
> Shall be one!
> The Worker's World![23]

In many of these poems the author projects no mere dream of change, but an urgency and a threat of violence. This urgency, present in "Let America Be America Again," dominates "Park Bench" and "Pride." In "Park Bench" Hughes says:

> I beg a dime for dinner—
> You got a butler and a maid.
> But I'm wakin up!
> Say, ain't you afraid
>
> That I might, just maybe,
> In a year or two,
> Move on over
> To Park Avenue?[24]

Violence is even more explicit in "Pride."

> For honest work
> You proffer me poor pay,
> For honest dreams
> Your spit is in my face.
> And so my fist is clenched—
> Today—
> To strike your face.[25]

Apparently, Hughes had come to agree with the ideological line called for in 1937 by Richard Wright. Negro writers, Wright said, "must view society as something becoming rather than something fixed and admired, they must stand shoulder to shoulder with Negro

---

[22]*Ibid.*, p. 28.
[23]*Ibid.*, p. 25.
[24]*Ibid.*, p. 12.
[25]*Ibid.*, p. 16.

workers in mood and outlook."[26] According to this standard, literature by Negro writers must contain a practical message for the
working man. A poem like Hughes's "Song of Spain" addressed
directly to the workers was well suited to the philosophy:

> Workers, make no bombs again!
> Workers, mine no gold again!
> Workers, lift no hand again
> To build up profits for the rape of Spain!
> Workers, see yourself in Spain![27]

In these poems Hughes abandoned his usual objective commentary on Negro life in order to preach the doctrines of socialism.
As a result, *A New Song* is little more than a polemic for brother-
hood, justice, and union. The poems can only be recommended as
characteristic of the proletarian trend of the 1930's. As Malcolm
Cowley has suggested, this kind of poetry was perhaps "more diversi-
fied in manners and messages than proletarian fiction, but most of
it has become almost as hard to read."[28] Aside from "Let America
Be America Again" Hughes's protest poems of the 1930's are narrow
in concept and monotonous.

By 1940, in the midst of war prosperity, many writers found
the old proletarian themes no longer appropriate. In his poetry and
prose Hughes began to re-emphasize the foolishness and frustration
that make up American race relations. "Note on Commercial
Theatre," published in *The Crisis* in March 1940, is a sample of
this return to race material.

> You've taken my blues and gone—
> You sing 'em on Broadway
> And you sing 'em in the Hollywood Bowl,
> And you mixed 'em up with symphonies
> And you fixed 'em
> So they don't sound like me.
> Yep, you done taken my blues and gone.

[26]Richard Wright, "Blueprint for Negro Writing," *The New Challenge*, I
(Fall, 1937), p. 55.

[27]Hughes, *A New Song*, p. 22.

[28]Malcolm Cowley, "They All Waited for Lefty," *Saturday Review*, XLVIII
(June 6, 1964), p. 18.

>You also took my spirituals and gone.
>You put me in Macbeth and Carmen Jones
>And all kinds of Swing Mikados
>And in everything but what's about me—
>But someday somebody'll
>Stand up and talk about me,
>And write about me—
>Black and beautiful—[29]

As Hughes goes on to point out, he will be that somebody. After a none-too-successful sojourn emulating the poets of the masses, Hughes directed his major interests back to the world of the American Negro.

In the 1930's Hughes wrote chiefly prose. His favorite form was the short story. While he was in Russia, he says, he had a sudden vision of the potential of the short story after reading D. H. Lawrence's "The Lovely Lady," and "The Rocking Horse Winner."

>A night or two after I had read the Lawrence stories, . . . I began to write a short story. I had been saying to myself all day, "If D. H. Lawrence can write such psychologically powerful accounts of folks in England, that send shivers up and down my spine, maybe I could write stories like his about folks in America."[30]

The first product to come from this new interest in fiction was "Cora Unashamed." Like many of his later efforts this was an examination of a Negro-white relationship.

Cora, a Negro cook, laments the loss of life when her employer's daughter is forced to have an abortion. Shortly, she has further cause for grief when the young mother herself dies. Cora speaks out against the hypocrisy of the white folks and consequently loses her job. As Redding points out, however, "Cora knows neither victory nor defeat—simply nullification."[31] The society that should have accepted her cast her out without apology. As a symbol of the Negro, unloved and misunderstood, Cora has no place in the white man's world.

"Cora Unashamed" is a good story from many points of view. Cora dominates the story from beginning to end with a subtle, per-

[29]Hughes, *Selected Poems*, p. 190.
[30]Hughes, *I Wonder as I Wander*, p. 213.
[31]Redding, *To Make A Poet Black*, p. 51.

suasive strength. Essentially, she is one of a long line of characters cast from Hughes's conception that the lives of the common folk provide the most legitimate source material for the American Negro writer. Wise and humble, she is the prototype of the uneducated Negroes used to people his most effective writing. She is related both to the early blues "heroes" and to lively characters of more recent date, such as Madam Alberta K. Johnson and Jessie B. Semple.

Once started in the short story genre Hughes pursued it with vigor and success. *Esquire, The American Mercury,* and *Scribner's Magazine* accepted his first stories written in Moscow. Aside from the help these publications undoubtedly gave Hughes's literary reputation, "the money," he comments, "came in handy."[32]

Back in the United States after a year and a half abroad, Hughes settled down to write prose at Noel Sullivan's comfortable home in Carmel-by-the-Sea. It was a productive period:

> At Carmel I worked ten or twelve hours a day, and turned out at least one story or completed article every week, sometimes more. . . . To Noel Sullivan I am indebted for the first long period in my life when I was able, unworried and unhurried, to stay quietly in one place and devote myself to writing.[33]

Hughes's observations of various aspects of Asian culture appeared in *Travel, Asia,* and *Theatre Arts.* His largest fee came from *The Woman's Home Companion* for an article describing the harems he had seen in southern Asia.

More interesting than these descriptive articles, however, are a group of realistic short stories centered on Negro-white relationships. "A Good Job Gone," for example, treats the issue of miscegenation. The narrator, who is neither very bright nor noble, works as a house boy for Mr. Lloyd, a wealthy white man. His pleasant job ends abruptly after Pauline, a Harlem beauty, enters the white man's life. Pauline is no easy conquest for Mr. Lloyd. Independent and proud, she drives her erstwhile lover into acute alcoholism and melancholia. When Mr. Lloyd sees Pauline with her Harlem boy friend, "a tall black good-looking guy with a diamond on his finger,"[34] his spirit

[32]Hughes, *I Wonder As I Wander,* p. 214.

[33]*Ibid.,* p. 285.

[34]Langston Hughes, *Something in Common and Other Stories* (New York: Hill and Wang, 1963), p. 37.

is broken. As the story ends, Mr. Lloyd is removed to a sanitorium.

In theme, this story is closely allied to "Luani of the Jungle" since both center on white men who can't accept the loss of their loved one to a black man. Luani and Pauline have much in common; they are both black and beautiful, both strong-minded and proud. Pauline speaks for Luani when she says, "No white man's gonna own me."[35] In total effect, however, the two stories are very different. Luani's rejection of her husband seems contrived and unmotivated while Pauline's protest appears inevitable. As Pauline says, "Hell, I'm from Arkansas where the crackers lynch niggers in the streets. How could I like 'em?"[36] Luani is a weak symbol; Pauline is a real person. Between 1926 and 1934 Hughes had developed a conception of characterization and plot development which enabled him to recast "Luani of the Jungle" into a tightly knit, compelling story. In "A Good Job Gone" Hughes records the emotions of whites and blacks with sureness and insight.

It is not surprising that several of Hughes's early stories deal with patronage. While some Negro artists achieved a good understanding with their white sponsors, many knew the kind of absurd relationship Hughes described in "Slave on the Block." As the story opens an artistic couple, Michael and Anne Carraway, invite a young Negro boy to live with them as part time butler, part time muse. According to the Carraways' uncritical standards Luther is black and therefore beautiful:

> "He *is* the jungle," said Anne when she saw him.
> "He's 'I Couldn't Hear Nobody Pray'," said Michael.[37]

At first Luther seems happy to pose for Anne and to sing spirituals for guests, but gradually he reveals more of his true self by working as little as possible and sleeping with Mattie, the cook. When Michael's forthright mother accuses Luther of impudence, he and Mattie quit. As the story ends Mattie puts things into proper perspective:

[35]*Ibid.*, p. 38.
[36]*Ibid.*
[37]Langston Hughes, *The Langston Hughes Reader* (New York: Braziller, 1958), p. 12.

"I does my work," said Mattie. "After that I don't want to be painted or asked to sing songs, nor nothing like that."[38]

This story asks for understanding based on mutual interest and honesty. Nothing is gained, as Hughes say in "Slave on the Block," by loving the Negro race indiscriminately.

Hughes reserved his bitterest comments on racial intolerance to stories of the South. In "Father and Son," for example, he describes how the southern caste system can lead to violence and death. Bert, the son of a plantation owner and a colored kitchen maid, returns home from college determined not to be what he calls "a white folks' nigger."[39] As the story unfolds Bert refuses to fall into the stereotypes of the past. An incident in the town post office, where Bert is accused of talking back to a white woman, touches off the final tragedies of the story. In a moment of rage Bert strangles his father and then commits suicide as the mob comes to lynch him. Their blood lust is satisfied with the lynching of Bert's innocent brother Willie. Hughes closes the story with a newspaper account of the death of the father. "The dead man," it says, "left no heirs."[40]

The extremes of violence described in this story produce little meaning. Bert and his father, more symbolic than real, fail to arouse much sympathy or anger. It is obvious from the first that no good can come of Bert's return to the plantation. His mother urges:

"Why didn't you act right, son? Oh-o-o!" moaned Cora. "You can't get nothin' from white folks if you don't act right." "Act like Willie, you mean, and the rest of these cotton pickers? Then I don't want anything."[41]

In a florid passage Hughes compares Bert's return to the plantation to the explosive ingredient poured into a test tube:

Oh, test tube of life! Crucible of the South, find the right powder and you'll never be the same again—the cotton will blaze and the cabins will burn and the chains will be broken and men, all of a sudden, will shake hands, black men and white men, like steel meeting steel![42]

[38]*Ibid.*, p. 14.
[39]Hughes, *Something in Common*, p. 119.
[40]*Ibid.*, p. 136.
[41]*Ibid.*, p. 125.
[42]*Ibid.*, p. 119.

At the end of "Father and Son" black and white are no nearer a handshake than at the beginning. The story is a sermon on the evils of the southern system, a sermon that seems too long and too melodramatic to be effective. "Father and Son" deals with an important topic, but its slow pace and stereotyped characters leave the serious reader dissatisfied.

In "Home," on the other hand, Hughes describes a believable incident in the life of Roy Williams, a Negro musician. The hero, after some considerable success abroad, returns to his home seriously ill. His arrival in the little southern town is chronicled with a sure sense of reality:

> "An uppity nigger," said the white loafers when they saw him standing, slim and elegant, on the station platform in the September sunlight, surrounded by his bags with the bright stickers. Roy had got off a Pullman—something unusual for a Negro in those parts.
> "God damn!" said the white loafers.[43]

Roy finds the one person at home who understands his music is Miss Reese, the white music teacher at the high school. This friendship leads to Roy's death. One evening as he walks through the business district, Miss Reese stops him with a greeting; he bows and extends his hand, "They smiled at each other, the sick young colored man and the aging music teacher."[44] This is more than the local ruffians can stand. Roy is struck down, trampled, and dragged off to the woods. There, his body was left hanging "strung from a tree at the edge of town, . . . like a violin for the wind to play."[45]

All the deficiencies of "Father and Son" are corrected in "Home." In the first place, Roy Williams is credible and lifelike while Bert and his father are mere puppets. "Home" is directed to a single point while "Father and Son" introduces extraneous background information, rambles through a psychological study of motives, and generally exhausts itself in diversity. Reading "Father and Son" is like watching a tedious melodrama; "Home" strikes the reader as both realistic and dramatic. One anthologist has pointed

[43]Langston Hughes, "Home" *Many Colored Fleece*, ed. Sister Mary Gable (New York: Sheed and Ward, 1950), p. 136.
[44]*Ibid.*, p. 144.
[45]*Ibid.*, p. 145.

out how "powerfully" this simple story projects "the stark-naked sinfulness, horror, ugliness and stupidity of the white man's refusal to accept his pigmented brother in Christ."[46]

Several stories written at this time deal with sex relationships between the races. "Mother and Child," "Red-Headed Baby," and "Little Dog" all explore the various complications of interracial hypocrisy and lust. In "Little Dog," perhaps the most sensitive of the group, Hughes describes the surging emotional attraction a white spinster feels for her Negro janitor. At the end of the story the spinster decides to move to another apartment. Hughes handles these potentially sensational themes with extreme delicacy.

Since Hughes has never overlooked dishonest or weak conduct in his own race, some of his stories turn the rasp of satire against Negro behavior. Dr. Brown, in "Professor," visits a white philanthropist to obtain funds for his small college, although he knows that by accepting he will prolong Jim Crow education. At the dinner table Dr. Brown says all the right things:

> "The American Negro must not be taken in by communism," Dr. Bulwick was saying with great positiveness as the butler passed the peas. "He won't," agreed Dr. Brown. "I assure you, our leadership stands squarely against it." . . . "America has done too much for the Negro," said Mr. Chandler, "for him to seek to destroy it." Dr. Brown bobbed and bowed.[47]

He is willing to sacrifice his ideals so "he might take his family to South America in the summer where for three months they wouldn't feel like Negroes."[48] In this story Hughes shows his profound disenchantment for the so-called "race leaders" who selfishly betray their own people.

Again, in "Trouble With the Angels," Hughes lampoons Negro timidity. The story describes how a group of influential Negroes attempt to gain admission to a segregated performance of a play with an all-Negro cast. Only Logan, who holds a minor part in the play, reacts to the injustice of the situation and attempts to organize a strike. The other actors, who consider Logan an agitator, not only

---

[46]Sister Mary Gable, ed. *Many Colored Fleece*, p. 134.
[47]Langston Hughes, "Professor," *Anvil*, II (May/June, 1935), p. 7.
[48]*Ibid.*, p. 8.

refuse to strike but they leave him to face the sheriff alone. The story concludes as Logan is taken to jail:

> Most of the actors *wanted* to think Logan was crying because he was being arrested—but in their souls they knew that was not why he wept.[49]

Logan is the man we all would wish to be while the lesser angels reflect what we often are. It is a particular cause for sadness, Hughes reminds us, when a race has suffered too long to be brave.

Late in 1933 Mrs. Knopf responded warmly to the suggestion that a group of Hughes's stories might make a worthwhile book.

> I held your letter over until I received the manuscript and read it. I think it is absolutely top notch and superb. Some of the stories of course, are infinitely better than some of the others, but as a whole they are grand and I congratulate you. . . . I am very excited about these and delighted that you have done them.[50]

Early the following year the book of stories appeared under the appropriate title, *The Ways of White Folks.* Taken as a whole the collection points out how the worst characteristics of white folks often come to the surface as they deal with their Negro brothers. Horace Gregory in his review of the book recognized Hughes's objectives and considered the result a victory for the artist. Concluding his review with high praise Gregory said, "I suspect Langston Hughes is revealing here that mysterious quality in writing that we call genius."[51] Sherwood Anderson called some of Hughes's white folks "caricatures," but generally approved the style and content of the stories. "Mr. Hughes has a fine talent," Anderson said, "I do not see how anyone can blame him for his hatreds."[52]

The best stories in *The Ways of White Folks,* "Cora Unashamed," "Slave on the Block," "Home," and "A Good Job Gone,"

[49]Langston Hughes, "Trouble With The Angels," *New Theatre,* VII (July, 1935), p. 7.

[50]Letter from Blanche Knopf to Langston Hughes dated December 18, 1933. Yale University Library.

[51]Horace Gregory, Review of *The Ways of White Folks,* by Langston Hughes, *New York Herald Tribune Books* (July. 1, 1934), p. 4.

[52]Sherwood Anderson, Review of *The Ways of White Folks,* by Langston Hughes, *The Nation,* CXXXIX (July 11, 1934), p. 50.

convey the truth about Negro-white relationships with feeling and artistry. Although, as Gregory points out, "Langston Hughes never allows his readers to forget his central purpose,"[53] he is, at the same time, able to transmit that purpose with well-rounded characterization and dramatic situation. Hughes makes his message palatable with an ability to write terse, believable prose.

In most of these stories, as in Hughes's other writing, the emphasis is on everyday life. The hero may be a fine musician, as in "Home," but more often he is an ordinary fellow trying to keep a job or get a girl. If the Negroes come out better than their white associates it is only because of the essential dishonesty of the white man's position in race relations. This is the very point Hughes wishes to stress. In "Slave on the Block" and "Little Dog" the whites love the Negroes for the wrong reasons. In "Home" and "Father and Son" they hate them with a similar imbalance. In effect, *The Ways of White Folks* calls for a reasonable treatment of the Negro, for tolerance and common sense.

In spite of the favorable reviews the book failed to sell. Eight months after it came out Alfred Knopf wrote:

> Book sales are pretty sad these days and it doesn't look as if either of us would make anything out of THE WAYS OF WHITE FOLKS. But I still think it has not done too badly, for a book of stories and it has certainly solidified your reputation.[54]

However well established Hughes's reputation may have been, conservative editors continued to reject his work. In a letter to Maxim Lieber, Hughes's agent, an *Atlantic* editor said:

> Why is it that authors think it is their function to lay the flesh bare and rub salt in the wound? The Langston Hughes story [Home] is powerful and delicate, but we cannot forget that most people read for pleasure and certainly there is no pleasure to be found here.[55]

This was criticism Hughes had received before. The white press, in

[53]Gregory, H., Review of *The Ways of White Folks, New York Herald Tribune Books* (July 1, 1934), p. 4.

[54]Letter from Alfred Knopf to Langston Hughes dated August 14, 1934. Yale University Library.

[55]Letter from an *Atlantic Magazine* editor [name withheld] to Maxim Lieber dated January 8, 1934. Yale University Library.

some cases, didn't want to print the facts of life, while the Negro journals avoided any portrayal that might be unflattering. Fortunately, there were magazines like *Esquire* and publishers like Knopf who were willing to take a chance with controversy.

Occasionally, however, Hughes's efforts were not accepted by the Knopfs. They, of course, maintained the right to reject any manuscript at any time even from an old friend. This happened for the first time in 1934, when Hughes offered his travel impressions on Russia. Mrs. Knopf put the decision as delicately as possible:

> I have read the nine chapters of the Russia book that you sent me, and, although I can't tell everything from nine chapters, I am disappointed. What you have done is charming and pleasant, but it is not fresh and it is not new and I don't think it is the kind of book the public expects to come from you. . . . You are writing with more and more facility and can tackle almost anything and do it frightfully well and I can't see readers awaiting just a nice book about Russia from *your* pen.[56]

This rejection may have resulted in some coolness, for Mrs. Knopf wrote late in 1936:

> I haven't heard from you in such a long time that I am beginning to worry and wonder. What about a new book from you? Have you any plans or thoughts about one or has the theatre got you? Do let me hear.[57]

Writing constantly, Hughes had no time to sulk over the rejection of one book. He turned out plays for the Gilpin Players of Cleveland, lectured extensively, and continued to produce stories and poems.[58] In 1937 he accepted the post of war correspondent in Spain for the *Baltimore Afro-American*.

[56]Letter from Blanche Knopf to Langston Hughes dated August 3, 1934. Yale University Library.

[57]Letter from Blanche Knopf to Langston Hughes dated September 28, 1936. Yale University Library.

[58]In answer to Mrs. Knopf's letter of September 28, 1936, Hughes wrote on March 1, 1937, "I have been meaning for a very long time to answer your note about the possibilities of a new book. The truth of the matter is that I have been devoting a great deal of my time to plays, and have five in manuscript. The one advantage of living in Cleveland is that here we have the only permanent Negro dramatic theatre, the Gilpin Players, who do six plays regularly every season, and who are quite willing to put on all of mine,—which is a great help to one trying to be a playwright. One of them, a comedy,

After writing poetry, short stories, a novel, and plays Hughes decided to attempt the story of his own life. This project had evidently been under consideration for some time, as indicated in a letter to Mrs. Knopf:

> Another idea I've had recently is to do the autobiographical book that you once thought might be amusing, and for which I now feel I have sufficient objectivity, and many more adventures like Russia, and Japan to put inside it.[59]

Mrs. Knopf agreed that the autobiography might be successful and in the fall of 1939 she approved the first draft:

> I have now finished THE BIG SEA and Harold Strauss in our office has, and we agree absolutely 1) that it is a fine perform-ance and 2) that it needs certain revisions. I congratulate you on the job and am really delighted with what it is and what it is going to be. . . . You have written an autobiography and every-thing that you write that has happened to you seems to be good. However, when you make courtesy gestures it seems to us to be quite out of order and not any longer fresh and important. . . . I also think it is too full of Carl, Thurman, Toomer, Hurston etc. excepting for the later adventures with Miss Hurston; . . . I think you have done a very good job and with these changes will have something important and possibly that we can really sell, which is what you are after and we are.[60]

Hughes cut the manuscript as directed, although he insisted on retaining references to important personalities of the twenties:

> Also the people to whom the most space is devoted there, Carl Van Vechten, Wallace Thurman, Zora Hurston, Rev. Becton were people who were certainly very much a part of that era, their names known to thousands of folks. . . . One could not write about life in Negro Washington without including the names I mention therein and who are nationally known to most

LITTLE HAM, was quite successful last spring, having a run of three weeks. . . . Would you, by any chance, be interested in publishing a volume of my plays? There are so few plays available for Negro amateur and college groups, and most of the old ones, like O'Neill's EMPEROR JONES have been produced so much that they no longer create any interest."

[59]Letter from Langston Hughes to Blanche Knopf dated March 1, 1937. Yale University Library.

[60]Letter from Blanche Knopf to Langston Hughes dated November 28, 1939. Yale University Library.

colored people, . . . I mention this so that you won't think they're being included as a "courtesy gesture," . . . although I hope most of my book will be interesting to the general public regardless of color, some small portions of it may have vital meaning only to my own people. But that, it seems to me, would only add to the final integrity and truth of the work as a whole. And I am trying to write a truthful and honest book.[61]

In *The Big Sea* Hughes traces his life from his early years in the Midwest through his travels abroad down to 1929, when the depression ended the Negro Renaissance. The protagonist of *The Big Sea* is a warmly human person whose chief characteristic is a vast curiosity about the world and its people. "The peculiar flavor of this book," as Edwin Embree commented, "is not that the boy was a Negro, but that he was a poet. . . . It is written in beautiful English and is a fine tale."[62] Throughout the book Hughes is as honest about the difficult times in his life as he is about his many successes. The unhappy period with his father in Mexico and the break with his patron are handled with restraint. Again, when he discusses his controversial relationship with Van Vechten, he is both natural and convincing.

The Big Sea is valuable not only as the story of a man's life but as a candid look at an era which, according to Richard Wright, Hughes analyzed with "humor, urbanity and objectivity."[63] Hughes's autobiography is a superb inside view of the Harlem Renaissance. He knew the important people, wrote for the best journals, and enjoyed the fun and frolic of cabaret society. His report on Harlem in the twenties is unequaled for honesty and breadth.

On another level, *The Big Sea* shows how, through gradual perception, the Negro artist forms his ideas on racial problems. Hughes's life story is a vivid example of this process. In *The Saturday Review of Literature* Oswald Villard said, "This is a moving, a well worthwhile book which should have been written; a most valuable contribution to the struggle of the Negro for life and justice

[61]Letter from Langston Hughes to Blanche Knopf dated February 8, 1940. Yale University Library.

[62]Edwin Embree, Review of *The Big Sea*, by Langston Hughes, *Survey Graphic*, XXX (February, 1941), p. 96.

[63]Richard Wright, Review of *The Big Sea*, by Langston Hughes, *The New Republic*, CIII (October 28, 1940), p. 600.

and freedom and intellectual liberty in America."[64] Basically, Hughes's autobiography tells the story of an interesting life simply and without pretense.

During the 1930's Hughes joined many other writers, white and black, in an emphasis on social realism. His short stories about racial misunderstandings and his poems on political and economic problems indicate a serious concern with man in society. Two poems of similar theme, "Advertisement for the Waldorf Astoria," and "Let America Be America Again," the first written at the beginning of the decade the second at the end, provide significant testimony to Hughes's preoccupation with the fate of the common man. The hope of democracy, Hughes says in both poems, lies with the common man, while its past failures stem directly from mishandling by the privileged few. Speaking for all believers in freedom and human dignity Hughes transmits a powerful affirmation of faith in democracy. His writing of the 1930's emphasizes the ability and right of the ordinary man to govern his own affairs and those of the nation with wisdom and justice. Jean Wagner has remarked, "Ni Harlem, ni sa race ne sauraient d'ailleurs revendiquer Langston Hughes tout entier, car au delà des frontières de sa couleur, il a chanté les aspirations éternelles de tous les hommes épris de liberté."[65]

The decade of the depression brought Hughes success in several new mediums. He was no longer known solely as a poet, but as a writer with a variety of talents at his disposal. The poems he wrote during this time are in harmony with the proletarian movement, but because of their narrow concept are less memorable than the poetry he wrote in the twenties. His best work of the decade, a series of powerful short stories and an enlightening autobiography, strengthened his position as an interpreter of the Negro. He was, as Richard Bardolph says, "already in the early 1930's, as he remains today, the unofficial laureate of the race, perennially young, ebullient and amused."[66]

[64]Oswald Villard, Review of *The Big Sea*, by Langston Hughes, *Saturday Review of Literature*, XXII (August 31, 1940), p. 12.

[65]Wagner, *Les Poètes Nègres des Etats-Unis*, p .533.

[66]Richard Bardolph, *The Negro Vanguard* (New York: Random House, 1961), p. 203.

chapter four

Mature Years 1941—1965

From river to river
Up town and down,
There's liable to be confusion
When a dream gets kicked around.
    You talk like
    they don't kick
    dreams around
    Downtown.
I expect they do—
But I'm talking about
Harlem to you!
        "Lenox Avenue Mural."

"I done got my feet caught in the sweet
flypaper of life—and I'll be dogged if
I want to get loose."
        "Sweet Flypaper of Life."

In the 1940's, 1950's, and early 1960's, Hughes continued to write poetry, short stories, and drama, but he also took on several new tasks such as editing anthologies and translating works by French and Spanish authors. In contrast to his earlier emphasis on protest, Hughes's work since 1940 has concentrated on lighter themes and life within the Negro group, not on conflict with outside groups. Because of his ability to write well for both children and adults, publishers have accepted a wide variety of books on Negro life. Among his more important achievements during this period are *The Poetry of the Negro, 1746–1949, Fight for Freedom, An African Treasury, The Sweet Flypaper of Life*, and a series of children's books on jazz, Africa, and the Negro. Between 1941 and 1965 he has also completed a second volume of autobiography, five collections of poems, one of short stories, a novel, and four volumes of sketches about that lovable, barroom philosopher, Jesse B. Semple. He has written librettos, song lyrics, plays, and a musical comedy. Hughes functions throughout this impressive volume of literature as a wry and sympathetic commentator on the world of the Negro.

Harlem is Hughes's principal subject and inspiration during recent years. Aside from two academic appointments he lived this period in New York, close to his favorite people, the urban Negroes.[1] His poetry, more than ever, reflects the rhythms of contemporary jazz, while his major literary figure, Jessie B. Semple, is drawn wholly from the street life of the city. No one can match Hughes's ability to transcribe the speech and emotions of the average Harlemite.

Aside from *Jim Crow's Last Stand*, a pamphlet of poems issued early in the 1940's, protest almost disappears from Hughes's writing. When it does appear it is likely to be embodied in humor rather than in bitterness. His poem "Me and the Mule" might be taken as a personal defense for this new approach to race:

> My old mule,
> He's got a grin on his face.
> He's been a mule so long
> He's forgot about his race.
>
> I'm like that old mule—
> Black—and don't give a damn!
> You got to take me
> Like I am.[2]

Blues frequently run through Hughes's recent poetry but the subjects are lighter in mood than those in his early blues. A poem like "Early Evening Quarrel" is typical of Hughes's post-war production.

> Where is that sugar, Hammond,
> I sent you this morning to buy?
> I say, where is that sugar

[1]Hughes spent the academic year 1947–1948 as Instructor of Creative Writing at Atlanta University and the academic year 1949–1950 as Poet-in-Residence at the Laboratory School, University of Chicago.
[2]Hughes, *Selected Poems*, p. 125.

> I sent you this morning to buy?
> Coffee without sugar
> Makes a good woman cry.[3]

Hughes wrote to Mrs. Knopf about this style of poetry as follows:

> I selected a number [of poems] that it seems to me might suit the public mood of the moment, the trend toward lighter things during the war, and the current interest in blues music and swing, Negro bands and singers.[4]

Mrs. Knopf agreed that such poetry would have a market and published the collection in 1942 as *Shakespeare in Harlem*. Hughes introduced the book with a note of explanation saying:

> A book of light verse. Afro-American in the blues mood. Poems syncopated and variegated in the colors of Harlem, Beale Street, West Dallas, and Chicago's South Side. Blues, ballads, and reels to be read aloud, crooned, shouted, recited and sung. Some with gestures, some not—as you like. None with a far away voice.[5]

Most of the poems in the collection are based on jazz rhythms or street songs of the city. "Declaration," for example, sounds like a children's skipping game.

> If I were a sea-lion
> Swimming in the sea,
> I would swim to China
> And you never would see me.
> No!
> You never would
> See me.[6]

"Free Man," another bit of street corner wisdom, could probably be heard on many Harlem doorsteps.

> You can catch the wind,
> You can catch the sea,
> But you can't, pretty mama,
> Ever catch me.

[3]*Ibid.*, p. 44.

[4]Letter from Langston Hughes to Blanche Knopf dated January 2, 1939. Yale University Library.

[5]Langston Hughes, *Shakespeare in Harlem* (New York: Alfred A. Knopf, 1942), p. iii.

[6]*Ibid.*, p. 22.

You can tame a rabbit,
Even tame a bear,
But you'll never, pretty mama,
Keep me caged up here.[7]

Other pieces, like "Little Lyric of Great Importance," are lightning flashes of wit:

I wish the rent
Was heaven sent.[8]

This is poetry for fun. It is difficult to understand Arthur Davis's evaluation of the book as containing "no bright colors . . . only the sombre and realistic shades appropriate to the depiction of a community that has somehow lost its grip on things."[9] The reviewer in *Poetry* came closer to the essence of the book when he remarked, "This is a book of light verse and, as such, the only demands that should be made upon it are those of entertainment. It has charm and spontaneity."[10]

In one section of the book called "Mammy Songs," however, the poet does become serious. Hughes intended to produce a book based on Harlem's gaiety, but couldn't entirely avoid the unpleasant side. The few poems of protest that appear here are as powerful as any Hughes wrote in the twenties. In "Merry-Go-Round" he presents the baffling problem a little colored girl faces at the carnival:

Where is the Jim Crow section
On this merry-go-round
Mister, cause I want to ride?
Down South where I come from
White and colored
Can't sit side by side.

Down South on the train
There's a Jim Crow car.
On the bus
We're put in the back—

[7]*Ibid.*, p. 31.
[8]*Ibid.*, p. 21.
[9]Arthur Davis, "The Harlem of Langston Hughes' Poetry," *Phylon*, XIII (Winter, 1952), p. 279.
[10]H. R. Hays, Review of *Shakespeare in Harlem*, by Langston Hughes, *Poetry*, LX (July, 1942), p. 223.

> But there ain't no back
> To a merry-go-round!
> Where's the horse
> For a kid that's black?[11]

Before reading this poem, in acceptance of the Spingarn Medal in 1960, Hughes said, "Perhaps today the capital P with which some of us spell problem, is larger than the capital A with which some others would spell art. Nevertheless, I think it permissible that a poem pose a problem."[12] In "Merry-Go-Round" Hughes demonstrates that his aim, to interpret Negro life, is in no way at odds with artistic craftsmanship.

Another of the "Mammy Songs," entitled "Share Croppers," permits Hughes to employ one of his favorite themes, the destruction of the lives of the poor through the economic system. He had treated this theme in one of his earliest poems about the mills in Cleveland:

> In the dawn
> They belch red fire.
> The mills—
> Grinding new steel,
> Old men.[13]

In "Share Croppers" he wrote:

> Year by year goes by
> And we are nothing more
>
> Than a herd of Negroes
> Driven to the field—
> Plowing life away
> To make the cotton yield.[14]

The only solution, as Hughes says in "West Texas," is to pack and leave:

> Pickin' cotton in de field
> Joe said I wonder how it would feel

[11]Hughes, *Selected Poems*, p. 194.

[12]Langston Hughes, "Remarks by Langston Hughes," One page processed copy of a talk given at the NAACP 51st Annual Convention, Northrop Auditorium, University of Minnesota, Minneapolis, Minnesota, June 26, 1960. Issued by NAACP National Office, New York, New York.

[13]Hughes, *The Big Sea*, p. 29.

[14]Hughes, *Shakespeare in Harlem*, p. 77.

> For us to pack up
> Our things
> And go?
>
> So we cranked up our old Ford
> And started down the road
> And where
>   We was goin'
> We didn't know—[15]

Most of the poems in *Shakespeare in Harlem* are characteristic
of Hughes's style since the war. They emphasize jazz rhythms and,
with a few exceptions, the light mood. Many of the poems are
amusing and ironic, but few have more than a momentary impact.
As one critical study summed up the book:

> Hughes's readers had been entertained, and sometimes shocked,
> by scenes of a brutalized and amoral life in Harlem, but
> Hughes's characters lacked the dignity and poise implied in
> James Weldon Johnson's Negro sermons, and that loss vitiates
> Hughes's avowedly light verses in *Shakespeare in Harlem*.[16]

It is not possible however to limit Hughes's poetic contribution
since 1940 entirely to the light and humorous. Occasionally, he
produced lyrics like "Wisdom."

> I stand most humbly
> Before man's wisdom,
> Knowing we are not
> Really wise:
> If we were
> We'd open up the kingdom
> And make earth happy
> As the dreamed of skies.[17]

And he could write delicate nature poems like "Snail."

> Little snail,
> Dreaming as you go
> Weather and rose
> Is all you know.

[15]*Ibid.*, p. 78.

[16]Horace Gregory and Marya Zaturenska, *A History of American Poetry, 1900–
1940* (New York: Harcourt, 1942), p. 396.

[17]Langston Hughes, *Fields of Wonder* (New York: Alfred A. Knopf, 1947),
p. 107.

> Weather and rose
> Is all you see,
> Drinking
> The dewdrop's
> Mystery.[18]

Fields of Wonder, a selection of these lyrics, received little praise from reviewers who, like Hubert Creekmore, charged the poems were largely derivative of Emily Dickinson, Stephen Crane, and E. A. Robinson.[19] Although the poems have a certain appeal, they lack the unique quality Hughes projected in his Harlem verse. Hughes himself agrees with this estimate, for in 1947, he stated:

> Beauty and lyricism are really related to another world, to ivory towers, to your head in the clouds, feet floating off the earth. Unfortunately, having been born poor—and also colored—in Missouri, I was stuck in the mud from the beginning. Try as I might to float off into the clouds, poverty and Jim Crow would grab me by the heels, and right back on earth I would land. A third floor furnished room is the nearest thing I have ever had to an ivory tower.[20]

Lyric poetry was an adjunct for Hughes, not one of his main concerns.

Hughes's next published volume of verse, *One Way Ticket*, contains a more typical mixture of pride and protest poetry. Some of the protest like "Lynching Song" is strident and bitter:

> Pull at the rope!
> O, pull it high!
> Let the white folks live
> And the black boy die.[21]

but more often, as in "Still Here," it is veiled in irony:

> I've been scarred and battered.
> My hopes the wind done scattered.
> Snow has frize me, sun has baked me.

[18]*Ibid.*, p. 4.

[19]Hubert Creekmore, Review of *Fields of Wonder*, by Langston Hughes, *New York Times* (May 4, 1947), p. 10.

[20]Langston Hughes, "My Adventures as a Social Poet," *Phylon*, VIII (Fall, 1947), p. 205.

[21]Langston Hughes, *One Way Ticket* (New York: Alfred A. Knopf, 1949), p. 58.

> Looks like between 'em
> They done tried to make me
> Stop laughin', stop lovin', stop livin'—
> But I don't care!
> I'm still here![22]

In this poem we feel the strong affirmation for life and the underlying sense of fun that are the components of Hughes's best work.
He states his philosophy clearly in the last verses of "Life is Fine."

> Since I'm here living,
> I guess I will live on.
> I could've died for love—
> But for livin' I was born.
>
> You may hear me holler,
> You may see me cry—
> But I'll be dogged, sweet baby,
> If you gonna see me die.
>   Life is fine!
>   Fine as wine!
>   Life is fine![23]

Perhaps Hughes's most delightful collection of views on life and
race are gathered in the poems about Madam Alberta K. Johnson.
He introduced Madam to readers of *Poetry* and *Common Ground* in
the early 1940's and later brought all the poems together in *One
Way Ticket.* "Madam's Past History" explains something of Madam's
wide experience:

> My name is Johnson—
> Madam Alberta K.
> The Madam stands for business.
> I'm smart that way.
>
> I had a
> HAIR-DRESSING PARLOR
> Before
> The depression put
> The prices lower.
>
> Then I had a
> BARBECUE STAND
> Till I got mixed up
> With a no good man.

[22]*Ibid.,* p. 49.
[23]*Ibid.,* p. 39.

Cause I had a insurance
The WPA
Said, We can't use you
Wealthy that way.

I said,
DON'T WORRY 'BOUT ME!
Just like the song,
You WPA folks take care of yourself—
And I'll get along.

I do cooking,
Day's work, too!
Alberta K. Johnson—
Madam to you.[24]

Madam is endowed with a shrewd outlook and a sense of humor that enable her to cope with whatever hardships may come her way. In "Madam and the Rent Man" she demonstrates her straightforward method of dealing with trouble:

The rent man knocked
He said, Howdy-do?
I said, What
Can I do for you?
He said, You know
Your rent is due.

I said, Listen,
Before I'd pay
I'd go to Hades
And rot away!

The sink is broke,
The water don't run,
And you ain't done a thing
You promised to've done.

Back window's cracked.
Kitchen floor squeaks,
There's rats in the cellar,
And the attic leaks.

He said, Madam,
It's not up to me.
I'm just the agent,
Don't you see?
I said, Naturally

[24]*Ibid.*, pp. 3–4.

> You pass the buck,
> If it's money you want
> You're out of luck.
>
> He said, Madam,
> I ain't pleased!
> I said, Neither am I.
> So we agrees![25]

David Daiches has ably explained Hughes's objectives in this kind of verse. The explanation serves to clarify much of Hughes's writing. Daiches wrote:

> The ultimate meaning, the subtle vision of reality, the oblique insight into man's personality and man's fate are not for him: he has a more urgent and immediate problem, to project the living American Negro onto the page. And he does so, on the whole, with success.[26]

Besides the poems about Madam Johnson, *One Way Ticket* includes Negro sermons, blues pieces, and shouts and chants about Florida, Georgia, and the South Side of Chicago. The book is a fresh and realistic portrait of the Negro.

In Hughes's next verse collection, *Montage of a Dream Deferred*, he underlines his commitment to Harlem and its music. The poems in this group, as he explained to Mrs. Knopf, "introduced for the first time (so far as I know) into American poetry the use of contemporary Be-Bop rhythms and motifs."[27] Mrs. Knopf's reply was polite but unenthusiastic:

> I don't think we should do the poetry but I think when we come to do a selected book of verse, this should be included in part. . . . I am writing this letter to you with great difficulty—we are old friends and have had a great deal of fun publishing together. This does not mean that we haven't a fine list of your books and that we do not want to do the selected poems at some time, too, I merely mean it for these two [the book of poems and a second volume of autobiography] projects you have in mind now.[28]

[25]*Ibid.*, pp. 9–10.

[26]David Daiches, Review of *One Way Ticket*, by Langston Hughes, *New York Herald Tribune Book Review* (January 9, 1949), p. 4.

[27]Letter from Langston Hughes to Blanche Knopf dated October 31, 1949. Yale University Library.

[28]Letter from Blanche Knopf to Langston Hughes dated November 10, 1949. Yale University Library.

Holt published *Montage on a Dream Deferred* in 1951 and in 1959, Mrs. Knopf kept her promise by devoting a lengthy section of the *Selected Poems* to Hughes's jazz verse.

The poems in *Montage on a Dream Deferred* lean heavily on jazz forms, particularly boogie-woogie and be-bop. These forms, influential for a time, soon decreased in popularity and were replaced by newer fads. It is not surprising that the poetry based on these rhythms seems as transitory as the music itself. The brief "Chord," for example, is hardly one of Hughes's more memorable efforts:

> Shadow faces
> In the shadow night
> Before the early dawn
> Bops bright.[29]

Other poems in *Montage on a Dream Deferred*, like "Argument," seem to be only colorful bits of conversation:

> White is right,
> Yellow mellow,
> Black, get back!
>   Do you believe that, Jack?
> Sure do!
>
> Then you're a dope
> for which there ain't no hope.
> Black is fine!
> And, God knows,
> It's mine![30]

It may be unfair to consider individual poems from this book because, as Hughes pointed out in the preface, he intended it to be taken as one long interrelated poetic jam session.

> In terms of current Afro-American popular music . . . this poem on contemporary Harlem, like be-bop, is marked by conflicting changes, sudden nuances, sharp and impudent interjections, broken rhythms, and passages sometimes in the manner of a jam session, sometimes the popular song, punctuated by riffs, runs, breaks, and disctortions [sic] of the music of a community in transition.[31]

[29]Hughes, *Selected Poems*, p. 264.

[30]Langston Hughes, *Montage on a Dream Deferred* (New York: Henry Holt, 1951), p. 62.

[31]*Ibid.*

The underlying theme and unity of the book is built around Harlem, a city with a dream deferred. The first poem, "Dream Boogie," sets the mood with a boogie-woogie rhythm.

> Good morning, daddy!
> Ain't you heard
> The boogie-woogie rumble
> Of a dream deferred?
>
> Listen closely:
> You'll hear their feet
> Beating out and beating out a—
>   You think
>   It's a happy beat?
>
> Listen to it closely:
> Ain't you heard
> Something underneath
> like a—
>   What did I say?
>
> Sure,
> I'm happy!
> Take it away!
>   Hey, pop!
>   Re-bop!
>   Mop!
> Y-e-a-h![32]

Hughes introduces "Buddy," "Sister," "Dancer," and "Be-Bop Boys" as well as a series of places like "Bar," "Movies," and "Cafe: 3 A.M." to fill out the picture of a waiting Harlem. There is no doubt, as Babette Deutsch commented, "Langston Hughes can write pages that throb with the abrupt rhythm of popular music."[33] Beyond this however, *Montage on a Dream Deferred* seems a rather unsatisfactory experiment. Taken as poetry, and it seems impossible to place a poetic jam session in another category, the contents of this book fail to arouse either sympathy or sustained interest. In his review of *The Selected Poems*, where the final grouping consisted entirely of this be-bop verse, James Baldwin said, "Every time I read Langston

[32]*Ibid.*, p. 3.
[33]Babette Deutsch, Review of *Montage on a Dream Deferred*, by Langston Hughes, *New York Times* (May 6, 1951), p. 23.

Hughes I am amazed all over again by his genuine gifts and depressed that he has done so little with them, . . . the book contains a great deal which a more disciplined poet would have thrown into the wastebasket (almost all of the last section, for example)."[34]

The thoughtful poems of pride and the blues are rare, but when they do occur, as in "Harlem," they still have power and beauty.

> What happens to a dream deferred?
> Does it dry up
> like a raisin in the sun?
> Or fester like a sore—
> And then run?
> Does it stink like rotten meat?
> Or crust and sugar over—
> like a syrupy sweet?
> Maybe it just sags
> like a heavy load.
> Or does it explode?[35]

In only a few selections does Hughes go below the surface to probe the more important aspects of race. Wagner objectively summarized the positive and negative features of this kind of writing:

> Techniques expérimentales louables et intéressantes, somme toute, que ces tentatives pour intégrer jazz et poésie, mais dont il faut déplorer malgré tout qu'elles aient parfois franchi avec une légèreté excessive les limites au delà desquelles on ne pouvait plus sincèrement espérer servir ni le jazz authentique, ni surtout la poésie.[36]

The final poem in the book reminds us that the dreams of Harlem are still deferred:

> Between two rivers
> North of the park
> Like darker rivers
> The streets are dark.

[34]James Baldwin, Review of *The Selected Poems*, by Langston Hughes, *New York Times* (March 29, 1959), p. 6.

[35]Hughes, *Montage of a Dream Deferred*, p. 71.

[36]Wagner, *Les Poètes Nègres des Etats-Unis*, p. 459.

Black and white
Gold and brown
Chocolate-custard
Pie of a town.

Dream within a dream
Our dream deferred
Good morning, daddy!

Ain't you heard?[37]

Much of the poetry in *Montage on a Dream Deferred* may be read to jazz, a popular night-club activity which Hughes himself indulged in from time to time. Unfortunately, this poetry often has serious defects, since a measure of beauty and depth is often given up for auditory effect.

In *Ask Your Mama*, published in 1961, Hughes went one step further in attempting to amalgamate poetry and jazz. Each poem includes a marginal note suggesting the proper musical accompaniment much like that supplied by Vachel Lindsay for "The Congo." The last verse of "Blues in Stereo," for example, describes Africa with words and drum:

IN A TOWN NAMED AFTER STANLEY
NIGHT EACH NIGHT COMES NIGHTLY drum
AND THE MUSIC OF OLD MUSIC'S   African
BORROWED FOR THE HORNS   beats
THAT DON'T KNOW HOW TO PLAY   over
ON LPs THAT WONDER   blues
HOW THEY EVER GOT THAT WAY   that
                                gradually
    WHAT TIME IS IT, MAMA?   mount
    WHAT TIME IS IT NOW?   in
    MAKES NO DIFFERENCE TO ME   intensity
    BUT I'M ASKING ANYHOW.   to
    WHAT TIME IS IT, MAMA?   end
    WHAT TIME NOW?[38]   in
                                climax.

In the title poem, "Ask Your Mama," Hughes ends with flute and blues:

[37]Hughes, *Montage of a Dream Deferred*, p. 75.
[38]Langston Hughes, *Ask Your Mama* (New York: Alfred A. Knopf, 1961), p. 37.

IN THE QUARTER OF THE NEGROES
WHERE NO SHADOW WALKS ALONE   Repeat high
LITTLE MULES AND DONKEYS SHARE   flute call
THEIR GRASS WITH UNICORNS.[39]   to segue into
                                     up tempo blues
                                     that continue
                                     behind the
                                     next sequence . .

The musical annotation in each case is intended to heighten the
effect of the poetry. No longer is the rhythm merely worked into the
lines of the poem; now it is also supplied by musicians. At last we
seem to have reached the ultimate in interrelating poetry and jazz.

In general, the results of this experimental technique seem less
successful than Hughes's early blues rhythms. Even his wry sense of
humor is less in evidence. Only occasionally, as in the closing lines
of "Blues in Stereo," do we hear that familiar ironic chuckle:

DOWN THE LONG HARD ROW THAT
    I BEEN HOEING
I THOUGHT I HEARD THE HORN OF PLENTY BLOWING.
BUT I GOT TO GET A NEW ANTENNA, LORD
MY TV KEEPS ON SNOWING.[40]

It is difficult to evaluate these poems by ordinary standards, as
Dudley Fitts says, "They are nonliterary—oral, vocal compositions to
be spoken or shouted . . . this is stunt poetry, a night club turn."[41]
At best, *Ask Your Mama* must be considered in the same category
as *Montage on a Dream Deferred*, a jam session that doesn't quite
live up to the author's talent.

Hughes's prose contributions have been so varied and numerous
since 1940 that it is difficult to treat them systematically. Perhaps
his most outstanding work has been the creation of the shrewd, fun-
loving rascal, Jesse B. Semple, known to his friends as Simple. One
evening in a neighborhood bar, Hughes says, he picked up the idea
for the Simple sketches. Talking with a young couple Hughes asked
where the man worked:

[39]*Ibid.*, p. 65.

[40]*Ibid.*, p. 37.

[41]Dudley Fitts, Review of *Ask Your Mama* by Langston Hughes, *New York
Times Book Review* (October 29, 1961), p. 16.

"In a war plant."

I said, "What do you make?"

He said, "Cranks."

I said, "What kind of cranks?"

He said, "Oh, man, I don't know what kind of cranks."

I said, "Well, do they crank cars, tanks, buses, planes or what?"

He said, "I don't know what them cranks crank."

Whereupon, his girl friend, a little put out at this ignorance of his job, said "You've been working there long enough. Looks like by now you ought to know what them cranks crank."

"Aw, woman," he said, "you know white folks don't tell colored folks what cranks crank."[42]

Hughes goes on to say "out of the mystery as to what the cranks of the world crank, to whom they belong and why, there evolved the character in this book."[43]

First appearing in the *Chicago Defender* of November 21, 1942, the adventures of Simple now fill five separately published volumes and promise to continue indefinitely.[44] The charm of Simple lies in his uninhibited pursuit of those two universal goals, understanding and security. As with most other humans, he usually fails to achieve either of these goals and sometimes once achieved they disappoint him. Simple has a tough resiliency, however, that won't allow him to brood over a failure for very long. Speaking as a typical Harlem resident Simple appears to be in harmony with the general trend in American humor. As Walter Blair has pointed out, "Our chief humorists until the 1920's were all rustic or western. Since the 1920's, by contrast, our famous humorists have been urban."[45] Simple is the very essence of the city. His language, mannerisms, and attitudes spring from the busy street-corner, the subway, and the air-conditioned bar.

[42]Langston Hughes, *The Best of Simple* (New York: Hill and Wang), p. viii.

[43]*Ibid.*

[44]The Alfred A. Knopf firm has had no connection with the Simple books. In a letter to the writer dated March 1, 1963 Hughes mentioned Mrs. Knopf's reaction to the sketches. "Blanche did not like my Simple stories, rejected them." *Simple Speaks His Mind, Simple Takes a Wife,* and *Simple Stakes a Claim* were published by Simon and Schuster. *Simple's Uncle Sam* and the anthology *The Best of Simple* were published by Hill and Wang.

[45]Walter Blair, "Urbanization of Humor," *A Time of Harvest,* ed. Robert Spiller (New York: Hill and Wang, 1962), p. 54.

Hughes's technique in these naratives is to set off Simple's direct, unsophisticated approach to life against the guarded viewpoints of an educated companion. The companion is a writer and quite likely represents Hughes himself. This dialogue between the moderate, educated wing of Negro thought and the man in the street serves to illustrate the cleavage in Negro life in America. Davis claims, with undoubted insight, that this is the chief reason the stories appeal to Negroes. He says, "as we read these dialogues, we often find ourselves giving lip-service to the sophisticated Hughes side of the debate while our hearts share Simple's cruder but more realistic attitude."[46] When Simple learns, for example, that Thoreau once threw out his bed and chairs he muses:

> "He really cleaned house," said Simple.
> "But there ain't a Negro living would throw out his bed. A Negro might throw out his rug if it was summertime. He might throw out his chairs if they broke down. But bed, uh-uh, no never would a Negro throw out his bed. It is too useful—even if it do have to be made up every morning and the sheets changed every week. Beds and Negroes go together. "You certainly are race-conscious," I said. "Negroes, Negroes, Negroes! Everything in terms of race. Can't you think just once without thinking in terms of color?"
> "I am colored," said Simple.[47]

In this flat statement of fact Simple goes to the heart of the race situation. He is colored and proud of it. Again we hear the repetition of Hughes's favorite theme—pride in race. Simple says:

> Some colored folks are ashamed to like watermelon. I told you about that woman who bought one in the store once and made the clerk wrap it up before she would carry it home, . . . Me, I would carry a watermelon unwrapped any day anywhere. I would eat one before the Queen of England.[48]

As a race man, Simple often rages about the absurd treatment he and other Negroes receive from white people, but he is no hate-monger. One can hardly picture him taking part in a protest march

[46]Arthur Davis, "Jesse B. Semple: Negro American," *Phylon*, XV (Spring, 1954), p. 22.

[47]Langston Hughes, *Simple Takes a Wife* (New York: Simon and Schuster, 1953), p. 22.

[48]*Ibid.*, p. 81.

for any cause. His feelings about whites, as Davis points out, "are neither morbid nor bitter, are not very deep, and as a matter of fact are not even consistent."[49] In a discussion of the second coming of Christ Simple says all white folks should be smitten down. "You don't mean all white folks, do you?" his friends asks. "No," says Simple, "I hope He lets Mrs. Roosevelt alone."[50] Besides the fun in this remark, it is a beautifully executed revelation of the ambivalence of the Negro attitude toward whites. Simple has an ingenious way of reducing any situation to its basic terms. His penetrating wit is in the high tradition of the so-called crackerbox philosophers, Josh Billings, Mr. Dooley, and Artemus Ward. If in Simple's case the crackerbox has been converted to a barstool the total effect is pleasantly the same.

While white behavior often fills Simple with wrath, Negro misdeeds bring down his utter scorn. Nothing is worse for the race, he feels, than Negro conduct that is rude or ignorant. In one story Simple derides the stuffy Negro attitude which refuses to cross the color line.

> "And everything was going fine at the formal until Jimboy—
> . . . brought his wife up to our box to introduce her to the ladies."
> "What happened then?"
> "The ladies friz up." said Simple.
> "Why?"
> "Jimboy's wife is white."
> "That's right," I said, "he did marry a white girl, didn't he? I haven't run into him since he got married."
> "Dorothea is not only white, she is pretty," said Simple. "There is nothing a colored woman hates more than to see a colored man married to a pretty white woman. If she's some old beat-up strumpet, they don't care much. But Jimboy's wife is a nice girl. So when he come up to our box with Dorothea, the womens just friz up, Joyce included."
> "That's not very polite," I said.
> "Of course it were not," said Simple, draining his beer, "It were right embarrassing."[51]

[49]Davis, "Jesse B. Semple: Negro American," *Phylon*, XV (Spring, 1954), p. 23.

[50]Hughes, *The Best of Simple*, p. 10.

[51]Hughes, *Simple Takes a Wife*, p. 65.

Simple is a well developed character, both believable and lovable. The situations he meets and discusses are so true to life everyone may enter the fun. This does not mean that Simple is in any way dull. He injects the ordinary with his own special insights. A perfect example occurs in a discussion of grammar. After Simple is corrected for using "ain't" because, as his friend says, "It's not Oxford or Boston or Washington English," Simple replies, "I am glad it ain't Washington English since I do not like that Jim Crow town. I do not know where Oxford is. And Boston I have never bean. [sic] So about them, I give less than a damn. I ain't bothered."[52]

In his conversation Simple reveals an insight born of the streets, of low-paying, back-breaking jobs, of Saturday night parties, and Sunday prayer meetings. His talk is Harlem argot, which Hughes knows how to transcribe with perfect register. As Davis says, "Simple like his creator is really a poet at heart, and when he gets aroused, his language glows."[53]

> "Buddy-o, daddy-o, pal, I do not want to argue with you this evening because I haven't got time. You are colored just like me, so set down and help me figure up my taxes for these white folks. What did you say that book says about taxation?"
> "Without representation, it's tyranny."
> "If you don't know how to add, subtract, multiply, erase, deduct, steal, stash, save, conceal, and long divide, it is worse than that," said Simple. "Taxes is hell! Buddy-o, here's our beer."[54]

Simple is a natural, unsophisticated man who never abandons his hope in tomorrow. Simple's fiancee, Joyce, his drinking partners, and his landlady make up a world that is often amusing, sometimes sad, but always very real. William Smith has said of Simple, "He has humor, sensitivity, intelligence, and something to say; he is the voice of the American Negro as few have heard him speak."[55]

The reality of Hughes's Harlem is quite different from the reality

[52]*Ibid.*, p. 40.

[53]Davis, "Jesse B. Semple: Negro American," *Phylon*, XV (Spring, 1954), p. 26.

[54]Hughes, *The Best of Simple*, p. 69.

[55]William Smith, Review of *Simple Speaks His Mind*, by Langston Hughes, *New Republic* CXXIII (September 4, 1950), p. 20.

as seen by James Baldwin or Richard Wright. Simple is the universal man in the street while Rufus, in *Another Country*, and Bigger in *Native Son* are tortured men in the gutter. Rufus seems to say to society, "Look at me, degenerate and hopeless, this is your fault!" Simple looks at society and chuckles over its stupidity. Both styles of writing have something to say about race—Baldwin and Wright attack with a hammer, Hughes chides with a sly dig in the ribs. Those who label Simple as the more conservative figure cannot deny his appeal and universality. Bone is correct in his judgment that the Simple sketches "are among his [Hughes's] finest literary creations."[56]

Simple's female counterpart, Madam Alberta K. Johnson, must have been prominent in Hughes's mind when he and Roy De Carava put together *The Sweet Flypaper of Life*, a photographic story of Harlem. A series of superb pictures with accompanying text describes the busy life of an average Harlem family. At the beginning of the story death's messenger rides up on a bicycle with a telegram for Sister Mary Bradley to come home. She is not ready to go because, as she tells the boy, "I might be a little sick, but as yet I ain't no ways tired."[57] While Sister Mary recovers her health the story of her children and grandchildren unfolds with photographs of the streets, bars, and tenements of Harlem. The significance of the title is explained in a conversation between Mary and her janitor:

> "Miss Mary, I hear tell you's down—but with no intentions of going out." I said, "You're right! I done got my feet caught in the sweet flypaper of life—and I'll be dogged if I want to get loose."[58]

Because of the new climate in race relations in the United States since World War II, protest themes no longer seemed quite as dramatic as in the past. In *The Sweet Flypaper of Life* Hughes tells the story of the Negro without hate or violence. Discerning Negro writers, Davis suggests, would do well to follow this lead and concentrate on "facets of Negro living—humorous, pathetic, and tragic

[56]Bone, *The Negro Novel in America*, p. 77.
[57]Langston Hughes and Roy De Carava, *The Sweet Flypaper of Life*, (New York: Simon and Schuster, 1955), p. 1.
[58]*Ibid.*, p. 92.

—which are not directly touched by the outside world."[59] These facets, as Hughes has proven, can be the basis of a literature of strength and beauty. Along with other Negro writers, such as Lorraine Hansberry, Gwendolyn Brooks and Owen Dodson, Hughes has shown, in his recent work, an increasing emphasis on non-protest writing. Wright related this trend toward non-protest writing to improved race relations in the United States. He notes that since the war there has been "a drastic reduction of racial content, a rise in preocupation with urban themes and subject matter both in the novel and the poem."[60] Further, he promises even greater assimilation with common literary themes and burdens when "a humane attitude prevails in America towards us."[61] Neither Wright nor Hughes means to deny racial conflict, but only to place it in perspective as one part of Negro life, to be understood along with many other parts.

The Sweet Flypaper of Life received generous praise from the reviewers. Comments such as "a small work of quality,"[62] "a little gem of a book,"[63] and "Astounding verisimilitude"[64] conveyed the general feeling of satisfaction. In *The Christian Century*, J. W. Parker epitomized the book with the comment, "The tone throughout, now quiet, now lively, is consistent with the ups and downs that characterize life in Harlem. Refreshing also is the growing emphasis upon humor one observes in this Hughes volume."[65]

Scraps of Hughes's humor are irresistible. Sister Mary describes her son-in-law's habits as follows:

One of Jerry's faults is, he don't come home every night. Melinda

---

[59]Arthur Davis, "Integration and Race Literature," *The American Negro Writer and His Roots* (New York: American Society of African Culture, 1960), p. 37.

[60]Richard Wright, "The Literature of the Negro in the United States" *White Man Listen* (New York: Doubleday, 1957), p. 147.

[61]*Ibid.*, p. 150.

[62]Robert Hatch, Review of *The Sweet Flypaper of Life*, by Langston Hughes, *Nation*, CLXXXI (December 17, 1955), p. 538.

[63]Rose Field, Review of *The Sweet Flypaper of Life*, by Langston Hughes, *New York Herald Tribune Book Review* (December 18, 1955), p. 3.

[64]Gilbert Milstein, Review of *The Sweet Flypaper of Life*, by Langston Hughes, *New York Times* (November 27, 1955), p. 5.

[65]John Parker, Review of *The Sweet Flypaper of Life*, by Langston Hughes *The Christian Century*, LXXIII (August 1, 1956), p. 905.

got the idea she can change him. But I tells Melinda, reforming some folks is like trying to boil a pig in a coffeepot—the possibilities just ain't there— . . .[66]

and later, when she talks about Mazie, her grandson's girl friend:

Mazie is somewhat like Jerry who don't give a parlor damn about paying Con-Edison. Mazie works just enough to get along: which is enough for some people. . . . Mazie is already kinder beat up by life which is like I were—so she knows what it's all about.[67]

The pages of *The Sweet Flypaper of Life* carry one up and down the Harlem streets:

Winter coal shoveled in.
Summer ice coming.
Some folks selling, other folks buyin:
Somebody always passing.
Coming and going.
Picket lines picketing:
And at night the street meetings on the corner—
Talking about "Buy Black":
"Africa for the Africans":
And "Ethiopia shall stretch forth her hand":
And some joker in the crowd always says,
"And draw back a nub!"[68]

All these events in the life of Harlem are heightened by a group of unusually intimate photographs. The book is completely successful in what it attempts—the realistic transcription of life in Harlem. Hughes knows his people and loves them with the unsentimental love of a wise father. On the surface the book is a delightful study of Harlem, underneath it is a warm affirmation in the dignity of the common man.

In addition to his other writing activities Hughes continued to produce short stories. Racial topics still carry the burden of exposition for most of the stories, but sometimes the theme is nonracial. Again, as in the poetry of this period, a light tone is predominant. Even in the stories of Negro-white relationships there is a tendency

[66]Hughes and De Carava, *The Sweet Flypaper of Life*, p. 57.
[67]*Ibid.*, pp. 90–91.
[68]*Ibid.*, pp. 74–83.

to substitute humor for bitterness. In "Who's Passing for Who" Hughes satirizes the Negro Renaissance when he and other young artists formed a literary Bohemia in Harlem. The story describes what happens during a tour of Harlem night clubs when an Iowa couple reveal to their dark friends that they are passing for white. Immediately, Hughes says, the party became more relaxed:

> All at once we dropped our professionally self-conscious "Negro" manners, became natural, ate fish, and talked and kidded freely like colored folks do when there are no white folks around.[69]

The story takes a final twist when the Iowa couple reveal they are not colored:

> "Listen boys! I hate to confuse you again. But to tell the truth, my husband and I aren't really colored at all. We're white. We just thought we'd kid you by passing for colored a little while—just as you said Negroes sometimes pass for white."[70]

In this tale Hughes demonstrates a pleasing ability to laugh at himself and the whole breed of literary giants of the twenties.

The story "I Thank You for This" describes an act of courtesy as a white man invites two colored soldiers into his compartment after they have been refused service on the train diner. It only requires one man of good will, as Hughes points out, to adjust the petty kind of injustice that occurs every day in America. The story ends quietly as the soldier from Georgia says to his white friend, "I thank you for this breakfast."[71] In "Something in Common" two old derelicts, one white, the other black, team up to defend the honor of America in a foreign land.

Many of the Hughes's recent stories deal with various aspects of love. "On the Way Home" describes the twisted love of a boy for his mother, "Patron of the Arts" the love of a young man for an older woman, and "Never Room With a Couple" the dangerous and somewhat amusing effects of illicit love. In only one of these "Patron of the Arts," had Hughes planned to identify the characters as

---

[69]Langston Hughes, *Laughing to Keep From Crying* (New York: Alfred A. Knopf, 1952), p. 46.
[70]*Ibid.*, p. 47.
[71]*Ibid.*, p. 227.

colored. Curiously, in "On the Way Home," an editor specifically requested that colored characters be added.[72]

Perhaps the strangest interworking of love and hate is found in "The Mysterious Madame Shanghai." A withdrawn and picturesque lady, whom her fellow boarders call Madame Shanghai, turns out to be an ex-lion tamer running away from a husband she once tried to kill in the circus ring. The conclusion is as melodramatic as the rest of the story. The husband finds his wife, gives her several slaps in the face and then kisses her. To Madam Shanghai, this means only one thing:

> "Jim!" she cried, "You love me—or you wouldn't be slapping me like this. You love me. You love me!"[73]

It is a strange adventure without any logic or point of view. One must accept it simply as a lesson on the relationship between love and hate.

"Powder White Faces," another story written in the 1940's, deals with prejudice against Orientals. Charlie Lee kills a white woman in a moment when:

> . . . all the hatred and anger of a lifetime had suddenly collected in his heart and gathered in his fingers at the sight of a white face and a red mouth on the pillow beneath him.[74]

It was difficult to decide why he had killed:

> But when he tried to figure it out, he kept remembering other white women (not the one he had killed, but other women), port-town women, taxi-dance-hall women, women with powder white faces who took all they could from him and then let him go, called him names, kicked him out or had him beaten up.[75]

Hughes can write sympathetically about Charlie Lee because he

---

[72]A comment written by Langston Hughes on the cover sheet of the revised manuscript draft of "On the Way Home" says, "Revised pages of this story making the characters colored at the request of Whit Burnett for *Story* magazine, who couldn't make out if they were colored or what and seemed worried. Why they just had to be described as "brown-skin," etc., I do not know. I am afraid many American white people have a color complex, even editors. July 27, 1945." In possession of Langston Hughes.

[73]Hughes, *Laughing to Keep From Crying*, p. 143.

[74]*Ibid.*, p. 227.

[75]*Ibid.*, p. 147.

knows the effect of accumulated hate and insult. As he asks in "Harlem,"

> What happens to a dream deferred?
> . . . .
> Maybe it just sags
> like a heavy load.
> Or does it explode?[76]

Prejudice also figures in "African Morning," the story of twelve-year old Maurai, son of a white father and a black mother. Tolerated by his father and openly despised by the natives, Maurai lives an unhappy life in a small African coastal town. During the day described in the story Maurai runs an errand for his father, is mistaken for a native guide by some sailors, and is beaten by the black dock boys. He considers suicide in a deep jungle pool but eventually, and with a heavy heart, he returns to the European enclosure. At the end of the story he can only think about his future in Africa "where nobody wanted him."[77] This is a particularly moving story since it focuses the attention of the reader on the fate of a helpless child. Davis has characterized "African Morning" as "restrained, finished and effectively written."[78] Possessing none of the sensationalism of Hughes's early stories of Africa, this tale of Maurai is a successful piece of realism.

The collection of stories published in 1952 under the title *Laughing to Keep From Crying* is not altogether satisfying. Although some of the stories are effective, none can compare with his earlier efforts like "Cora Unashamed" and "Slave on the Block." The reviewers generally agreed with Bucklin Moon who said, "Some of the shorter vignettes come alive with a sudden flash of imagery, . . . other stories are less successful."[79] Even if one feels that some of the stories fall below Hughes's earlier level, it can not be denied that the writing is lucid and tightly knit. Hughes is rarely guilty of using a superfluous word or phrase. As Stanley Cooperman stated, "It is

[76]Hughes, *Selected Poems*, p. 268.

[77]Hughes, *Laughing to Keep From Crying*, p. 20.

[78]Davis, "The Tragic Mulatto Theme in Six Works by Langston Hughes," *Phylon*, XVI (Winter, 1955), p. 202.

[79]Bucklin Moon, *Review of Laughing to Keep From Crying*, by Langston Huges, *New York Times* (March 23, 1952), p. 4.

the sort of lean, compact writing that implies as much as it states; an active, rhythmical prose without excess literary fat.[80]

Besides producing a quantity of poetry and prose, Hughes has devoted considerable time to editorial activities since 1940. Perhaps his most important work was *The Poetry of the Negro, 1746–1949*, undertaken with his old friend Arna Bontemps. The book filled a void since it was the first major anthology of Negro poetry to be issued since Cullen's *Caroling Dusk* appeared in 1925. Besides the work of colored poets of the United States the anthology included an unusual section of Caribbean verse and a group of poems about the Negro by white writers. While a few of the poems were the work of lesser known writers, most of them came from such familiar figures as Dunbar, Cullen, James Weldon Johnson, and Hughes himself. In a later anthology, *New Negro Poets U.S.A.*, Hughes presented a sample of the work of a score of younger writers without established literary reputations. Taken together, these anthologies provide a good index of Negro poetry up to 1960.

In another phase of editorial work Hughes undertook several projects in the 1960's involving African writing. Both *An African Treasury* and *Poems From Black Africa* provide American readers with a unique taste of native African literature. In explanation for the content of *An African Treasury* Hughes reveals his system of selection as follows, "Quite frankly, I have chosen to assemble here only those pieces which I enjoyed most and which I hope others will find entertaining, moving, possibly instructive, but above all readable."[81] Certainly, the collection achieves this goal. In *An African Treasury*, *Poems From Black Africa*, and *The First Book of Africa*, a survey for children, Hughes returns to an early interest in Africa. Happily, in these books he has abandoned his preoccupation with a primitive past and taken up a more vital concern with political and literary movements of the present.

Closely related to these editorial works on Negro poetry and Africa are a group of books Hughes produced for laymen on Negro music and history. *The Pictorial History of the Negro in America*, *Famous Negro Music Makers*, and *Famous American Negroes* are

[80]Stanley Cooperman, Review of *Laughing to Keep From Crying*, by Langston Hughes, *The New Republic*, CXXVI (May 5, 1952), p. 21.

[81]Langston Hughes, ed. *An African Treasury* (New York: Crown, 1960), p. x.

all readable and accurate interpretations of Negro life. They do not sanctify the race with overpraise, but merely describe important personalities and their achievements. For younger readers Hughes supplied the same kind of careful, readable prose in a series of books that included *The First Book of Negroes, The First Book of Jazz, The First Book of Rhythms,* and *Famous Negro Heroes of America.* Through the wide distribution of these books to schools and public libraries readers can obtain an honest evaluation of the contribution of the Negro to American life. They offer, therefore, not only useful but critically important information.

In 1962 Hughes produced his most important book on Negro history, *Fight for Freedom,* the story of NAACP. Through its support of legal action and non-violent protest, NAACP had become one of the best known organizations in America, in fact NAACP had won a new climate for the Negro. It was appropriate, therefore, to review the history of the organization and equally appropriate for Hughes, a long time advocate of racial justice, to write the book.

Hughes's history of NAACP is informative and lively. It presents the basic facts of the organization's founding, its early development, and its activities since World War II. Hughes skillfully weaves into his history such great Negro personalities as W. E. B. Du Bois, Walter White, Roy Wilkins, and Daisy Bates. The book is a worthwhile reading for all who want a better understanding of the American Negro. As Irving Dilliard has said, "Somebody ought to put it in every library in the country."[82]

In one further service to the American reading public Hughes completed several full length translations. His first work of this kind was a French novel, *Masters of the Dew,* by an old friend Jacques Roumain. Always interested in Spanish, Hughes followed the Roumain novel with a volume of poetry by Nicholas Guillen, a collection of Lorca's *Gypsy Ballads,* and a selection of the poetry by the Nobel prize winner Gabriela Mistral. He also frequently supplied periodicals with translations of the work of important Latin American writers who he felt deserved attention from English readers. It is significant that Hughes found time to devote to these translation projects in view of his extremely active production in other areas. He had

[82]Irving Dilliard, Review of *Fight for Freedom,* by Langston Hughes, *Saturday Review,* XLV (September 29, 1962), p. 33.

learned as a tutor in Mexico and later as a traveler that understanding another person's language is the first step toward understanding the person. These translations seem to be Hughes's modest offering toward better world understanding.

A much more personal project had been on Hughes's mind for several years, as he reveals in a letter to Blanche Knopf:

> I am now ready to begin work on this book [a second volume of autobiography] which will cover the years from the end of 1929 through World War II to the present, 1950. Geographically covering: Haiti, a cross country tour of America including a Northern Negro's impression of the South, around the World through Russia and China and Japan, the Civil War in Spain as a newspaper correspondent covering the activities of Negroes in the International Brigades for one of our biggest weeklies, Carmel, California, Jeffers, Martin Flavin, and other friends in the artists group there, the production of my plays, MULATTO, and the musical version of STREET SCENE, . . .[83]

The outline, however, didn't capture Mrs. Knopf's fancy. She wrote back the next month:

> The autobiography sounds to me in reading the outline pretty weighted and I don't feel in fairness to you, and certainly in fairness to ourselves, much as I regret having to say this to you, that we should make any commitment for it until you have written some of it so that we can read it. If this means that you feel that you should take it elsewhere, I think I will have to free you to do it with great regret. But the outline as it reads is not a book, in my opinion.[84]

Hughes's ambitious plan to include events through 1950 had to be cut back ten years in the final publication by Rinehart.[85] As a result, more than half of the book is devoted to a description of the trip to Russia and the Far East. Although the Russian journal is

[83]Letter from Langston Hughes to Blanche Knopf of October 31, 1949. Yale University Library.

[84]Letter of Blanche Knopf to Langston Hughes of November 10, 1949. Yale University Library.

[85]A letter from Blanche Knopf to Langston Hughes dated October 29, 1956, shows there were no bad feelings over this rejection. Mrs. Knopf wrote "Very many thanks for the beautifully inscribed copy of your book, which you asked Rinehart to send along. . . . I can only wish you all kinds of success with it." Yale University Library.

often good reading the book would have been strengthened by more information about Hughes himself. It seems reasonable to ask that the autobiography of a writer should furnish insights into writing aims and processes. In *The Big Sea* Hughes involved the readers in the career of a rising young author, but unfortunately, *I Wonder As I Wander* fails to sustain this interest. Roi Ottley felt Hughes had written "warmly and amusingly . . . with asides which give flashes of social and racial insights,"[86] but Saunders Redding complained that "neither events nor people are seen in depth."[87] When Hughes talks about his own work the book comes alive, but between these brief moments are vast sections of travelogue.

If Hughes's second volume of autobiography was less adroit than the first, his second novel, *Tambourines to Glory*, did nothing to balance the scales.[88] The story describes the rapid rise of Laura and Essie, two unemployed Harlem women who cleverly promote their street corner evangelism into a profitable business enterprise. The origin of the project was remarkably uncomplicated:

> "Money! I sure wish I had some. Say Essie, why don't you and me start a church like Mother Bradley's? We ain't doing nothing else useful, and it would beat Home Relief. You sing good. I'll preach. We'll both take up collection and split it."[89]

The main characters are, like Simple, a part of contemporary Harlem, but somehow they fail to project any warmth or individuality. It is difficult to become concerned with either the evangelists or their church. Laura wants to get spending money for her boy-friend, Big-Eyed Buddy; Essie wants to get her daughter up North. The novel ends melodramatically when Laura kills the unfaithful Buddy and tries to fix the blame on Essie. The forces of good triumph, however, and Essie returns to the church in a final scene to announce the engagement of her daughter to a choir boy. Aside from pro-

[86]Roi Ottley, Review of *I Wonder As I Wander*, by Langston Hughes, *Saturday Review*, XXXIX (November 17, 1956), p. 35.

[87]Saunders Redding, Review of *I Wonder As I Wander*, by Langston Hughes, *New York Herald Tribune* (December 23, 1956), p. 6.

[88]Hughes described the origin of the novel and the musical comedy which subsequently developed from it in *The New York Times* October 27, 1963, Sect. 2, p. 3.

[89]Langston Hughes, *Tambourines to Glory* (New York: John Day, 1958), pp. 19–20.

viding a delightful sample of Harlem conversation and some exuber-
ant gospel songs, *Tambourines to Glory* is slight and unsatisfying.

Writing for the theatre continued to claim much of Hughes's
time and energy. His dramatic production includes lyrics for the
musical adaptation of Elmer Rice's *Street Scene*, the libretto for
William Grant Still's *Troubled Island*, two gospel-song plays, *Black
Nativity* and *Jerico-Jim Crow*, and perhaps his most successful
theatrical venture, the musical comedy *Simply Heavenly*.[90] In a
general comment on Hughes's writing for the theatre, T. J. Spencer
has concluded, "Although the plays of Langston Hughes are about
Negroes, . . . he has never been a 'Negro playwright' in the sense
of advocating a cause or limiting his plays to a separate audience,
white or black. His writing consequently has honesty, sincerity and
vigor apparent to anyone who will read or attend his plays."[91]
Hughes's dramatic writing has the strength of his best poetry in that
it conveys the essence of the Negro point of view without lapsing
into mere racial propaganda.

To summarize, in the period beginning with 1941 Hughes has
written prolifically in a wide variety of forms for a wide variety of
journals and book publishers. Because much of his recent writing is
on a more popular level than his earlier work it is somewhat lacking
in appeal for the serious reader. The Simple sketches, *The Sweet
Flypaper of Life*, and some of the poems, however, are original and
sensitive. Further, editorial works such as *The Poetry of the Negro,
1746–1949*, *Fight for Freedom*, the picture books on Negro history,
and the children's books all have a place in defining the role of the
Negro in American culture. As always, Hughes's most significant
contributions cluster around the interpretation of Negro life in
America. His reputation no longer depends on poetry, as it did in
the 1920's, or short stories, as it did in the 1930's but on writing
itself in the broadest sense of that term. In a few sentences of self-
revelation he once summarized his feelings about writing as follows,

[90]Hughes's plays became available to readers for the first time in 1963 with
the publication of *Five Plays*, edited and with an introduction by Webster
Smalley at Indiana University Press. The plays included in this volume are:
Mulatto, Soul Gone Home, Little Ham, Simply Heavenly, and Tambourines to
Glory.

[91]T. J. Spencer and Clarence Rivers, "Langston Hughes, his Style and Optimism," *Drama Critique*, VII (Spring 1964), p. 102.

"Literature is a big sea full of many fish. I let down my nets and pulled. I'm still pulling."[92] This statement certainly characterizes Hughes's recent literary activity.

Hughes's writing has always been a barometer of social and economic pressures on the Negro. It is noteworthy that since World War II he adjusted his point of view to suit the shifting color line in America. As Bardolph remarked, "the old protestantism became anachronistic, for the nation was now officially on the Negro's side. . . . Perhaps only the very newest writers were at home in the changed social landscape, though the poets Hughes, Tolson, Hayden and Brooks successfully weathered the dislocations."[93] Specifically, in the Simple stories and in *The Sweet Flypaper of Life* Hughes de-emphasizes conflict and stresses life within the Negro group.

Between 1941 and 1965 Hughes continued to write actively on all phases of Negro life in America. The direction of his work is in the lighter vein and tending toward editorial projects to which his good taste and broad interests are well suited. Hughes emerges in the mid-sixties as one of the best known Negro writers in America. His most distinguished contributions have been the interpretations of his race with understanding, humor, and optimism.

[92]Hughes, *The Big Sea*, p. 335.
[93]Bardolph, *The Negro Vanguard*, p. 384.

Conclusion

Although most of Hughes's writing is based on Negro life, he is a writer first, a Negro writer second. As he has remarked: "For the general public, 'the blacker the berry, the sweeter the juice' may be true in jazz, but not in prose. These days I would hate to be a Negro writer depending on race to get somewhere."[1] Hughes has always given credit to the Negro people for his source material, but he has stamped this material with his own talent to make it come alive as literature. A writer of lesser skill would have merely incorporated racial detail into a tasteless polemic. In Hughes's case there has never been any need to substitute race for ability.

From the first Hughes's writing has been an integral part of the stream of American literature. He began as a disciple of the New Poetry giants, Sandburg and Lindsay, writing unrhymed verse in praise of the "little people." During the 1930's he joined the general outcry for reform with stories and poems that spoke of eviction notices, unemployment, and hunger. Later, when wartime tension had reduced, he turned to lighter themes, to jazz poems and the antics of Jesse B. Semple. Throughout, his work is a part of and not apart from American literature.

Hughes is never obscure and seldom despairing. The slow process of correcting racial misunderstanding angers him, but he never doubts the final victory of justice. While some of his work may be criticized as journalistic or merely entertaining it has a vitality and richness of expression that promises to keep it alive long after more serious treatments of "the problem" have been forgotten.

Few Negroes have been able to make their living as professional writers. Hughes has managed to achieve this goal by hard work and versatility. He writes pleasing poems for children and sophisticated plays for adults. In the same month one can read his translation of a Lorca poem in the *Beloit Poetry Chapbook*, a Simple sketch in the *Chicago Defender*, and an article on creative writing in *Phylon*. His publication history includes close association with highly selective

[1]Langston Hughes, "Writers: Black and White," *The American Negro Writer and His Roots* (New York: American Society of African Culture, 1960), p. 41.

poetry journals and discriminating commercial publishers. He has fished in most corners of his "big sea of literature" with critical and commercial success.

Richard Wright claims that Hughes has played a dual role as a writer. First, in *The Weary Blues* and *Fine Clothes to the Jew*, Wright says, Hughes set the stage for the rise of realism in Negro literature, and secondly, through his extensive publication he has been an important "cultural ambassador" for the Negro case.[2] While Hughes probably did no more than several others in the movement to promote realistic Negro writing, there is no question but that he is a cultural ambassador par excellence. He has supplied both Americans and foreigners with some of the most popular interpretations of the Negro.

Hughes's first collections of poems were well received by critics in the 1920's. His blues and his songs of pride and protest were all applauded by major white review journals, although they received scant praise from the conservative Negro press. "The Negro Speaks of Rivers," "Mother to Son," "The Weary Blues," "Cross," and "Brass Spittoons," for example, were heralded as artistic renderings of the Negroes' moods and aspirations. In direct, vigorous verse, Hughes projected a realistic image of the urban Negro. Besides his portraits of the "little people," Hughes captured the cabaret life of the 1920's in a delightful series of verses set to the rhythms of Negro music. With his circle of literary friends, his publication success, and his fresh realism, Hughes has been correctly characterized as the most representative and productive member of the New Negro movement.[3] The poetry Hughes wrote in the 1930's is not remarkable primarily because of the burden of social ideology it was forced to carry. Since 1940 he has concentrated on experimental themes set to the rhythms of boogie-woogie and be-bop. The result of this amalgamation of poetry and jazz, a poetic "jam session," seems less satisfying than the traditional blues verses Hughes wrote early in his career. It is these early poems for which Hughes is best known. One anthologist has commented, "With his prolific imagination and sensitive ear, Hughes raised to the level of art the material of the

---

[2]Richard Wright, Review of *The Big Sea*, by Langston Hughes, *New Republic*, CIII (October 28, 1940), p. 600.

[3]Redding, *To Make a Poet Black*, p. 115.

blues and the jazz idiom as well as the songs of the gospel singers and the 'shouts' of the rural South."[4] In a general comment on Negro poetry a British critic confirmed this view saying, "Where it strikes a pulsing rhythm and captures the inimitable tang of Negro speech, as in the blues of Langston Hughes . . . it is moving and successful."[5]

Not Without Laughter, the novel Hughes wrote in 1930, and *Tambourines to Glory*, written in 1958, contain the strong points of his best poetry, vigor, simplicity, and a sure sense of human relationships, but they lack a certain depth of characterization and unity. *Not Without Laughter* is certainly the better work of the two, transcribing as it does a warmly human picture of Negro life. This novel is also important for its emphasis on life within the Negro group. Jimboy, Annjee, and Aunt Hager are certainly aware of racial discrimination, but they live their own lives, not without laughter.

In the 1930's Hughes wrote a series of short stories on racial misunderstanding which appeared in leading literary magazines and afterwards received favorable attention in compiled form as *The Ways of White Folks*. They are dramatic and show penetrating insight, making the reader realize, as one commentator put it, "that there is a greater depth in Negro-white relationships of the most casual sort than other writers have suggested."[6] More recently Hughes has written stories on a variety of themes, race being but one. The collection entitled *Laughing to Keep From Crying*, published in 1952, shows Hughes's broadening interest in minority groups of all kinds, timid Negro leadership, and the curious workings of love and hate. Although both collections have strong and weak stories, *The Ways of White Folks*, with its subtle emphasis on Negro-white behavior, seems the superior book.

Closely related to his short stories are Hughes's sketches of Jesse B. Semple. These anecdotes of Harlem show Hughes's sense

[4]Hebert Hill, "Introduction" *Soon One Morning*, ed. Herbert Hill (New York: Alfred A. Knopf, 1963), p. 16.

[5]"Negro Writing," *American Writing Today*, ed. Allan Angoff (New York: New York University Press, 1957), p. 98.

[6]Sterling Brown, ed. *The Negro Caravan* (New York: Dryden Press, 1941), p. 16.

of humor at its lively best. In Simple, Hughes has etched a charming and well-developed character, perhaps one of his finest literary creations. Although Simple speaks the language of Harlem, he is understood around the world. In *The Sweet Flypaper of Life* Hughes offers another delightful panorama of Harlem, this time with photographs as well as words. Webster Smalley has summarized Hughes's contributions to American letters saying, "no writer has better interpreted and portrayed Negro life, especially in the urban North." Further, as Smalley points out, "no one has more faith in the strength and dignity of his people than does Hughes, . . ."[7] It is this faith that comes across so distinctly in the Simple stories and in *The Sweet Flypaper of Life.*

Aside from the writing already mentioned Hughes has contributed to the over-all understanding of the Negro with a series of well written books for children and young people, two selections of Negro poetry, a history of NAACP, and two anthologies of African writing. He has also translated the work of several well known Spanish and French authors.

Critics do not rank Hughes as a writer of the first class. He has done little with the deeper questions of life and often his work is confined to a certain predictable scope. In some cases he stresses the experimental at the expense of sound literary values while at other times he tends toward a journalistic facility. Considering the amount of work Hughes has done it is little wonder that some of his pieces are less polished than others. One might wish that he had spent more time in perfecting certain poems or stories rather than branching out into theatre work and editorial projects. After all this is said, however, one must admit that Hughes's writing is often effective and moving. A reading of his early poems and stories, his first volume of autobiography, and the Simple sketches reveals originality and understanding. Hughes has performed two major literary services; first, he has clarified for the Negro audience their own strength and dignity and, second, he has supplied the white audience with an explanation of how the Negro feels and what he wants.

Like most of the literature produced by the Negro in America,

[7]Webster Smalley, "Introduction," *Five Plays of Langston Hughes* (Bloomington: University of Indiana Press, 1963), p. vii.

Hughes's writing has been motivated by the immediate problems of the race. He has illuminated these problems with optimism and humor. Hughes believes the Negro has a right to share in the American dream of opportunity and freedom. In his writing he enunciates a hope that this dream will not be long deferred. In the meantime, he says:

> I, too, sing America.
> I am the darker brother.
> They send me to eat in the kitchen
> When company comes,
>
> But I laugh,
> And eat well,
> And grow strong.
> Tomorrow,
> I'll be at the table
> When company comes.
> Nobody'll dare
> Say to me,
> "Eat in the kitchen,"
> Then.
> Besides,
> They'll see how beautiful I am
> And be ashamed—
> I, too, am America.[8]

Hughes's problem has been to portray the American Negro with literary skill. He has done so in most cases with success. In seeking to play back the melodies and emotions of the Negro he has contributed a valuable component to American literature.

[8]Hughes, *Selected Poems*, p. 275.

appendix

Foreign Reception of Langston Hughes

Langston Hughes is well known to foreign readers. Because his poems, plays, and short stories have appeared in a dozen different languages from Arabic to Polish, it is not overstating the case to say that Hughes is accepted by people all over the world as the voice of the American Negro. The chief reasons for his popularity lie in his exposition of Negro music and American race relations—two topics of great interest throughout the world.

Hughes first became known abroad as a poet and it is for his poems that he continues to be best known today. In 1924 *Les Continents*, a Paris magazine, carried two of Hughes's poems. From this beginning, interest in his work spread throughout Europe. Anna Nussbaum included thirty-seven poems in her anthology *Africa Singt* in 1929, and in 1932 the Russians issued *Scottsboro Limited* in an edition of ten thousand copies. During the thirties the number of Hughes's contributions in Russian journals outdistanced all other American writers except those two perennial favorites, Erskine Caldwell and Ernest Hemingway.[1] His popularity in the Soviet Union continues strong in recent years.[2]

There is a remarkable contrast in the political motivation that sparked Hughes's popularity in Russia and that which prompted the Dutch underground to publish his poems in 1944. The Russians delighted in Hughes's critical comments on democracy while the Dutch found inspiration in his songs of freedom. It is appropriate that this poetry written in honor of a submerged people in America was

[1]Glendora Brown and Deming Brown, *A Guide to Soviet Russian Translations of American Literature* (New York: Columbia University Press, 1954), p. 21.

[2]Deming Brown, in his study *Soviet Attitudes Toward American Writing* (Princeton: Princeton University Press, 1962), says in the period between 1955 to 1960, "Langston Hughes continued to be the Russian's favorite contemporary American poet, . . ." p. 177. In 1964, a rather comprehensive listing of Hughes's publications entitled *Lengston Kh'yuz, Bibliograficheskii ukazatel'* appeared in Russian. This alone is a significant index of Hughes's importance to Soviet readers.

selected to bring a message of hope to a conquered people in Europe.[3]

Latin American editors also responded favorably to Hughes's poetry, particularly his protest verse like "Brass Spittoons," and "I, Too." As early as 1940 René Piquion published a critical biography in Haiti long before such evaluation was available in English. It is not surprising that Hughes wrote to Mrs. Knopf about translation of his autobiography into Spanish:

> So far I think I have forgotten to mention to you the fact that there might be some sales and translation possibilities for THE BIG SEA in Latin America. Many of my poems and several of my short stories have appeared in translation in various countries down there, and I am in two Latin American anthologies of Negro verse in Spanish.[4]

The Big Sea subsequently appeared in both Spanish and Portuguese.

Once Hughes's reputation was established as a poet, foreign publishers readily accepted prose and drama. The novel *Not Without Laughter* appeared first in Russian, then in Polish, Dutch, Swedish, Italian, Spanish, and Japanese. Individual short stories such as "Cora Unashamed" and "Slave on the Block" were accepted in European journals shortly after their publication in America. By 1951, *The Ways of White Folks* had been translated into four central European languages, and in 1958 Insel Verlag included *Laughing To Keep From Crying* in its famous Bucherei series.

The world knows the American Negro best through Hughes's sketches of Jesse B. Semple. Both the Germans and the Danes have published complete books of Simple stories while separate episodes have appeared in papers and magazines around the world. An analysis of Simple's popularity in Germany closes with this statement:

> Simple ist ein Mann aus dem Volke, der angeborene Natürlichkeit mit gesundem Menschenverstand paart. Er ähnelt in gewisser Hinsicht dem "Simplicius Simplicissimus" von Grimmelshausen.[5]

[3]A letter in Hughes's personal copy of *Lament for Dark Peoples* is inscribed "To the author this clandestinely anthology with feelings of friendship and admiration and with a bad conscience. February 17, 1946."

[4]Letter from Langston Hughes to Blanche Knopf dated August 5, 1940. Yale University Library.

[5]Heinz von Rogge, "Die Figur des Simple im Werke von Langston Hughes," *Die Neueren Sprachen*, Heft 12, 1955, pp. 565–566.

Although *Not Without Laughter* came out in Japan in 1941 it is only within the last five years that Hughes's writing has been available in quantity in the Eastern hemisphere. Since 1958 seven of Hughes's books have been translated into Japanese and five into various Indian dialects. In Japan, according to Hughes's translator, the principal interest is in poetry.[6] Indian readers, on the other hand, seem to favor Hughes's prose. Several of the "First Books" have been issued in India by the United States Information Service, and *Famous American Negroes* is available in Hindi, Bengali, and Marathi.

Hughes is widely known abroad as an interpreter of the American Negro. His stories, novels, plays, and poems explain the facts of our caste system as well as psychological complexities it often produces. In his explanations Hughes is seldom violent and never pedantic. He delivers his message with the delicate instruments of humor and irony. Furthermore, the message is clothed in the rhythms of Negro music, one American product approved around the world. With his gift for exposition and his insights on Negro life Hughes has won an enviable international reputation.

[6]In a letter to the writer dated July 27, 1962 Mr. Hajime Kijima states, "In general Mr. Hughes's works have been well received in Japan. Especially poetry-loving younger men and women like his writing."

Epilogue

Langston Hughes died after a brief illness on May 22, 1967. His travels were extensive and work continued to pour from his typewriter up to the time of his hospitalization. In March, 1967, a trip to the University of California at Los Angeles followed by appointments in New York and Paris seemed only routine.

Posthumous works have included *Panther and the Lash*, a book of poems; *Black Magic*, a pictorial history of the Negro in American entertainment; *Best Short Stories of Negro Writers*; and, most recently, *The Poetry of the Negro, 1746–1970*, an anthology compiled with Arna Bontemps. No doubt the list of Hughes's published works will continue to grow as editors review the rich and extensive body of his work.

Since Hughes's death, a substantial amount of critical and biographical material has appeared. Two biographies are available for younger readers (Meltzer and Rollins) while a sound critical study (Emanuel) supplies good background for the mature reader (see pages 249–255). Serious interest in Hughes as a writer has increased and will no doubt continue to develop. Few writers have concerned themselves over such a long period and in so many varied forms with the condition of the black man in white America. Hughes's story was seldom pleasant but he told it with understanding and hope. The voice of black America is nowhere better recorded than in the writings of Langston Hughes.

part two

BIBLIOGRAPHY

An Explanation

This bibliography of Langston Hughes's writing includes all publications in English and foreign languages up to 1965 as far as they could be identified. It does not include his publication in newspapers, his lyrics for published music, or his readings on phonograph recordings.

The bibliography is divided into eight sections as follows:

   I   Books by Langston Hughes. Books are arranged by date of first edition. Foreign and later editions are listed following the original edition. The source of bibliographic information is given for editions not seen.

  II   Books edited by Langston Hughes.

 III   Book-length translations by Langston Hughes.

 IV   Works of Langston Hughes appearing in foreign languages for which there is no English edition.

  V   Collections indexed for contributions by Langston Hughes. Collections are listed alphabetically by title.

 VI   Prose and drama by Langston Hughes. Each item is listed alphabetically by title with a chronological arrangement for its publication.

VII   Poems by Langston Hughes. Each poem is listed alphabetically by title with a chronological arrangement for its publication.

VIII   Works about Langston Hughes.

Whenever a listing has not been personally examined an asterisk (*) is placed before the number and information given in the entry as to the source of bibliographic information.

Books by Langston Hughes

1. THE WEARY BLUES, First Edition, 1926

   The Weary Blues. Introduction by Carl Van Vechten. New York: Alfred A. Knopf, 1926. 109p.

   Contents (in seven sections): THE WEARY BLUES: The Weary Blues — Jazzonia — Negro Dancers — The Cat and the Saxaphone — Young Singer — Cabaret — To Midnight Nan at LeRoy's — To a Little Lover Lass, Dead — Harlem Night Club — Nude Young Dancer — Young Prostitute — To a Black Dancer — Song for a Banjo Dance — Blues Fantasy — Lenox Avenue: Midnight — DREAM VARIATIONS: Dream Variation — Winter Moon — Poème d'Automne — Fantasy in Purple — March Moon — Joy — THE NEGRO SPEAKS OF RIVERS: The Negro Speaks of Rivers — Cross — The Jester — The South — As I Grew Older — Aunt Sue's Stories — Poem — BLACK PIERROT: A Black Pierrot — Harlem Night Song — Songs to the Dark Virgin — Ardella — Poem — When Sue Wears Red — Pierrot — WATER FRONT STREETS: Water Front Streets — A Farewell — Long Trip — Port Town — Sea Calm — Caribbean Sunset — Young Sailor — Seascape — Natcha — Sea Charm — Death of an Old Seaman — SHADOWS IN THE SUN: Beggar Boy — Troubled Woman — Suicide's Note — Sick Room — Soledad — To the Dark Mercedes of "El Palacio de Amor" — Mexican Market Woman— After Many Springs — Young Bride — The Dream Keeper — Poem — OUR LAND: Our Land — Lament for Dark Peoples — Afraid — Poem — Summer Night — Disillusion — Dance Africaine — The White Ones — Mother to Son — Poem — Epilogue.

   Notes: An edition of 1500 copies constituted the first issue, according to the publisher.

   Yale University Library has copies inscribed to Carl Van Vechten, Walter White, James Weldon Johnson and Hughes's mother.

   Dedication: To My Mother

   Introducing Langston Hughes to the Reader by Carl Van Vechten pp. 9–13.

   A cheap edition was issued in 1931 with same pagination and same title page as first edition, lacking half-title and in smaller format.

1a. THE WEARY BLUES, Danish Edition, 1945

> Blues. Translated by Ole Sarvig. Kobenhavn: Rosendahl og Jorgensens, 1945. 101p.
>
> *Note*: Illustrated with photographs by A. Mertz and J. Roos.

1b. THE WEARY BLUES, Japanese Edition, 1958

> Niguro to Kawa. Translated by T. Saito. Tokyo: Kokobunsha, 1958. 143p.

2. FINE CLOTHES TO THE JEW, First Edition, 1927

> Fine Clothes to the Jew. New York: Alfred A. Knopf, 1927. 90p.
>
> *Contents* (in six sections): BLUES: Hey! — Hard Luck — Misery — Suicide — Bad Man — Gypsy Man — Po' Boy Blues — Homesick Blues — RAILROAD AVENUE: Railroad Avenue — Brass Spittoons — Ruby Brown — The New Cabaret Girl — Closing Time — Prize Fighter — Crap Game — Ballad of Gin Mary — Death of Do Dirty — Elevator Boy — Porter — Sport — Saturday Night — GLORY HALLELUIAH: Judgement Day — Prayer Meeting — Feet o' Jesus — Prayer — Shout — Fire — Moan — Angels Wings — Sinner — BEALE STREET LOVE: Beale Street Love — Cora — Workin' Man — Bad Luck Card — Baby — Evil Woman — A Ruined Gal — Minnie Sings Her Blues — Dressed Up — Black Gal — FROM THE GEORGIA ROADS: Sun Song — Magnolia Flowers — Mulatto — Red Silk Stockings — Jazz Band in a Parisian Cabaret — Song for a Dark Girl — Mammy — Laughers — AND BLUES: Lament Over Love — Gal's Cry for a Dying Lover — Young Gal's Blues — Midwinter Blues — Listen Here Blues — Hard Daddy — Bound No'th Blues — Ma Man — Hey! Hey!
>
> *Notes*: An edition of 1546 copies constituted the first issue, according to the publisher.
>
> Yale University Library has copies inscribed to Carl Van Vechten, James Weldon Johnson and Hughes's mother.
>
> Dedication: To Carl Van Vechten
>
> A Note on the Blues p. 13

3. NOT WITHOUT LAUGHTER, First Edition, 1930

> Not Without Laughter. New York: Alfred A. Knopf, 1930. 324p.
>
> *Notes*: An edition of 2500 copies constituted the first issue, according to the publisher.
>
> Yale University Library has copies inscribed to Carl Van Vechten and James Weldon Johnson.
>
> Dedication: To J. E. and Amy Spingarn.
>
> A cheap edition was issued in 1933 with same pagination and same title page as first edition, lacking half-title and in smaller format.

3a. NOT WITHOUT LAUGHTER, English Edition, 1930
Not Without Laughter. London: Allen and Unwin, 1930, 324p.

3b. NOT WITHOUT LAUGHTER, English Edition, 1969.
Not Without Laughter. Introduction by Arna Bontemps. New
York: Collier, 1969. 304p.

3c. NOT WITHOUT LAUGHTER, Argentinian Edition, 1945
Pero con Risas. Translated by Nestor R. Ortis Oderigo. Buenos
Aires: Editorial Futuro, 1945. 252p.

*3d. NOT WITHOUT LAUGHTER, Dutch Edition, 1941
Niet Zonder Lachen. Translated by Manuel van Loggem. Amster-
dam: F. G. Kroonder, 1941. 255p.
Brinkmans 1941. Source of bibliographic information.

3e. NOT WITHOUT LAUGHTER, Dutch Edition, 1951
Niet Zonder Lachen. Translated by Manuel van Loggem. Amsterdam: N. V. Em. Querido's Uitgeversmij, 1951. 200p.

3f. NOT WITHOUT LAUGHTER, French Edition, 1934
Sandy. Translated by Gabriel Beauroy. Paris: Editions Rieder,
1934. 304p.

3g. NOT WITHOUT LAUGHTER, Italian Edition, 1947
Piccola. Translated by M. Monti. Milano: Longanesi, 1947. 374p.

*3h. NOT WITHOUT LAUGHTER, Japanese Edition, 1941
Waramanu Domo Nashi. Translated by Y. Yokemura. Tokyo:
Hakasuisha, 1940. 430p.
Information supplied by H. Kijima, translator of Hughes's books
into Japanese.

*3i. NOT WITHOUT LAUGHTER, Japanese Edition, 1961
Warai Naki Ni Arazu. Translated by T. Hamamoto. Tokyo:
Hayakawa Shobô, 1961.
Information supplied by H. Kijima, translator of Hughes's books
into Japanese.

3j. NOT WITHOUT LAUGHTER, Russian Edition, 1932
Smech Skvoz Slezy. Translated by Vera Stanevic. Moskva:
Goslitizdat, 1932. 237p.

3k. NOT WITHOUT LAUGHTER, Swedish Edition, 1948
Tant Hagers Barn. Translated by Martin Edlund. Stockholm: KF's
Bokförlag, 1948. 341p.
Note: Paper bound edition published in same format in 1948.

*31. NOT WITHOUT LAUGHTER, Swedish Edition, 1961

Sandy och Harriett. Translated by Martin Edlund. Stockholm: Folket i Bild, 1961. 254p.

Index Translationum.

3m. NOT WITHOUT LAUGHTER, Swiss Edition, 1949

Vater und Sohn. Zurich: Universum Verlag, 1949. 61p.

4. DEAR LOVELY DEATH, First Edition, 1931

Dear Lovely Death. Amenia, New York: Troutbeck Press, 1931. 20 unnumbered pages.

Contents: Drum — The Consumptive — Dear Lovely Death — Tower — Two Things — Flight — Afro American Fragment — Demand — Sailor — Florida Road Workers — Poem — Aesthete in Harlem

Notes: Verso of last leaf says One hundred copies printed at the Troutbeck Press for private distribution only. Cover design by Zell Ingram. Frontispiece by Amy Spingarn, Handmade paper by Dard Hunter.

Yale University Library has a copy inscribed to Carl Van Vechten. Kansas University Library has inscribed copy.

5. THE NEGRO MOTHER, First Edition, 1931

The Negro Mother and Other Dramatic Recitations. Decorations by Prentiss Taylor. New York: Golden Stair Press, 1931. 20p.

Contents: The Colored Soldier — Broke — The Black Clown — The Big Timer — Dark Youth

6. THE DREAM KEEPER, First Edition, 1932

The Dream Keeper and Other Poems. Illustrations by Helen Sewell. New York: Alfred A. Knopf, 1932. 77p.

Contents (in five sections): THE DREAM KEEPER: The Dream Keeper — Winter Moon — Fairies — Autumn Thoughts — Dreams — April Rain Song — After Many Springs — Winter Sweetness — Quiet Girl — Poem — Joy — SEA CHARM: Water Front Streets — Long Trip — Sea Calm — Sailor — Seascape — Mexican Market Woman — Beggar Boy — Parisian Beggar Woman — Irish Wake — Death of an Old Seaman — Sea Charm — DRESSED UP: A Note on Blues — Dressed Up — Reasons Why — Negro Dancers — The Weary Blues — Homesick Blues — Wide River — Minstrel Man — A Black Pierrot — Bound No'th Blues — Song — Passing Love — When Sue Wears Red — Po' Boy Blues — Song for a Banjo Dance — Night and Morn — FEET O' JESUS: Feet O' Jesus — Sinner — Prayer — Judgement

Day — Ma Lord — Baby — Lullaby — Prayer Meeting —
WALKERS WITH THE DAWN: Walkers With the Dawn — African
Dance — Aunt Sue's Stories — Alabama Earth — My People —
Lincoln Monument: Washington — Dream Variation — Sun Song
— The Negro Speaks of Rivers — The Negro — Mother to Son
— As I Grew Older — I Too — Youth

Notes: An edition of 500 copies constituted the first issue, according to the publisher.

Dedication: To My Brother

By Way of Introduction [unpaged] by Effie Power, Director of Work with Children, Cleveland Public Library

7.   SCOTTSBORO LIMITED, First Edition, 1932

Scottsboro Limited, Four Poems and a Play. Illustrations by
Prentiss Taylor. New York: Golden Stair Press, 1932. 18 unnumbered pages.

Contents: Justice — Scottsboro — Christ in Alabama — Town
of Scottsboro — Scottsboro Limited

Notes: Yale University Library has No. 3 of 30 large paper
copies signed by the author and artist with lithographs
printed from the original stones.

7a. SCOTTSBORO LIMITED, Russian Edition, 1932

Skottsboro. Translated by A. Grefsa and A. Mejers. Moskva:
CK Mopr, 1932. 23p.

8.   POPO AND FIFINA, First Edition, 1932

Popo and Fifina. By Arna Bontemps and Langston Hughes.
Illustrations by E. Simms Campbell. New York: Macmillan,
1932. 100p.

Note: An edition of 4000 copies constituted the first issue, according to the publisher.

*8a. POPO AND FIFINA, Czechoslovakian Edition, 1961

Popo and Fifina. Translated by J. Markovic. Praha: Státni Naklad-
telstvi Detské Kniby, 1961. 106p.

Information supplied by *Claus Dressler, translator of Negro
poetry into German.

8b. POPO AND FIFINA, French Edition

Popo et Fifine. Translated by René Piquion. Port au Prince, Haiti:
Imprimerie de L'Etat, [n. d.] 81p.

In Langston Hughes's collection.

*8c. POPO AND FIFINA, Japanese Edition, 1957

    Popo to Fifina. Translated by H. Kijima. Tokyo: Iwanani Shoten, 1957. 182p.

    Information supplied by H. Kijima, translator of Hughes's books into Japanese.

*8d. POPO AND FIFINA, Russian Edition, 1962

    Dity z Gajiti. Translated by V. Mytrofanov. Kiev: Detizdat, 1962. 88p.

    Index Translationum

9.   THE WAYS OF WHITE FOLKS, First Edition, 1934

    The Ways of White Folks. New York: Alfred A. Knopf, 1934. 248p.

    Contents: Cora Unashamed — Slave on the Block — Home — Passing — A Good Job Gone — Rejuvenation Through Joy — The Blues I'm Playing — Red Headed Baby — Poor Little Black Fellow — Little Dog — Berry — Mother and Child — One Christmas Eve — Father and Son

    Notes: An edition of 2500 copies constituted the first issue, according to the publisher.

        Yale University Library has copies inscribed to Carl Van Vechten and James Weldon Johnson.

    Dedication: To Noel Sullivan

9a.   THE WAYS OF WHITE FOLKS, Czechoslovakian Edition, 1951

    To Jsou Bílí. Translated by K. Bem. Praha: Mladá Fronta, 1951. 150p.

9b.   THE WAYS OF WHITE FOLKS, English Edition, 1934

    The Ways of White Folks, London: Allen and Unwin, 1934. 248p.

9c.   THE WAYS OF WHITE FOLKS, French Edition, 1946

    Histoires de Blancs. Translated by Hélène Bokanowski. Paris: Editions de Minuit, 1946. 258p.

*9d. THE WAYS OF WHITE FOLKS, Russian Edition, 1936

    Nravy Belyh. Translated by N. S. Nadezdina. Leningrad: Goslitizdat, 1936, 268p.

    Index Translationum.

*9e. THE WAYS OF WHITE FOLKS, Yugoslavian Edition, 1951

    Takvi su Beli Ljudi. Translated by S. Brkíc. Beograd: "Rad," 1951. 174p.

    Index Translationum.

10. A NEW SONG, First Edition, 1938

   A New Song. Introduction by Michael Gold. Frontispiece by Joe
   Jones. New York: International Workers Order, 1938. 31p.

   Contents: Let America Be America Again — Justice — Park
   Bench — Chant for Tom Mooney — Chant for May Day —
   Pride — Ballad of Ozie Powell — Kids Who Die — History —
   Ballads of Lenin — Song of Spain — A New Song — Sister
   Johnson Marches — Open Letter to the South — Negro Ghetto
   — Lynching Song — Union

11. THE BIG SEA, First Edition, 1940

   The Big Sea. New York: Alfred A. Knopf, 1940. 335p.

   Notes: An edition of 3200 copies constituted the first issue,
   according to the publisher.

   Yale University Library has a copy inscribed to Carl Van
   Vechten.

   Dedication: To Emerson and Toy Harper.

11a. THE BIG SEA, Reprint Edition, 1963

   The Big Sea. New York: Hill and Wang, 1963. 335p.

11b. THE BIG SEA, Argentinian Edition, 1944

   El Imenso Mar. Translated by L. Rivaud. Buenos Aires: Editorial Lautaro, 1944. 308p.

11c. THE BIG SEA, Brazilian Edition, 1944

   O Imenso Mar. Translated by F. Burkinski. Rio de Janeiro: Editorial Vitória, 1944. 458p.

11d. THE BIG SEA, English Edition, 1940

   The Big Sea. London: Hutchinson, 1940. 254p.

11e. THE BIG SEA, French Edition, 1947

   Les Grandes Profondeurs. Paris: Editions Seghers, 1947. 415p.

11f. THE BIG SEA, German Edition, 1963

   Ich Werfe Meine Netze Aus. Translated by Paridam von dem
   Knesebeck. München: Nymphenburger Verlag, 1963. 240p.

11g. THE BIG SEA, Italian Edition, 1948

   Nel Mare Della Vita. Translated by A. Ghirelli. Rome: Einaudi,
   1948. 439p.

11h. THE BIG SEA, Polish Edition, 1949

   Wielkie Morze. Translated by J. Kydrynski. Warszawa: "Czytelnik,"
   1949. 282p.

12. SHAKESPEARE IN HARLEM, First Edition, 1942

Shakespeare in Harlem. Drawings by E. McKnight Kauffer. New York: Alfred A. Knopf, 1942. 124p.

Contents (in eight sections): SEVEN MOMENTS OF LOVE: Twilight Reverie — Supper Time — Bed Time — Daybreak — Sunday — Pay Day — Letter — DECLARATIONS: Evil — Hope — Young Negro Girl — Harlem Sweeties — Little Lyric — Declaration — Kid Sleepy — Snob — Statement — Me and the Mule — Present —· Free Man — If-ing — Aspiration — BLUES FOR MEN: Six Bits Blues — Evenin' Air Blues — Out of Work — Brief Encounter — Morning After — Mississippi Levee — In a Troubled Key — Only Woman Blues — Hey Hey Blues — DEATH IN HARLEM: Death in Harlem — Wake — Cabaret Girl Dies on Welfare Island — Sylvester's Dying Bed — Crossing — Death Chant ,— MAMMY SONGS: Southern Mammy Sings — Share Croppers — West Texas — Merry Go Round — Ku Klux — BALLADS: Ballad of the Sinner — Ballad of the Killer Boy — Ballad of the Fortune Teller — Ballad of the Girl Whose Name is Mud — Ballad of the Gypsy — Ballad of the Pawnbroker — Ballad of the Man Who's Gone — BLUES FOR LADIES: Down and Out — Love Again Blues — Midnight Chippie's Lament — Widow Woman — LENOX AVENUE: Shakespeare in Harlem — Fired — Early Evening Quarrel — Announcement — 50, 50 — Evil Morning — Lover's Return — Black Maria — Reverie on the Harlem River — Love

Notes: An edition of 3300 copies constituted the first issue, according to the publisher.

Yale University Library has a copy inscribed to Carl Van Vechten.

Dedication: To Louise

*12a. SHAKESPEARE IN HARLEM, Japanese Edition, 1962

Shishu-Kokujingai No Shakespeare. Translated by T. Saito. Tokyo: Kokobunsha, 1962. 171p.

Information supplied by H. Kijima, translator of Hughes's books into Japanese.

13. FREEDOM'S PLOW, First Edition, 1943

Freedom's Plow. New York: Musette Publishing Company, 1943. 14p.

Notes: Verso of title page says, "copyright 1943. This poem was read by Paul Muni over the Blue Network on Monday, March 15, 1943 from 3:45 to 4:00 P.M. Eastern War Time. Background music was furnished by organ accompaniment and the Golden Gate Quartette."

14. JIM CROW'S LAST STAND, First Edition, 1943

> Jim Crow's Last Stand. Atlanta: Negro Publication Society of America, 1943. 30p.
>
> *Contents*: The Black Man Speaks — Democracy — Color — Freedom — Red Cross — Note to All Nazis — How About it Dixie — Blue Bayou — The Bitter River — October 16 — Motherland — Brothers — To Captain Mulzac — Still Here — Visitors to the Blackbelt — Ballad of the Landlord — Big Buddy — Ballad of Sam Solomon — Note on Commercial Theatre — Daybreak in Alabama — Me and My Song — Good Morning Stalingrad — Jim Crow's Last Stand
>
> *Note*: On Contents page "black" and "Belt" upside down in title "Visitors to the Blackbelt."

*15. STREET SCENE, First Edition, 1948

> Street Scene, an American opera based on Elmer Rice's play. Lyrics by Langston Hughes. New York: Chappell, 1948. 273p.
>
> *Note*: Two act musical drama.
>
> Music by Kurt Weill.

16. FIELDS OF WONDER, First Edition, 1947

> Fields of Wonder. New York: Alfred A. Knopf, 1947. 114p.
>
> *Contents* (in nine sections): FIELDS OF WONDER: Heaven — Snail — Big Sur — Moonlight Night: Carmel — Snake — New Moon — Birth — BORDER LINE: Border Line — Night: Four Songs — Dustbowl — Burden — One — Beale Street — Gifts — Circles — Grave Yard — Convent — Poppy Flower — Gypsy Melodies — Montmartre — Fragments — Desert — End — HEART ON THE WALL: Heart — Remembrance — Havana Dreams — Girl — For Dead Mimes — SILVER RAIN: In Time of Silver Rain — Fulfilment — Night Song — Silence — Carolina Cabin — Songs — Sleep — DESIRE: Desire — Dream — Juliet — Man — TEARLESS: Vagabonds — Luck — Exits — Walls — Chippy — Dancers — Grief — Prayer — MORTAL STORM: A House in Taos — Old Sailor — Genius Child — Dream Dust — Strange Hurt — Little Song — Personal — Jaime — Faithful One — Sailing Date — There — STARS OVER HARLEM: Trumpet Players: 52nd Street — Harlem Dance Hall — Dimout in Harlem — Motherland — Communion — Migration — Stars — WORDS LIKE FREEDOM: Refugee in America — Earth Song — Wisdom — Dusk — When the Armies Passed — Today — Oppression — Spirituals — Reprise
>
> *Notes*: An edition of 2500 copies constituted the first issue according to the publisher.
>
> Dedication: To Arna and Alberta Bontemps

17. TROUBLED ISLAND, First Edition, 1949

Troubled Island, an opera in 3 acts by William Grant Still. Libretto by Langston Hughes. New York: Leeds Music Corporation, 1949. 38p.

Note: verso of title page says "World premiere Thursday, March, 31st, 1949 at New York City Opera Company.

18. ONE WAY TICKET, First Edition, 1949

One Way Ticket. Illustrated by Jacob Lawrence. New York: Alfred A. Knopf, 1949. 136p.

Contents (in nine sections): MADAM TO YOU: Madam's Past History — Madam and Her Madam — Madam's Calling Cards — Madam and the Rent Man — Madam and the Number Writer — Madam and the Phone Bill — Madam and the Charity Child — Madam and the Fortune Teller — Madam and the Wrong Visitor — Madam and the Minister — Madam and her Might Have Been — Madam and the Census Man — LIFE IS FINE: Mama and Daughter — S-sss-ss-sh — Sunday Morning Prophecy — Life is Fine — Honey Babe — Stranger in Town — DARK GLASSES: Seashore Through Dark Glasses — Lincoln Theatre — Song for Billie Holiday — Still Here — SILHOUETTES: Blue Bayou — Flight — Silhouette — Lynching Song — ONE WAY TICKET: One Way Ticket — Restrictive Covenants — Visitors to the Black Belt — Juice Joint — Negro Servant — Puzzled — Who But the Lord? — The Ballad of Margie Polite — MAKING A ROAD: Note on Commercial Theatre — Daybreak in Alabama — Man Into Men — Roland Hayes Beaten — Democracy — October 16 — Florida Road Workers — TOO BLUE: Late Last Night — Little Old Letter — Curious — Bad Morning — Lonesome Corner — Could Be — Yesterday and Today — Too Blue — MIDNIGHT RAFFLE: Midnight Raffle — Monroe's Blues — White Felts in Fall — Raid — Little Green Tree — Blues on a Box — HOME IN A BOX: Request for Requiems — Deceased — Final Curve — Boarding House — Funeral — SOUTH SIDE: CHICAGO: Summer Evening — Migrant — Graduation — Third Degree — Jitney — Interne at Provident

Notes: An edition of 3500 copies constituted the first issue, according to the publisher.

Yale University Library has a copy inscribed to Carl Van Vechten.

Dedication: To Nathaniel and Geraldine White.

19. SIMPLE SPEAKS HIS MIND, First Edition, 1950

Simple Speaks His Mind. New York: Simon and Schuster, 1950. 231p.

> *Notes*: Verso of dedication page says "The author and publisher of *Simple Speaks His Mind* are grateful to the *Chicago Defender* where these stories originated, the *New Republic* and *Phylon* for permission to reprint material in this book."
>
> Yale University Library has uncorrected proofs.
>
> Dedication: To Zell and Garnett
>
> Paper covered edition issued in 1950 with same pagination and title page.

19a. SIMPLE SPEAKS HIS MIND, English Edition, 1951

> Simple Speaks His Mind. London: Gollancz, 1951. 231p.

19b. SIMPLE SPEAKS HIS MIND, Danish Edition, 1954

> Simple Siger Sin Mening. Translated by Michael Tejn. Kobenhavn: Gyldendal, 1954. 228p.
>
> *Note*: Verso of title page says: 4000 copies.

19c. SIMPLE SPEAKS HIS MIND, German Edition, 1960

> Simple Spricht Sich Aus. Translated by Günther Klotz. Berlin: Aufbau Verlag, 1960. 277p.

20. MONTAGE OF A DREAM DEFERRED, First Edition, 1951

> Montage of a Dream Deferred. New York: Henry Holt, 1951. 75p.
>
> *Contents* (in six sections): BOOGIE SEGUE TO BOP: Dream Boogie — Parade — Children's Rhymes — Sister — Comment on Stoop — Preference — Necessity — Question — Figurine — Buddy — Juke Box — Song — Ultimatum — Warning — Croon — New Yorkers — Wonder — Easy Boogie — DIG AND BE DUG: Movies — Tell Me — Not a Movie — Neon Signs — Numbers — What? So Soon? — Comment Against a Lamp Post — Figurette — Motto — Dead in There — Situation — Dancer — Advice — Green Memory — Wine O — Relief — Ballad of the Landlord — Corner Meeting — Projection — EARLY BRIGHT: Flatted Fifths — Tomorrow — Mellow — Live and Let Live — Gague — Bar — Cafe: 3 AM — Drunkard — Street Song — 125th Street — Dive — Warning Augmented — Up-Beat — Jam Session — Be-Bop Boys — Tag — VISA VERSA TO BACH: Theme for English B — College Formal — Low to High — Boogie: 1 AM — High to Low — Lady's Boogie — Freedom Train — Request — Shame on You — World War II — DREAM DEFERRED: Mystery — Sliver of Sermon — Testimonial — Passing — Nightmare Boogie — Sunday by the Combination — Casualty — Night Funeral in Harlem — Blues at Dawn — Dime — Argument — Neighbor — Evening Song — Chord — Fact — Joe

Lewis — Subway Rush Hour — Brothers — Likewise — Sliver
— Hope — Dream Boogie: Variation — LENOX AVENUE MURAL:
Harlem — Good Morning — Same in Blues — Comment on
Curb — Letter — Island
Note: Dedication: To Ralph and Fanny Ellison

21. LAUGHING TO KEEP FROM CRYING, First Edition, 1952
Laughing to Keep From Crying. New York: Henry Holt, 1952.
206p.
Contents: Who's Passing For Who? — Something in Common
— African Morning — Pushcart Man — Why, You Reckon? —
Saratoga Rain — Spanish Blood — Heaven to Hell — Sailor
Ashore — Slice Him Down — Tain't So — One Friday Morning
— Professor — Name in the Papers — Powder White Faces —
Rouge High — On the Way Home — Mysterious Madame
Shanghai — Never Room With a Couple — Little Old Spy —
Tragedy at the Baths — Trouble With the Angels — On The
Road — Big Meeting
Note: Dedication: To Dorothy

21a. LAUGHING TO KEEP FROM CRYING, Argentinian Edition,
1955
Riendo Por no Llorar. Translated by Julio Galer. Buenos Aires:
Ediciones Siglo Veinte, 1955. 184p.

21b. LAUGHING TO KEEP FROM CRYING, German Edition, 1958
Lachen um Nicht zu Weinen. Translated by Paridam von dem
Knesebeck. Berlin: Insel Verlag, 1958.

22. FIRST BOOK OF NEGROES, First Edition, 1952
The First Book of Negroes. Pictures by Ursula Koering. New
York: Franklin Watts, 1952. 69p.
Note: Yale University Library has copies inscribed to Carl Van
Vechten and Walter White.

22a. THE FIRST BOOK OF NEGROES, English Edition, 1956
The First Book of Negroes. Pictures by Ursula Koering. London:
Bailey, 1956. 69p.

23. SIMPLE TAKES A WIFE, First Edition, 1953
Simple Takes a Wife. New York: Simon and Schuster, 1953.
240p.

23a. SIMPLE TAKES A WIFE, English Edition, 1954
Simple Takes a Wife. London: Gollancz, 1954. 240p.

24. FAMOUS AMERICAN NEGROES, First Edition, 1954
Famous American Negroes. New York: Dodd Mead, 1954. 125p.
Note: Yale University Library has a copy autographed by all
living subjects of the biographical sketches.

24a. FAMOUS AMERICAN NEGROES, Reprint Edition, 1962
Famous American Negroes. New York: Popular Library, 1962.
125p.

*24b. FAMOUS AMERICAN NEGROES, Arabic Edition, 1961
Mashaher al-zunuj. 'umar al-Iskandari. al-Qaherah: Mu'assasit
al-Matbu'at al-Hadithah. 214p.
Index Translationum.

24c. FAMOUS AMERICAN NEGROES, Brazilian Edition, 1957
Negroes Famosas da America do Norte. Translated by H. R.
Gandelman and M. H. Muus. Sao Paulo: Editora Classico-
Cientifica, 1957. 114p.

24d. FAMOUS AMERICAN NEGROES, French Edition, 1962
Le dur Chemin de la Gloire: Portraits de Noirs Americains.
Translated by J. Recqueville. Paris: Istra, 1962. 205p.

24e. FAMOUS AMERICAN NEGROES, Indian Edition (Bengali) 1958
Pankmanthi Pragtelan. Bombay: Anant Desai, 1958.
Note: Verso of title page says 2000 copies printed.

*24f. FAMOUS AMERICAN NEGROES, Indian Edition (Bengali)
1957
America Negro manisha. Krishnager: Homashikha Prakashani
Vibhag, 1957. 178p.
Index Translationum.

24g. FAMOUS AMERICAN NEGROES, Indian Edition (Hindi) 1957
Prasiddha Amariki Nigro. Allahabad: Indian Press, 1957. 161p.

*24h. FAMOUS AMERICAN NEGROES. Indian Edition (Marathi)
1957
Smriti ani gaurav. Bombay: Majestic Book Stall, 1957. 66p.
Index Translationum.

*24i. FAMOUS AMERICAN NEGROES, Indian Edition (Marathi)
1957
Pwiva divya jyanche. Bombay: Majestic Book Stall, 1957. 63p.
Index Translationum.

*24j. FAMOUS AMERICAN NEGROES, Pakistan Edition, n.d.

 Swappa yader safal holo. Translated by S. Mannan. Dacca: Khosroj Kitab Mahal, n.d. 175p.

 Index Translationum.

25. FIRST BOOK OF RHYTHMS, First Edition, 1954

 The First Book of Rhythms. Pictures by Robin King. New York: Franklin Watts, 1954. 63p.

25a. FIRST BOOK OF RHYTHMS, English Edition, 1956

 The First Book of Rhythms. Pictures by Robin King. London: Bailey, 1956. 63p.

26. FIRST BOOK OF JAZZ, First Edition, 1955

 The First Book of Jazz. Pictures by Cliff Roberts. New York: Franklin Watts, 1955. 65p.

*26a. FIRST BOOK OF JAZZ, Arabic Edition, n.d.

 Musiqa al-jaz. 'abd al-aziz. al-Qahirah: Maktabat al-Nahdah al-Misriyyah. n.d. 83p.

 Index Translationum.

26b. FIRST BOOK OF JAZZ, English Edition, 1957

 The First Book of Jazz. Pictures by Cliff Roberts. London: Bailey, 1957. 65p.

*26c. FIRST BOOK OF JAZZ, French Edition, 1962

 Une Introduction au Jazz. Translated by Sim Copans and P. Koechlin. Paris: Istra, 1962. 101p.

 Index Translationum.

*26d. FIRST BOOK OF JAZZ, German Edition, 1955

 Das Buch vom Jazz. Translated by Paridem von dem Knesebeck. Feldafing: Birchheim Verlag, 1955. 94p.

 Index Translationum.

*26e. FIRST BOOK OF JAZZ, Japanese Edition, 1960

 Jazu. Translated by H. Kijima. Tokyo: Iisuka Shoten, 1960. 189p.

 Note: Also contains parts of *Langston Hughes Reader* and *Famous American Negroes.*

 Index Translationum.

26f. FIRST BOOK OF JAZZ, Yugoslavian Edition, 1959

 Pocetnica O Jazzu. Translated by Slobadan Drenovac. Rijeka: Otokar Kersovani, 1959. 59p.

27. FAMOUS NEGRO MUSIC MAKERS, First Edition, 1955
   Famous Negro Music Makers. New York: Dodd Mead, 1955. 179p.

27a. FAMOUS NEGRO MUSIC MAKERS, Swedish Edition, 1956
   Black Music Fran Blues Till Bop. Stockholm: Wennerbergs Forlag, 1956. 112p.
   Notes: Photograph of Lena Horne on cover.
   Hughes spelled Huges on cover.

28. THE SWEET FLYPAPER OF LIFE, First Edition, 1955
   The Sweet Flypaper of Life. Photographs by Roy DeCarava. New York: Simon and Schuster, 1955. 98p.
   Note: Paper covered edition issued in 1955 with same pagination.

28a. THE SWEET FLYPAPER OF LIFE, German Edition, 1956
   Harlem Story. Translated by Paridem von dem Knesebeck. Ebenhausen: Langewiesche-Brandt, 1956. 92 unnumbered pages.

29. I WONDER AS I WANDER, First Edition, 1956
   I Wonder As I Wander. New York: Rinehart, 1956. 405p.
   Note: Yale University Library has galley proofs.
   Dedication: To Arthur and Marion Spingarn

29a. I WONDER AS I WANDER, Reprint Edition, 1964
   I Wonder As I Wander. New York: Hill and Wang, 1964. 405p.

29b. I WONDER AS I WANDER, Argentinian Edition, 1959
   Yo Viajo por un Mundo Encantado. Translated by Julio Galer. Buenos Aires: Compañia General Fabril, 1959. 417p.

30. PICTORIAL HISTORY OF THE NEGRO IN AMERICA, First Edition, 1956
   A Pictorial History of the Negro in America. By Milton Meltzer and Langston Hughes. New York: Crown, 1956. 316p.

30a. PICTORIAL HISTORY OF THE NEGRO IN AMERICA, Revised Edition, 1963
   A Pictorial History of the Negro in America. By Milton Meltzer and Langston Hughes. New York: Crown, 1963. 337p.

30b. PICTORIAL HISTORY OF THE NEGRO IN AMERICA, Third Edition, 1968.
   A Pictorial History of the Negro in America. By C. Eric Lincoln and Milton Meltzer. New York: Crown, 1968

31. FIRST BOOK OF THE WEST INDIES, First Edition, 1956
     The First Book of the West Indies. Pictures by Robert Bruce.
     New York: Franklin Watts, 1956. 63p.

31a. FIRST BOOK OF THE WEST INDIES, English Edition, 1956
     The First Book of the West Indies. Pictures by Robert Bruce.
     London: Baily, 1956. 63p.

31b. FIRST BOOK OF THE WEST INDIES, English Edition, 1965.
     The First Book of the Caribbean. London: Ward, 1965. 63p.

32. SIMPLE STAKES A CLAIM, First Edition, 1957
     Simple Stakes a Claim. New York: Rinehart, 1957. 191p.
     Note: Dedication: To Adele Glasgow
        pp. 9–12 "Let's Laugh a Little"

32a. SIMPLE STAKES A CLAIM, English Edition, 1958
     Simple Stakes a Claim. London: Gollancz, 1958. 191p.

33. FAMOUS NEGRO HEROES OF AMERICA, First Edition, 1958
     Famous Negro Heroes of America. Illustrated by Gerald McCann.
     New York: Dodd Mead, 1958. 202p.
     Note: Dedication: To my namesake cousin, Langston.

34. TAMBOURINES TO GLORY, First Edition, 1958
     Tambourines to Glory. New York: John Day, 1958. 188p.
     Note: Yale University Library has uncorrected galley proofs and
        seven manuscript drafts.
     Dedication: To Irene

34a. TAMBOURINES TO GLORY, English Edition, 1959
     Tambourines to Glory. London: Gollancz, 1959. 188p.

*34b. TAMBOURINES TO GLORY, Dutch Edition, 1961
     Op De Klank Der Tamboerijnen. Translated by M. Gerritsen.
     Bussum: Kroonder, 1960. 192p.
     Information supplied by Langston Hughes.

34c. TAMBOURINES TO GLORY, German Edition, 1959
     Trommeln zur Seligkeit. Translated by Paridem von dem Knese-
     beck. München: Kindler Verlag, 1959. 268p.

35. LANGSTON HUGHES READER, First Edition, 1958
     The Langston Hughes Reader. New York: Braziller, 1958. 501p.
     Contents (in nine sections): SHORT STORIES: Cora Unashamed —
     Slave on the Block — Red Headed Baby — Little Dog — Who's

Passing For Who? — Something in Common — Spanish Blood
— On the Way Home — Tain't So — One Friday Morning —
Tragedy at the Baths — Big Meeting — Thank You, M'am —
Patron of the Arts — POEMS: Weary Blues — The Negro Speaks
of Rivers — Dream Boogie — Parade — Children's Rhymes —
Sister — Preference — Necessity — Question — Figurine —
Buddy — Juke Box Love Song — Ultimatum — Warning —
Croon — New Yorkers — Wonder — Easy Boogie — Movies —
Tell Me — Not a Movie — Neon Signs — Numbers — What?
So Soon! — Comment Against Lamp Post — Figurette — Motto
— Dead in There — Situation — Dancer — Advice — Green
Memory — Wine O — Relief — Ballad of the Landlord —
Corner Meeting — Projection — Flatted Fifths — Tomorrow —
Mellow — Live and Let Live — Gauge — Bar — Cafe: 3 A.M.
— Drunkard — Street Song — 125th Street — Dive — Warning:
Augmented — Up Beat — Jam Session — Theme for English B
— College Formal — Low to High — Boogie: 1 A.M. — High
to Low — Lady's Boogie — Deferred — Request — Shame on
You — World War II — Mystery — Sliver of a Sermon —
Testimonial — Passing — Nightmare Boogie — Sunday by
the Combination — Casualty — Night Funeral — Blues at
Dawn — Dime — Argument — Neighbor — Evening Song
— Chord — Fact — Joe Lewis — Subway Rush Hour —
Brothers — Likewise — Sliver — Hope — Harlem — Good
Morning — Same in Blues — Letter — Island — Ballad of
Mary's Son — Acceptance — Pastoral — Dear Lovely Death —
Poet to Bigot — Testament — Conservatory Student Struggles
With Higher Instrumentation — Elderly Politicians — Freedom's
Plow — Epigram by Lanusse — Verse Written in the Album of
Mademoiselle by Dalcour — Flute Players by Rabearivelo —
Guinea by Roumain — She Left Herself One Evening by Damas
— Opinions of the New Student by Pedroso — Dead Soldier by
Guillen — CHILDREN'S POETRY: Children and Poetry — There's
Always Weather — New Flowers — Year Round — Country —
Grandpa's Stories — Piggy Back — Shearing Time — Brand
New Clothes — Problems — Not Often — Grocery Store — Poor
Rover — The Blues — Silly Animals — Old Dog Queenie —
Little Song — Friendly in a Friendly Way — Shepherd's Song
at Christmas — SONG LYRICS: Songs Called the Blues — NOVELS
AND HUMOR: Not Without Laughter — Simple Speaks His Mind
— Simple Takes a Wife — Simple Stakes a Claim — PLAYS:
Soul Gone Home — Simply Heavenly — AUTOBIOGRAPHY: The
Big Sea — I Wonder As I Wander — PAGEANT: Glory of Negro
History — ARTICLES AND SPEECHES: The Writer's Position in
America — Memories of Christmas — My Most Humiliating Jim
Crow Experience — Ten Thousand Beds — How to be a Bad

Writer — Jazz as Communication — Sweet Chariots of the World
— Fun of Being Black — My America

Note: Dedication To My Uncle John

36. SELECTED POEMS OF LANGSTON HUGHES, First Edition,
1959

Selected Poems of Langston Hughes. Drawings by E. McKnight
Kauffer. New York: Alfred A. Knopf, 1959. 297p.

Contents (in thirteen sections): AFRO AMERICAN FRAGMENTS:
Afro American Fragment — Negro Speaks of Rivers — Sun
Song — Aunt Sue's Stories — Danse Africaine — Negro —
American Heartbreak — October 16 — As I Grew Older — My
People — Dream Variations — FEET OF JESUS: Feet of Jesus —
Prayer — Shout — Fire — Sunday Morning Prophecy — Sinner
— Litany — Angels Wings — Judgement Day — Prayer Meet-
ing — Spirituals — Tambourines — SHADOW OF THE BLUES: The
Weary Blues — Hope — Late Last Night — Bad Morning —
Sylvester's Dying Bed — Wake — Could Be — Bad Luck Card
— Reverie on the Harlem River — Morning After — Early
Evening Quarrel — Evil — As Befits a Man — SEA AND LAND:
Havana Dreams — Catch — Water Front Streets — Long Trip
— Seascape — Moonlight Night: Carmel — Heaven — In Time
of Silver Rain — Joy — Winter Moon — Snail — March Moon
— Harlem Night Song — To Artina — Fulfillment — Gypsy
Melodies — Mexican Market Woman — A Black Pierrot —
Ardella — When Sue Wears Red — Love — Beale Street —
Port Town — Natcha — Young Sailor — Sea Calm — Dream
Dust — No Regrets — Troubled Woman — Island — DISTANCE
NOWHERE: Border Line — Garden — Genius Child — Strange
Hurt — Suicide's Note — End — Drum — Personal — Juliet
— Desire — Vagabonds — One — Desert — A House in Taos —
Demand — Dream — Night: Four Songs — Luck — Old Walt
— Kid in the Park — Song for Billie Holiday — Fantasy in
Purple — AFTER HOURS: Midnight Raffle — What? — Gone Boy
— 50-50 — Maybe — Lover's Return — Miss Blues Child —
Monroe's Blues — Stony Lonesome — Black Maria — LIFE IS
FINE: Life is Fine — Still Here — Ballad of the Gypsy — Me
and the Mule — Kid Sleepy — Little Lyric — Fired — Midnight
Dancer — Blue Monday — Ennui — Mama and Daughter —
Delinquent — S-sss-ss-s — Homecoming — Final Curve — Little
Green Tree — Crossing — Widow Woman — LAMENT OVER LOVE:
Misery — Ballad of the Fortune Teller — Cora — Down and Out
— Young Gal's Blues — Ballad of the Girl Whose Name is Mud
— Hard Daddy — Midwinter Blues — Little Old Letter —

Lament Over Love — MAGNOLIA FLOWERS: Daybreak in Alabama
— Cross — Magnolia Flowers — Mulatto — Southern Mammy
Sings — Ku Klux — West Texas — Share Croppers — Ruby
Brown — Roland Hayes Beaten — Uncle Tom — Porter — Blue
Bayou — Silhouette — Song for a Dark Girl — The South —
Bound No'th Blues — NAME IN UPHILL LETTERS: One Way
Ticket — Migrant — Summer Evening — Graduation — Interne
at Provident — Railroad Avenue — Mother to Son — Stars —
To Be Somebody — Note on Commercial Theatre — Puzzled —
Seashore Through Dark Glasses — Baby — Merry go Round
— Elevator Boy — Who But the Lord — Third Degree — Ballad
of the Man Who's Gone — MADAM TO YOU: Madam's Past History
— Madam and her Madam — Madam's Calling Cards — Madam
and the Rent Man — Madam and the Number Writer — Madam
and the Phone Bill — Madam and the Charity Child — Madam
and the Fortune Teller — Madam and the Wrong Visitor —
Madam and the Minister — Madam and Her Might Have Been
— Madam and the Census Man — MONTAGE OF A DREAM DE-
FERRED: Dream Boogie — Parade — Children's Rhymes — Sister
— Preference — Necessity — Question — Buddy — Juke Box
Love Song — Ultimatum — Warning — Croon — New Yorkers
— Wonder — Easy Boogie — Movies — Tell Me — Not a Movie
— Neon Signs — Numbers — What? So Soon! — Motto —
Dead in There — Situation — Dancer — Advice — Green
Memory — Wine O — Belief — Ballad of the Landlord — Corner
Meeting — Projection — Flatted Fifths — Tomorrow — Mellow
— Live and Let Live — Gauge — Bar Cafe: 3 A.M. —
Drunkard — Street Song — 125th Street — Dive — Warning:
Augmented — Up Beat — Jam Session — Be Bop Boys — Tag
— Theme for English B — College Formal — Low to High —
Boogie: 1 A.M. — High to Low — Lady's Boogie — So Long —
Deferred — Request — Shame on You — World War II —
Mystery — Sliver of Sermon — Testimonial — Passing — Night-
mare Boogie — Sunday by the Combination — Casualty — Night
Funeral — Blues at Dawn — Dime — Argument — Neighbor
— Evening Song — Chord — Fact — Joe Lewis — Subway Rush
Hour — Brothers — Likewise — Sliver — Hope — Dream
Boogie; Variation — Harlem — Good Morning — Same in Blues
— Comment on Curb — Letter — Island — WORDS LIKE FREE-
DOM: I Too — Freedom Train — Georgia Dusk — Lunch in a
Jim Crow Car — In Explanation of Our Times — Africa —
Democracy — Consider Me — Negro Mother — Refugee in
America — Freedom's Plow

Note: An edition of 5650 copies constituted the first issue,
　　according to the publisher.
　　Dedication: To My Cousin Flora.

37. SIMPLY HEAVENLY, First Edition, 1959
     Simply Heavenly. Music by David Martin. Book and Lyrics by
     Langston Hughes. New York: Dramatists Play Service, 1959. 86p.

38. THE FIRST BOOK OF AFRICA, First Edition, 1960
     The First Book of Africa. Illustrated with Photographs. New
     York: Franklin Watts, 1960. 66p.

38a. THE FIRST BOOK OF AFRICA, Revised Edition, 1964
     The First Book of Africa. Illustrated with Photographs. New
     York: Franklin Watts, 1964. 82p.

38b. THE FIRST BOOK OF AFRICA, English Edition, 1961
     The First Book of Africa. Illustrated with Photographs. London:
     Mayflower, 1961. 82p.

39. ASK YOUR MAMA, First Edition, 1961
     Ask Your Mama. New York: Alfred A. Knopf, 1961. 92p.
     Contents: Cutural Exchange — Ride, Red, Ride — Shades of
     Pigmeat — Ode to Dinah — Blues in Stereo — Horn of Plenty
     — Gospel cha cha — Is it True? — Ask Your Mama — Bird in
     Orbit — Jazztet Muted — Show Fare, Please

40. THE BEST OF SIMPLE, First Edition, 1961
     The Best of Simple. Illustrated by Bernhard Nast. New York:
     Hill and Wang, 1961. 245p.
     Note: Available both in paperback and hardback edition.

40a. THE BEST OF SIMPLE, French Edition, 1967
     L'ingenu de Harlem. Translated by F. J. Roy. Paris: Laffont,
     1967. 379p.
     Index Translationum

40b. THE BEST OF SIMPLE, Italian Edition, 1967
     Due Negri al bar. Translated by Augusta Mattioli. Milano: Mon-
     dadori, 1967. 344p.
     Index Translationum

41. FIGHT FOR FREEDOM, First Edition, 1962
     Fight for Freedom. Forward by Arthur Spingarn. New York:
     Norton, 1962. 224p.

41a. FIGHT FOR FREEDOM, Reprint Edition, 1962
     Fight for Freedom. Forward by Arthur Spingarn. New York:
     Berkley Publishing, 1962. 224p.

42. FIVE PLAYS OF LANGSTON HUGHES, First Edition, 1963
     Five Plays of Langston Hughes. Edited and with an Introduction

by Webster Smalley. Bloomington, Indiana: Indiana University Press, 1963. 258p.

Contents: Mulatto — Soul Gone Home — Little Ham — Simply Heavenly — Tambourines to Glory

43. SOMETHING IN COMMON AND OTHER STORIES, First Edition, 1963

Something in Common and Other Stories. New York: Hill and Wang, 1963. 236p.

Contents: Thank You, M'am — Little Dog — Rock, Church — Little Old Spy — A Good Job Gone — Who's Passing for Who? — African Morning — Pushcart Man — Why, You Reckon? — Saratoga Rain — Spanish Blood — Gumption — Heaven to Hell — Sailor Ashore — Slice Him Down — His Last Affair — Tain't So — Father and Son — Professor — Sorrow for a Midget — Powder White Faces — Rouge High — The Gun — Fine Accommodations — No Place to Make Love — On the Way Home — Mysterious Madame Shanghai — Patron of the Arts — Early Autumn — Never Room with a Couple — Tragedy at the Baths — Trouble With the Angels — On the Road — Big Meeting — Breakfast in Virginia — Blessed Assurance — Something in Common

Note: Available both in paperback and hardback edition.

44. SIMPLE'S UNCLE SAM, First Edition, 1965

Simple's Uncle Sam. New York: Hill and Wang, 1965. 192p.

Note: Available both in paperback and hardback edition.

44a. SIMPLE'S UNCLE SAM. Large type Edition, 1965

Simple's Uncle Sam. Large type edition, complete and unabridged. New York: Watts, 1965. 180p.

45. BLACK MAGIC, A PICTORIAL HISTORY OF THE NEGRO IN AMERICAN ENTERTAINMENT, First Edition, 1967

Black Magic. By Langston Hughes and Milton Meltzer. New York: Prentice Hall, 1967. 375p.

Dedication: To Langston with love. Milton Meltzer

46. THE PANTHER AND THE LASH, First Edition, 1967

The Panther and the Lash. New York: Alfred A. Knopf, 1967. 101p.

Contents (in seven sections): WORDS ON FIRE: Corner Meeting — Harlem — Prime — Crowns and Garlands — Elderly Leaders —Backlash Blues — Lenox Avenue Bar — Motto — Junior Addict — Dream Deferred — Death in Yorkville — Who But the Lord? — Third Degree — Black Panther — Final Call — AMER-

ICAN HEARTBREAK: American Heartbreak — Ghosts of 1619 —
October 16: the Raid — Long View: Negro — Frederick
Douglass: 1817–1895 — Still Here — Words Like Freedom —
THE BIBLE BELT: Christ in Alabama — Bible Belt — Militant —
Office Building: Evening — Florida Road Workers — Special
Bulletin — Mississippi — Ku Klux — Justice — Birmingham
Sunday — Bombings in Dixie — Children's Rhymes — Down
Where I Am — THE FACE OF WAR: Mother in Wartime — With-
out Benefit of Declaration — Official Notice — Peace — Last
Prince of the East — The Dove — War — AFRICAN QUESTION
MARK: Oppression — Angola Question Mark — Lumumba's
Grave — Color — Question and Answer — History — DINNER
GUEST: ME: Dinner Guest: Me — Northern Liberal — Sweet
Words on Race — Un-American Investigators — Slave — Under-
tow — Little Song on Housing — Cultural Exchange — Frosting
—▸Impasse — DAYBREAK IN ALABAMA: Freedom — Go Slow —
Merry-Go-Round — Dream Dust — Stokely Malcolm Me —
Slum Dreams — Georgia Dusk — Where? When? Which? —
Vari-colored Song — Jim Crow Car — Warning — Daybreak in
Alabama.
Dedication: To Rosa Parks of Montgomery.

47. BLACK MISERY, First Edition, 1969
Black Misery. Illustrated by Arouni. New York: P. S. Erikson,
1969. 60p.

48. DON'T YOU TURN BACK, First Edition, 1969.
Don't You Turn Back, Poems by Langston Hughes. Selected by
Lee Hopkins, Woodcuts by Ann Grifalconi, with an Introduction
by Arna Bontemps. New York: Alfred A. Knopf, 1969. 78p.
Contents: MY PEOPLE: My People — Aunt Sue's Stories — Sun
Song — The Negro Speaks of Rivers — Mexican Market Woman
—Troubled Woman — Baby — April Rain Song — Lullaby —
Hope — Mother to Son — Ennui — Stars — Alabama Earth —
Poem — Youth — Walkers With the Dawn — PRAYERS AND
DREAMS: Prayer Meeting — Shout — Feet o' Jesus — Tambou-
rines — Prayer — Heaven — Dream Keeper — Dream Variation
— Dream Dust — Dreams — Snail — OUT TO SEA: Long Trip
— Moonlight Night: Carmel — Winter Moon — Sea Calm —
Suicide's Note — Island — Wonder — Water front Streets —
Sailor — Seascape — I AM A NEGRO: As I Grew Older — The
Negro — Merry-Go-Round — Color — I, Too — Brothers —
Daybreak in Alabama.
A collection made up of poems especially enjoyed by students.

Books Edited by Langston Hughes

1. FOUR LINCOLN UNIVERSITY POETS. Foreword by President William Hallock Johnson. Edited by Langston Hughes. Waring Cuney, William Allyn Hill, Edward Silvera, Langston Hughes. Lincoln University, 1930.

2. THE POETRY OF THE NEGRO 1746–1949. Edited by Langston Hughes and Arna Bontemps. Garden City: Doubleday, 1949.

2a. THE POETRY OF THE NEGRO 1746–1970. Edited by Langston Hughes and Arna Bontemps. Garden City: Doubleday, 1970.

3. LINCOLN UNIVERSITY POETS. Edited by Waring Cuney, Langston Hughes, and Bruce McWright. New York: Fine Editions Press, 1954.

4. THE BOOK OF NEGRO FOLKLORE. Edited by Langston Hughes and Arna Bontemps. New York: Dodd, Mead, 1958.

5. AN AFRICAN TREASURY, ARTICLES, ESSAYS, STORIES, POEMS BY BLACK AFRICANS. Selected by Langston Hughes. New York: Crown, 1960.

5a. AN AFRICAN TREASURY, ARTICLES, ESSAYS, STORIES, POEMS BY BLACK AFRICANS. Selected by Langston Hughes. New York: Pyramid Books, 1961.

5b. AN AFRICAN TREASURY, ARTICLES, ESSAYS, STORIES, POEMS BY BLACK AFRICANS. Selected by Langston Hughes. London: Victor Gollancz, 1961.

5c. TRESOR AFRICAIN. ANTHOLOGIE. Paris: Editions Seghers, 1962.

5d. ANTHOLOGIE AFRICAINE ET MALGACHE. Paris: Editions Seghers, 1962.
This includes a selection of African literature written in French.

5e. MIN-RAWA I AL-ADAB AL-AFRIQI. al-Qahirah: al-Dar al-Qawmiyyah lil-Tiba ah wal-Nashr, 1962.

5f. ANTHOLOGIE AFRICAINE ET MALGACHE. Verviers: Marabout, 1962.

6. POEMS FROM BLACK AFRICA, ETHIOPIA AND OTHER COUNTRIES. Bloomington, Indiana: University of Indiana Press, 1963.

7. NEW NEGRO POETS USA. Foreword by Gwendolyn Books. Bloomington, Indiana: University of Indiana Press, 1964.

8. BOOK OF NEGRO HUMOR. New York: Dodd, Mead, 1965.

9. THE BEST SHORT STORIES BY NEGRO WRITERS. Edited and with an Introduction by Lanston Hughes. New York: Little Brown, 1967.

Book-length Translations

by Langston Hughes

Garcia Lorca, Federico. GYPSY BALLADS. Translated by Langston Hughes. Beloit, Wisconsin: Beloit College, 1951. (Beloit Poetry Chapbook No. 1)

Guillen, Nicolas. CUBA LIBRE. Translated by Langston Hughes and Benjamin Carruthers. Los Angeles: Anderson and Ritchie, 1948.

Mistral, Gabriela. SELECTED POEMS OF GABRIELA MISTRAL. Translated by Langston Hughes. Bloomington: Indiana University Press. 1957. (paperback edition issued in 1965 by Indiana University Press)

Roumain, Jacques. MASTERS OF THE DEW. Translated by Langston Hughes and Mercer Cook. New York: Reynal and Hitchcock, 1947.

————. MASTERS OF THE DEW. Translated by Langston Hughes and Mercer Cook. New York: Liberty Book Club, 1957.

Works of Langston Hughes

in Foreign Languages

(for which there is no corresponding published English edition)

DRAMA

MULATTO, DRAMA IN DUE ATTI E TRE SCENE. Translated by A. Ghirelli. Milano: A. Mondadori, 1949. 159p.

MULATO, DRAMA EN DOS ACTOS. Translated by J. Galer. Buenos Aires: Editorial Quetzal, 1954. 57p.

MULAT. Translated by B. Becher. Praha: Dilia, [n.d.] 157p.

POETRY

ZDRAVSTVUI REVOLUTSIIA. Translated by U. Anisimov. Moskva: Goslitizdat, 1933. 103p.

DOS GESANG FUN NEGER-FOLK. Translated by Z. Bagish. Chicago: M. Ceshinsky, 1936. 44p.

LAMENT FOR DARK PEOPLE. Selected and introduced by an amateur. Amsterdam: privately printed, 1944. 45p.
> *Note*: 300 copies printed, 50 on special paper.
> Yale University Library has copy 12.

O AMERICE ZPIVAM. Translated by J. Boucek. Praha: Mlada Fronta, 1950. 89p.

POEMES. Translated by F. Dodat. Paris: Seghers, 1955. 89p.
> *Note*: Poems appear in French and English.

POEMAS. Translated by J. Galer. Buenos Aires: Lautaro, 1952. 147p.

CERNOCH SI ZPIVA BLUES. Translated by J. Valja. Praha: Statni nakadatelstvi krasne literatury, 1957. 198p.

HUGHES SHISHU. Translated by H. Kijima. Tokyo: Eureka, 1959. 108p.

IZBRANNYE STIKKI. Selected and arranged by M. Becker. Moskva: Izdatelstvo inostrannoi literatury. 1960. 167p.

GEDICHTE. Translated by E. Hesse and P. von dem Knesebeck. Berlin: Langewiesche, Brandt, 1960. 62p.

IO SONO UN NEGRO. Translated by S. Piccinato. Milano: Avanti, 1960. 103p.

MEMLEKET OZLEMI. Istanbul: Kitabevi, 1961. 45p.

HARLEMSKY ZPEVNIK PRELOZIL. Translated by J. Valja. Praha: Mlada Fronta, 1963. 120p.

IZBRANNYE STIKKI. Translated by M. Becker. Moskva: "Progress," 1964. 342p.

LANGSTON HUGHES SHISHU. Translated by H. Kajima. Tokyo: Shichosha, 1967. 248p.

JASS NO HON. Translated by H. Kajima. Tokyo: Shobunsha, 1968. (Includes *First book of jazz, Famous Negro music makers, Famous American Negroes, Langston Hughes Reader*)

PROSE

NEPRIJATNOE PROISSESTVIE S ANGELAMI I DRUGIE RASSKAZY. Translated by T. Sinkar. Moskva: Izdatelstvo inostrannoi literatury, 1955. 128p.

ARU KINYOBI NO ASA. Translated by H. Kijima. Tokyo: Iizuka-shoten, 1959. 298p.

ONE SUNDAY MORNING AND OTHER STORIES. Edited and annotated by H. Kijima and T. Hamamoto. Tokyo: Eihosha, 1960.

WEISSGEPUDERTE GESICHTER. Translated by P. von dem Knesebeck. Munchen: Nymphenburger Verlag, 1961. 150p.

SCHEREREI MIT DEN ENGELN. Translated by P. von dem Knesebeck. Leipzig: Reclam, 1963. 109p.

I TOO SING AMERICA, Famous American Negroes. Ausgewählt und bearbeit von . . . Heinz Rogge. Dortmund: Verlag Lambert Lensing, 1964. 72 p. [Reprinted from *Story of the Negro* by Arna Bontemps and *Famous American Negroes* by Langston Hughes.]

Collections Indexed for Contributions

by Langston Hughes

(Collections with but one contribution are given only
under the title of the specific poem or story)

AS   AFRICA SINGT. ed. A. Nussbaum. Wien: Speidel Verlag,
1929

Negro — African Dance — Negro Speaks of Rivers —
Poem — Yes? — I Too Sing America — Afraid — Our
Land — Lenox Avenue: Midnight — Sun Song — Prize
Fighter — Porter — Ruby Brown — Brass Spittoons —
Ihr Weissen — Song for a Dark Girl — Lament for Dark
People — African Boy — Cross — Aunt Sue's Stories —
Knowing — Fire — Harlem Night Club — New Cabaret
Girl — Gin Mary — Harlem Night Song — As I Grew
Older — Tomorrow — Homesick — Suicide's Note —
Meiner — Ubler Bursche — Bound North Blues — Misery
— Po' Boy Blues — Bad Luck Card — Gal's Cry for a
Dying Lover

AM   AMERICAN AUTHORS TODAY. ed. W. Burnett. New
York: Ginn, 1947

Poem — April Rain — Dreams — As I Grew Older —
Weary Blues

AML   AMERICAN LITERATURE BY NEGRO AUTHORS. ed.
H. Dreet. New York: Macmillan, 1950

Dreams — Joy — Night and Morn — Weary Blues —
Mother to Son

ANACD   AMERICAN NEGRO ART. ed. C. Dover. London: Studio,
1960
Negro Speaks of Rivers—Esthete in Harlem

ANP   AMERICAN NEGRO POETRY. ed. A. Bontemps. New
York: Hill and Wang, 1963

Brass Spittoons — Cross — Jazzonia — The Negro
Speaks of Rivers — I, Too — Bound No'th Blues —
Personal — Dream Variation — Mother To Son —
Harlem — Good Morning — Same in Blues — Letter —
Island — Pennsylvania Station — I Dream a World —
Without Benefit of Declaration

152

APA   ANTHOLOGIE DE LA POESIE AMERICAINE. ed. A.
           Bosquet. Paris: Librairie Stock, 1956
           Dream Variation — Cross — Negro Speaks of Rivers

APNA   ANTOLOGIA DE LA POESIA NEGRA AMERICANA. ed.
           I. Valdes. Santiago de Chile. Ediciones Ercilla, 1936
           Negro — I Too — Cross — Ardella — Negro Speaks of
           Rivers — Port Town — Joy — Song for a Dark Girl —
           Always the Same — Union — Mulatto

AMV26   ANTHOLOGY OF MAGAZINE VERSE 1926. ed. W.
           Braithwaite. Boston: Brimmer, 1926
           Gypsy Man — Midwinter Blues — My Man — Strange
           Hurt She Knew

AMV28   ANTHOLOGY OF MAGAZINE VERSE 1928. ed. W.
           Braithwaite. Boston: Brimmer, 1928
           I Thought it was Tangiers I Wanted — Being Old

AnMaVe   ANTHOLOGY OF MAGAZINE VERSE 1938–1942. ed. A.
           Pater. New York: Pasbar, 1942
           Air Raid Barcelona — Roar China

ANL   ANTHOLOGY OF AMERICAN NEGRO LITERATURE.
           ed. V. Calverton. New York: Modern Library, 1929
           I Too — Mulatto — Song for a Dark Girl — Weary Blues

AANL   ANTHOLOGY OF AMERICAN NEGRO LITERATURE. ed.
           S. Watkins. New York: Modern Library, 1944.
           One Friday Morning — What the Negro Wants

ASA   AMERIKA SINGE AUCH ICH. ed. H. Meuter. Dresden:
           Jess Verlag, 1932
           An earth song — Negro — I Too

AsP   AS I PASS, O MANHATTAN. ed. E. McCullough. New
           York: C. Taylor, 1956
           Harlem Sweeties — Trumpet Player: 52nd Street —
           Mother to Son — Weary Blues

BNH   BEST OF NEGRO HUMOR. ed. J. Johnson. New York:
           Negro Digest, 1945
           White Folks Do the Funniest Things — Simple and Dogs
           — Simple and the Ladies

BLB   BLACK AND UNKNOWN BARDS. Aldington, Kent: Hand
           and Flower Press, 1958
           Weary Blues — Mother to Son — Merry-Go-Round —
           Negro Speaks of Rivers — When Sue Wears Red —
           Ballad of a Man That's Gone — Lenox Avenue Mural —
           Letter — Island

BlMa   BLACK MANHATTAN. by J. W. Johnson. New York:
           Knopf, 1930
           Cross — Negro Speaks of Rivers

BANP   BOOK OF AMERICAN NEGRO POETRY. ed. J. W.
           Johnson. New York: Harcourt, Brace, 1931
           As I Grew Older — Brass Spittoons — Cross — Esthete
           in Harlem — Fantasy in Purple — Hard Daddy — Jazz
           Band in a Parisian Night Club — Jazzonia — Negro
           Speaks of Rivers — Po' Boy Blues

BoChLi   BOOK OF CHILDREN'S LITERATURE. ed. L. Hollowell.
           New York: Rinehart, 1950
           Dreams — Mother to Son

BCSS   BOOK OF CONTEMPORARY SHORT STORIES. ed D.
           Brewster. New York: Macmillan, 1936
           Professor — Rejuvenation Through Joy

BNF   BOOK OF NEGRO FOLKLORE. ed. L. Hughes. New York:
           Dodd, Mead, 1958
           Young Gal's Blues — Ma Lawd — Blues at Dawn — Bad
           Morning — Wake — Request for Requiems — Motto —
           Dead in There — Jam Session — House Rent Parties —
           Simple on Military Integration — Simple on Bop Music
           — Simple on Gospel Singers — Simple on Indian Blood
           — Simple on House Cleaning — Simple on Country Life

BrA   BROWN AMERICANS. by E. Embree. New York: Viking,
           1943
           Brass Spittoons — Let America Be America Again —
           Merry-Go-Round

CDC   CAROLING DUSK. ed. C. Cullen. New York: Harper, 1927
           Dream Variation — Fantasy in Purple — Homesick Blues
           — House in Taos — I Too — Mother to Son — Negro
           Speaks of Rivers — Poem — Prayer — Song for a Dark
           Girl — Suicide's Note

CP   CERNOSSKA POESIE. ed. A. Capek. Praha: Nase Vojsko, 1958

I Too — Negro Speaks of Rivers — Brass Spittoons — Zpev Cernosske Pradlene — Weary Blues — Song for a Dark Girl — Kolotoc — Mother To Son — Kdyz Jsem Vyrustal — Let America Be America Again — Na Vysvetlenou Nasi Doby — Africa

CR   CROSS SECTION. ed E. Seaver. New York: L. Fischer, 1944

Madam and the Minister — Madam and Her Might Have Been — Madam and the Wrong Visitor

DSp   DEMOCRATIC SPIRIT. ed. B. Smith. New York: Knopf, 1941

Cross — I Too — Let America Be America Again

EbR   EBONY RHYTHM. ed B. Murphy. New York: Exposition Press, 1948

For Billie Holliday — From Selma — Wisdom and War

ECR   ECRIVAINS ET POETES DES ETATS-UNIS D'AMERI-QUE. ed. J. Wahl. Paris: Fontaine, 1945.

Drum — Homesick Blues — Crossing Jordan — Blues — Hommage to Three Poets — Song for a Dark Girl

FANP   FAMOUS AMERICAN NEGRO POETS. by C. Rollins. New York: Dodd, Mead, 1965.

Cross — Negro Speaks of Rivers — Merry-go-round

FP   FAVORITE POEMS OLD AND NEW. Selected by H. Ferris. New York: Doubleday, 1957

April Rain Song — Snail — Cycle — City — African Dance

FOUR   FOUR NEGRO POETS. ed. A. Locke. New York: Simon and Schuster, 1927

Weary Blues — Jazzonia — Nude Young Dancer — Midwinter Blues — Negro Dancers — Young Gal's Blues — Sport — Minstrel Man — Jester — Mother to Son — Cross — Song — Dream Variation — Sun Song — Mammy — Feet O' Jesus — Song for a Dark Girl — I Too — Our Land — Negro Speaks of Rivers — Youth

GoSl   GOLDEN SLIPPERS. ed. A. Bontemps. New York: Harper,

Alabama Earth — City: San Francisco — Cycle —

Dreams — Dressed Up — Florida Road Workers —
Garment — Havanna Dreams — Heaven — In Time of
Silver Rain — Ma Lord — Mother to Son — Negro
Speaks of Rivers — Sailor — Snail — Song of a Negro
Wash Woman — Trip: San Francisco — When Sue
Wears Red — Winter Sweetness — Youth

IHP   AN INHERITANCE OF POETRY. ed G. L. Adshead.
Boston: Houghton Mifflin, 1948

Dreams — Mother to Son

IZ   IK ZAG HOC ZWART IK WAS. ed. R. Pool. Den Haag:
Daamen, 1958

Harlem — Comment on Curb — Letter — Island

LIU4   FOUR LINCOLN UNIVERSITY POETS. ed. L. Hughes.
Lincoln University, 1930

Negro Speaks of Rivers — Being Walkers With the
Dawn — Feet O' Jesus — Cross — Youth — Mother to
Son

LIU   LINCOLN UNIVERSITY POETS. ed. L. Hughes. New
York: Fine Editions Press, 1954

Lincoln University 1954 — Heaven — College Formal —
Draftees — Juke Box Love Song — Trumpet Player —
Oppression — Azikiwe in Jail — Poet to Bigot — House
in Taos — Mother to Son — Negro Speaks of Rivers —
Youth

LA   LYRIC AMERICA 1630-1930. ed. A. Kreymborg. New
York: Coward McCann, 1930

Cross — To Midnight Nan at Leroy's

MBOP   BOOK OF POETRY. ed. E. Markham. New York: Wise,
1926

Dream Variation — Negro

MPB   TO MAKE A POET BLACK. by J. Redding. Chapel Hill:
University of North Carolina Press, 1939

Negro Dancers — Afraid

MaAnDe   MAN ANSWERS DEATH. ed. C. Lamont. New York: Phi-
losophical Library, 1952

Dear Lovely Death — Drum — Two Things

MPN   MAPA DE LA POESIA NEGRA AMERICANA. ed. E. Bal-
lagas. Buenos Aires: Editorial Pleamar, 1946

Negro — I Too — Song for a Dark Girl — Poem

MoAmPo   MODERN AMERICAN POETRY. ed. L. Untermeyer. New York: Harcourt, Brace, 1930
        Brass Spittoons — Homesick Blues — Saturday Night

MoAmPox ——————— 1936
        Homesick Blues — Brass Spittoons — Saturday Night — Jazz Band — Drum — Florida Road Workers

MS   MORK SANG. ed. T. Jonsson. Stockholm: Bonniers Forlag, 1949
        Negro — Little Green Tree Blues — Mother to Son — Negro Speaks of Rivers — Song for a Dark Girl

NANC   NEGRO. ed. N. Cunard. London: Wishart, 1934
        I Too — Florida Road Workers — House in the World — To Certain Negro Leaders — Always the Same — Goodby Christ

NeCa   NEGRO CARAVAN. ed. S. Brown. New York: Dryden, 1941
        Let America Be American Again — Minstrel Man — Negro Speaks of Rivers — Song for a Dark Girl — Song to a Negro Wash Woman — To Midnight Nan at LeRoy's — Weary Blues — Young Gal's Blues — Guitar — Slave on the Block

New Negro   THE NEW NEGRO. ed. A. Locke. New York: Boni, 1925
        Negro Speaks of Rivers — An Earth Song — Poem — Youth — Song — Dream Variation — Minstrel Man — Our Land — I Too — Jazzonia — Nude Young Dancer

NIA   NEGRO IN AMERICA. ed. L. Cuban. Chicago: Scott, Foresman, 1964.
        Negro Artist and the Racial Mountain — Conversation — Song To a Negro Wash-Woman

NP   NEW POEMS BY AMERICAN POETS. ed. R. Humphries. New York: Ballantine, 1957
        Two Somewhat Different Epigrams — Acceptance — Testament — Late Corner — Where? When? Which?

NPT   NEGRO POETS AND THEIR POEMS. ed. R. Kerlin. Washington: Associated Press, 1923
        Negro

NPTP ———————— 2nd ed., 1935
Negro — Negro Speaks of Rivers — I Too

NPTPo ———————— 4th ed., 1947
Negro — Negro Speaks of Rivers — I Too — Poem —
Suicide — Po' Boy Blues — Mulatto — Song for a Dark
Girl — Let America Be America Again

Npo NEW POETRY. ed. H. Monroe. New York: Macmillan,
1932
Feet O' Jesus — Fire — Hard Luck

PWD PEOPLE THAT WALK IN DARKNESS. by J. Nordholt.
New York: Ballantine, 1960
Song for a Dark Girl — Homesick Blues

PJU POEMS OF JUSTICE. ed. T. Clark. Chicago: Willett,
Clark and Colby, 1929
Negro — I Too — Being Walkers With the Dawn

PoMeSp POETRY FOR MEN TO SPEAK CHORALLY. ed. M.
Robinson. Boston: Expression, 1939
Ballad of Lenin — Drum — Fire

PoWoSp POETRY FOR WOMEN TO SPEAK CHORALLY. ed.
M. Robinson. Boston: Expression, 1940
Moon — Rain — Sun — Wind

PoNe POETRY OF THE NEGRO. ed. L. Hughes. New York:
Doubleday, 1949
Afro-American Fragment — Cross — Dream Variation
— Harlem Sweeties — Havanna Dreams — I Too —
Let America Be America Again — Little Green Tree
Blues — Merry-Go-Round — Mother to Son — Negro
Speaks of Rivers — Personal — Song for a Dark Girl —
Weary Blues

PortC PORTRAITS IN COLOR. by M. Ovington. New York:
Viking, 1927
Brass Spittoons — Ruined Gal — Feet O' Jesus

PreP PREFACE TO POETRY. ed. C. Cooper. New York: Harcourt, 1946
Epilogue — Poem

PWF   PRIMER FOR WHITE FOLKS. ed. B. Moon. New York: Doubleday, 1945

Slave on the Block — What Shall We Do About the South?

PrLt   PROLETARIAN LITERATURE IN THE UNITED STATES. ed. G. Hicks. New York: International, 1935

Ballad of Lenin — Sharecroppers — Park Bench

RFN   READINGS FROM NEGRO AUTHORS. ed. O. Cromwell. New York: Harcourt, 1931.

Poem — Poem (We Have Tomorrow) — Sea Charm — Troubled Woman — Aunt Sue's Stories — Mother to Son — Dream Variation — Cabaret

SePoSe   SEVEN POETS IN SEARCH OF AN ANSWER. ed. T. Yoseloff. New York: B. Ackerman, 1944

Barrel House: Industrial City — Bitter River — Black Man Speaks — Dear Mr. President — Dimout in Harlem — Good Morning Stalingrad — Moonlight in Valencia — Question — Silhouette — The Underground

SIN   SINGERS IN THE DAWN. ed. R. Eleazer. Atlanta: Commission on Interracial Cooperation, 1934

Minstrel Man — Mother to Son — I Too

SOM   SOON ONE MORNING. ed. H. Hill. New York: Knopf, 1963

Moscow Movie — Rock Church — Blues in Stereo — Ask Your Mama — Jazztet Muted — Dream Boogie — Parade — Children's Rhymes — Night Funeral in Harlem — Harlem — Same in Blues

ThAo   THIRTEEN AGAINST THE ODDS. by E. Embree. New York: Viking, 1944

Rain — Breath of a Rose — Negro Speaks of Rivers — Brass Spittoons — Cross — Merry-Go-Round

THI   THIS IS MY BEST. ed. W. Burnett. New York: Dial, 1942

Negro — Weary Blues — I Too

TSD   TIEF IM SUDEN DIXIES. ed. E. Kaiser. Berlin: Bermen Verlag, 1960

Song for a Dark Girl — Negro Speaks of Rivers

TiPo   TIME FOR POETRY. ed. M. Arbuthnot. Chicago: Scott
            Foresman, 1952
            African Danse — April Rain Song — Heaven — In Time
            of Silver Rain — Mexican Market Woman — Snail —
            Wisdom

TiPoa   ——————— 2nd ed., 1959
            April Rain Song — Heaven — In Time of Silver Rain
            — Mexican Market Woman — Snail — Wisdom

TCPD   TWENTIETH CENTURY POETRY. ed. J. Drinkwater.
            New York: Houghton Mifflin, 1929
            Gypsy Man — Weary Blues

VS   VIDENTES E SONAMBULOS. ed. O. Marques. Rio de
            Janeiro: Ministerio de Educacao e Cultura, 1955
            I Too — Negro — Jazzonia

WOK   WAY OF KNOWING. ed. G. McDonald. New York:
            Crowell, 1959
            Life is Fine — Homesick Blues — There are Words
            Like Freedom

Prose and Drama by

Langston Hughes

ABOUT THE USSR
International Literature, No. 2, 1933, p. 155.

ADVENTURES OF A POET *see* MY ADVENTURES AS A SOCIAL POET

AFRICAN MORNING
Pacific Weekly, Aug. 31, 1936, pp. 137–138
The African, April 1945, p. 5, 14, 15 "Outcast"
Laughing,* 1952, pp. 15–20
Something in Common, 1963, pp. 45–49

AIR RAID OVER HARLEM
New Theatre, Feb. 1936, p. 19

AMERICA'S MOST POWERFUL NEGRO (Article on Walter White)
Bronzeville, Oct. 1954, pp. 12–18

AMERICA'S MOST UNIQUE NEWSPAPER
Negro Digest, Oct. 1945, pp. 23–24

AN AMERICAN LOOKS AT AMERICA *see* MY AMERICA

AN APPEAL FOR JACQUES ROMAIN (Letter to the editor)
New Republic, Dec. 12, 1934, p. 130
New Masses, Jan. 1935, p. 34

ATLANTA: ITS NEGROES HAVE MOST CULTURE BUT SOME OF WORST GHETTOS IN THE WORLD by Langston Hughes and John Alston
Ebony, Jan. 1948, pp. 19–24

AUNT SARA'S WOODEN GOD *see* Forward

BANQUET IN HONOR (included in Simple Speaks His Mind)
Negro Quarterly, Summer 1942, pp. 176–178

BESSIE SMITH, EMPRESS OF THE BLUES (From Famous Negro Music Makers)
125th Anniversary Anthology. New York: Dodd, 1964.

*Laughing to keep from crying

BERRY
> *Abbott's Weekly*, Feb. 24, 1934, pp. 2, 14
> *Ways of White Folks*, 1934, pp. 171–182
> *International Literature*, No. 9, 1935, pp. 61–64

BIG MEETING
> *Scribner's Magazine*, July 1935, pp. 22–26
> *Laughing*, 1952, pp. 191–206
> *L. H. Reader,** 1958, pp. 66–76
> *Something in Common*, 1963, pp. 212–224

BLACK MISERY (From *Black Misery*)
> *Good Housekeeping*, July 1969. pp. 78–79
> *Reader's Digest*, November 1969. pp. 131

BLESSED ASSURANCE
> *Something in Common*, 1963, pp. 227–232

BLUES I'M PLAYING
> *Scribner's Magazine*, May 1934, pp. 345–351
> *Ways of White Folks*, 1934, pp. 96–120
> *Antologia del Cuento Norteamericano.* ed. L. Franulic. Santiago:
> Ediciones Ercilla, 1943, pp. 327–342

BODIES IN THE MOONLIGHT
> *The Messenger*, April 1927, pp. 105–106

(Book Review) of SAILOR'S RETURN by DAVID GARNETT
> *Crisis*, Nov. 1925, p. 33

BOOKER T. WASHINGTON IN ATLANTA
> *Radio Drama in Action*, ed. E. Barnow. New York: Farrar, 1945, pp.
> 283–294

BOY DANCERS OF UZBEKISTAN
> *Travel*, Dec. 1934, p. 36

BREAKING OF BREAD *see* I THANK YOU FOR THIS

BREAKFAST IN VIRGINIA *see* I THANK YOU FOR THIS

BRIGHT CHARIOTS
> *Negro Digest*, April 1951, pp. 58–62
> *L. H. Reader*, 1958, pp. 494–498 "Sweet Chariots"

BRONCOS OVER THE BORDER by Langston Hughes and Arna
Bontemps
> *Jack and Jill*, July 1956, pp. 20–30

BROWN AMERICA IN JAIL
Opportunity, June 1932, p. 174
*Langston Hughes reader.

BURUTU MOON, AN EVENING IN AN AFRICAN VILLAGE
Crisis, June 1925, p. 64

THE CASE AGAINST SEGREGATION
Negro Digest, July 1943, pp. 45–46

CEASELESS RINGS OF WALT WHITMAN
Preface to I Hear the People Singing. ed. L. Hughes. New York:
Young World Books, 1946, pp. 7–10

CHILDREN AND POETRY
Borzoi Battledore, July 1946, pp. 4–8
Something Shared. by P. Fenner. New York: Day, 1949, pp. 95–98

AU COIN DE LA 125 RUE (Three Simple columns)
La Revue de Poche, June 1965, p. 111

CONVERSATION
Fight Against War and Fascism, Oct. 1936, p. 21
NIA, 1964, pp. 112–117

CORA UNASHAMED
American Mercury, Sept. 1933, pp. 19–24
Ways of White Folks, 1934, pp. 3–18
Best Short Stories of 1934. ed. M. Foley. New York: Houghton, pp.
188–197
Literaturny Sovremennik, No. 10, 1935, pp. 133–155
Konsument Bladet, Oct. 1936, pp. 2–5, 18
Drum, Feb. 1956, pp. 50–57

COWARDS FROM THE COLLEGES
Crisis, Aug. 1934, pp. 226–228

A CUBAN SCULPTOR (article on Ramos Blanco)
Opportunity, Nov. 1930, p. 334

CULTURE VIA THE BACK DOOR
Negro Digest, July 1946, pp. 47–48

DEATH IN HARLEM
Literary America, June 1935, pp. 437–440

DEVILS IN DIXIE AND NAZILAND
Negro Digest, Nov. 1942, pp. 43–44

DO BIG NEGROES KEEP LITTLE NEGROES DOWN?
Negro Digest, Nov. 1951, pp. 79–82

DON'T HIT A WOMAN
Direction, No. 6, 1940, pp. 12–13

DON'T YOU WANT TO BE FREE?
One Act Play Magazine, Oct. 1938, pp. 359–393

DOWN UNDER IN HARLEM
New Republic, March 27, 1944, pp. 404–405
Negro Digest, June 1944, pp. 7–9

EARLY AUTUMN
Something in Common, 1963, pp. 189–190

EBONY'S NATIVITY
Ebony, Nov. 1965, pp. 40–46

FAMILY TREE (From Simple Speaks His Mind)
Best Humor of 1949–50. ed. L. Untermeyer. New York: Holt, 1950,
    pp. 113–116

FAREWELL TO MAHOMET
Travel, Feb. 1935, pp. 28–31

FASCINATION OF CITIES
Crisis, Jan. 1926, pp. 138–140

FATHER AND SON
Ways of White Folks, 1934, pp. 200–248
Literaturny Sovremennik, No. 10, 1935, pp. 115–125
Something in Common, 1963, pp. 106–136

FINE ACCOMMODATIONS
Something in Common, 1963, pp. 161–166

FOLKS AT HOME *see* HOME

FOOLING OUR WHITE FOLKS
Negro Digest, April 1950, pp. 38–41

(Forward) to AUNT SARA'S WOODEN GOD by MERCEDES GILBERT
Boston: Christopher, 1938, p. vii
    p. vii

FUN OF BEING BLACK
L. H. Reader, 1958, pp. 498–500

FUTURE OF THE NEGRO
 New World, Aug. 1943, pp. 21–23
 Negro Digest, Nov. 1944, pp. 3–6

GLORY OF NEGRO HISTORY
 L. H. Reader, 1958, pp. 465–480

GOING SOUTH IN RUSSIA
 Crisis, June 1934, pp. 162–163

GOLD PIECE
 Brownie's Book, July 1921, pp. 191–194
 Sadsa Encore, Spring 1949, pp. 30–32

GOOD JOB GONE
 Esquire, April 1934, pp. 46, 142, 144
 Ways of White Folks, 1934, pp. 54–65
 30 Dnei, No. 11, 1938, pp. 89–90
 Kostyor, No. 4, 1939, pp. 60–61
 Bedside Esquire, ed. A. Gingrich. New York: Grosset, 1940, pp. 97–103
 Strange Barriers, ed. J. Shea. New York: Lion Editions, 1955, pp. 44–50
 Duke, June 1957, pp. 55, 56, 58 "Sugar Brown"
 Something in Common, 1963, pp. 33–40

GREETINGS TO SOVIET WORKERS
 New Masses, Dec. 1930, p. 23

GUITAR (from Not Without Laughter)
 NC, 1941, pp. 224–230
 America in Literature, ed. T. McDowell. New York: Crofts, 1944, pp. 378–383
 Caravan of Music Stories, ed. N. Fabricant. New York: Fell, 1947, pp. 71–79

 L. H. Reader, 1958, pp. 167–173

GUMPTION *see* OYSTER'S SON

THE GUN
 Something in Common, 1963, pp. 154–161.

HARLEM HOUSE RENT PARTIES (From The Big Sea)
 New York City Folklore, ed. B. Botkin. New York: Random House, 1956, pp. 291–295
 BNF, 1958, pp. 596–600

HARLEM LITERATI IN THE TWENTIES
 Saturday Review of Literature, June 22, 1940, pp. 13–14

Saturday Review Gallery, ed. J. Beatty. New York: Simon and Schuster, 1959, pp. 207–212

HAUNTED SHIP (from The Big Sea)
On Our Way, ed. R. Patterson. New York: Holiday, 1952, pp. 178–186

HEAVEN TO HELL
Laughing, 1952, pp. 47–49
Something in Common, 1963, pp. 73–75

HIS LAST AFFAIR
Something in Common, 1963, pp. 93–101

HOLD FAST TO DREAMS
Lincoln University Bulletin, "Langston Hughes Issue," 1964, pp. 1–8

HOLIDAY IN THE TROPICS
Ebony, Nov. 1948, pp. 44–50

HOME
Esquire, May 1934, pp. 56, 57, 93–94 "The Folks at Home"
Ways of White Folks, 1934, pp. 32–48
International Literature, No. 9, 1935, pp. 55–60
Literaturny Sovremennik, No. 10, 1935, pp. 126–132
Krasnaya Nov, No. 11, 1935, pp. 46–51
Zemlya, Jan. 1937, pp. 49–60
Many Colored Fleece, ed. M. Gable. New York: Sheed and Ward, 1950, pp. 134–145

HOW TO BE A BAD WRITER
Harlem Quarterly, Spring 1950, pp. 13–14
L. H. Reader, 1958, pp. 491–492

I REMEMBER THE BLUES
Missouri Reader, ed. F. L. Mott. Columbia: University of Missouri Press, 1964, pp. 152–155

I THANK YOU FOR THIS
Common Ground, Oct. 1944, pp. 27–28
Negro Digest, Dec. 1944, pp. 53–55 "Breaking of Bread"
Something in Common, 1963, pp. 224–227 "Breakfast in Virginia"

IN A MEXICAN CITY
Brownie's Book, April 1921, pp. 102–105

IN AN EMIR'S HAREM
Woman's Home Companion, Sept. 1934, p. 12

INFLUENCE OF NEGRO MUSIC ON AMERICAN ENTERTAINMENT
Theatre Spotlight, Sept. 1955, pp. 6, 15

(Introduction) to BOOTSIE AND OTHERS by OLLIE HARRINGTON
New York: Dodd Mead, 1958, p. i–ii

(Introduction) to PUDD'NHEAD WILSON by MARK TWAIN
New York: Bantam, 1959, p. vii–xiii

(Introduction) to UNCLE TOM'S CABIN by HARRIET STOWE
New York: Dodd, Mead, 1952, p. i–iii

INVESTMENT IN FREE INDIVIDUALS
Southern Atlantic Quarterly, Spring 1961, p. 9

IS HOLLYWOOD FAIR TO NEGROES?
Negro Digest, April 1943, pp. 19–21

JAZZ AS COMMUNICATION
L. H. Reader, 1958, pp. 492–494

JEFFERS; MAN, SEA AND POETRY
Carmel Pine Cone, Jan. 10, 1941, p. 10

JOKES NEGROES TELL ON THEMSELVES
Negro Digest, June 1951, pp. 21–25
Negro Digest, July 1962, p. 63–66

JOLLY GENIUS OF JAZZ (article on Fats Waller)
Popular Album News, July 1958, pp. 9, 13

JUST TRAVELING
Carmel Pine Cone, May 2, 1941, pp. 6–7

LANGSTON HUGHES SPEAKS
Crisis, May 1953, pp. 279–280

LAUGHTER IN MADRID
Nation, Jan. 29, 1938, pp. 123–124
Reader's Digest, March 1938, pp. 51–52

A LETTER FROM HAITI
New Masses, July 1931, p. 9

LISTEN BOY (from Not Without Laughter)
Revista de la Habana, July/Aug. 1930, pp. 77–84

LITTLE DOG
Ways of White Folks, 1934, pp. 156–170
L. H. Reader, 1958, pp. 22–29
Something in Common, 1963, pp. 5–14

LITTLE HAM
Five Plays, 1963, pp. 43–112

LITTLE OLD SPY
  Esquire, Sept. 1934, pp. 47, 150, 152
  Laughing, 1952, pp. 153–163
  Something in Common, 1963, pp. 24–32
  Tuvrhenpozt, April 21, 1962, pp. 24–29

THE LITTLE VIRGIN
  The Messenger, Nov. 1927, pp. 327–328

LOVE IN MEXICO (from The Big Sea)
  Opportunity, April 1940, p. 107

LUANI OF THE JUNGLE
  Harlem, Nov. 1928, pp. 7–11

MEMORIES OF CHRISTMAS
  L. H. Reader, 1958, pp. 485–488

MR. HUGHES VISITS THE SCHOOLS
  Common Ground, Winter 1943, pp. 88–90

MEXICAN GAMES
  Brownie's Book, Jan. 1921, p. 18

MOSCOW AND ME
  International Literature, July 1933, pp. 61–66

MOSCOW MOVIE (From I Wonder as I Wander)
  SOM, 1963, pp. 107–136

MOSCOW ROMANCE (from I Wonder as I Wander)
  Scarlet Treasury of Great Confessions, ed. W. Burnett. New York:
    Pyramid Books, 1958, pp. 54–60

MOTHER AND CHILD
  Ways of White Folks, 1934, pp. 183–191

MULATTO
  Five Plays, 1963, pp. 1–35

MULE BONE by Langston Hughes and Zora Hurston (excerpt)
  Drama Critique, Spring 1964, pp. 103–107

MY ADVENTURES AS A SOCIAL POET
  Phylon, Fall 1947, pp. 205–212
  Negro Digest, Jan. 1948, pp. 12–14 "Adventures of a Poet"

MY AMERICA
  Journal of Educational Sociology, Feb. 1943, pp. 334–336

What the Negro Wants, ed. R. Logan. Chaple Hill: University of North
   Carolina Press, 1944, pp. 299–307
This Way to Unity, ed. A. Herrick. New York: Oxford, 1945, pp. 31–34
   "An American Looks at America"
L. H. Reader, 1958, pp. 500–501

MY MOST HUMILIATING JIM CROW EXPERIENCE
Negro Digest, May 1945, pp. 33–34
L. H. Reader, 1958, pp. 488–489

MYSTERIOUS MADAME SHANGHAI
Afro Magazine, March 15, 1952, pp. 6–7
Laughing, 1952, pp. 133–143
Something in Common, 1963, pp. 177–185

NAME IN THE PAPERS
Laughing, 1952, pp. 107–109

NAME, RACE AND GIFT IN COMMON
Voices, Winter 1950, pp. 54–56

NEED FOR HEROES
Crisis, June 1941, pp. 184–185, 206

THE NEGRO
Hunger and revolt, by J. Burck. New York: Daily Worker, 1935, pp.
   141–142

NEGRO ARTIST by Langston Hughes and Sidney Kingsley
American Writer, April 1953, pp. 16–17

NEGRO ARTIST AND THE RACIAL MOUNTAIN
Nation, June 23, 1926, pp. 692–694
NIA, 1964, pp. 110–111

NEGRO IN THE DRAWING ROOM *see* FINE ACCOMMODATIONS

NEGRO TROOPS
Fighting Words, ed. D. Stewart. New York: Harcourt, 1940, pp. 58–63

NEGRO WRITERS HAVE BEEN ON A BLACKLIST ALL OUR LIVES
Mainstream, July 1957, pp. 46–48

NEGROES IN MOSCOW
International Literature, No. 4, 1933, pp. 78–81

NEVER ROOM WITH A COUPLE
Laughing, 1952, pp. 145–151
Something in Common, 1963, pp. 191–195

NO PLACE TO MAKE LOVE
  Something in Common, 1963, pp. 166–169

ON THE ROAD
  Esquire, Jan. 1935, pp. 92, 154
  Democratic Spirit, ed. B. Smith. New York: Knopf, 1941, pp. 814–818
  Short Story Craft, ed. L. Gilkes. New York: Macmillan, 1949, pp. 167–172
  Laughing, 1952, pp. 183–189
  Christ Erscheint am Kongo, ed. P. Sulzer. Heilbronn: Salber Verlag, 1958, pp. 235–241
  Something in Common, 1963, pp. 207–212

ON THE WAY HOME
  Story Magazine, May/June 1946, pp. 70–74
  Story, ed. W. Burnett. New York: Dutton, 1949, pp. 450–457
  Laughing, 1952, pp. 121–131
  L. H. Reader, 1958, pp. 44–50
  Something in Common, 1963, pp. 169–177
  Story Jubilee, ed. W. Burnett. New York: Doubleday, 1965, pp. 244–249

ONE CHRISTMAS EVE
  Opportunity, Dec. 1933, pp. 362–368
  Ways of White Folks, 1934, pp. 192–199
  Fireside Book of Christmas Stories, ed. E. Wagenknecht. New York: Bobbs, 1945
  Our Lives, ed. J. Gaer. New York: Boni, 1948, pp. 158–162

ONE FRIDAY MORNING
  Crisis, July 1941, pp. 216–218
  AANL, 1944, pp. 30–38
  Kirchenblatt, Dec. 27, 1947, pp. 8, 13–14; Jan. 10, 1948, pp. 13–15
  Short Stories for Our Time, ed. S. Certner. New York: Houghton, 1950, pp. 151–161
  Laughing, 1952, pp. 83–95
  Girls, Girls, Girls, ed. H. Fersis. New York: Watts, 1956, pp. 83–95
  Schwarze Ballade, ed. J. Jahn. Dusseldorf: Diederichs Verlag, 1957, pp. 166–177
  Das Amerikanische Jahrhundert, ed. M. Lieber. Leipzig: List Verlag, 1957, pp. 274–280
  L. H. Reader, 1958, pp. 54–62
  La Procellaria, Sept./Oct. 1959, pp. 13–18
  Egy Péntek Délelött. ed. E. Máthé. Bueapest: Terra, 1959, pp. 1-36

OUTCAST *see* AFRICAN MORNING

OYSTER'S SON
  New Yorker, Jan. 12, 1935, pp. 51–54
  30 Dnei, No. 4, 1938, pp. 71–75
  Something in Common, 1963, pp. 67–72 as "Gumption"

PARTY FOR WHITE FOLKS
  New Masses, July 1930, p. 6

PASSING
  Ways of White Folks, 1934, pp. 49–53

PATRON OF THE ARTS
  L. H. Reader, 1958, pp. 80–83
  Something in Common, 1963, pp. 185–189

PEOPLE WITHOUT SHOES
  New Masses, Oct. 1931, p. 12

POOR LITTLE BLACK FELLOW
  American Mercury, Nov. 1933, pp. 326–335
  Ways of White Folks, 1934, pp. 129–155
  Commune, April 1937, pp. 897–914

POWDER WHITE FACES
  Laughing, 1952, pp. 111–118
  Something in Common, 1963, pp. 147–153

PRAYER FOR PUBLIC SERVICE (from Simple Speaks His Mind)
  15 Million Negroes and 15 Billion Dollars, ed. W. Bell. New York:
  W. Bell, 1956, pp. 78–80

PRIVATE JIM CROW
  Negro Story Magazine, May/June 1945, pp. 3–9

PROBLEMS OF THE NEGRO WRITER: THE BREAD AND BUTTER
SIDE
  Saturday Review, April 20, 1963, pp. 19–20

PROFESSOR
  Anvil, May/June 1935, pp. 5–8
  BCSS, 1936, pp. 413–420
  Literaturny Sovremennik, No. 6, 1938, pp. 101–105
  Laughing, 1952, pp. 97–105
  Something in Common, 1963, pp. 136–143

PUDD'NHEAD WILSON *see* Introduction

PUSHCART MAN
  Laughing, 1952, pp. 21–24
  Something in Common, 1963, pp. 49–51

RED HEADED BABY
  Ways of White Folks, 1934, pp. 121–128
  L. H. Reader, 1958, pp. 18–22

REJUVENATION THROUGH JOY
  Ways of White Folks, 1934, pp. 66–95
  BCSS, 1936, pp. 205–226

RICHARD ALLEN: FOUNDER OF A CHURCH
  Crisis, Dec. 1933, pp. 605–607

ROCK CHURCH
  SOM, 1963, pp. 231–241
  Something in Common, 1963, pp. 14–24

ROUGE HIGH
  Laughing, 1952, pp. 119–120
  365 Days, ed. K. Boyle. New York: Harcourt, 1936, p. 189
  Something in Common, 1963, pp. 153–154

SAILOR AND THE STEWARD
  Anvil, July/Aug. 1935, pp. 28–30

SAILOR ASHORE
  Laughing, 1952, pp. 51–57
  Something in Common, 1963, pp. 75–79

SARATOGA RAIN
  Negro Story, March/April 1945, pp. 46–47
  Laughing, 1952, pp. 33–34
  Something in Common, 1963, pp. 57–58

SAVED FROM THE DOGS
  Direction, Feb./March 1944, pp. 4–5
  Negro Digest, May 1944, pp. 17–19
  Lionel Hampton Swing Book. New York: Negro Story, 1946, pp.
  146–147

SCOTTSBORO LIMITED
  New Masses, Nov. 1931, pp. 18–21
  Scottsboro Limited, by L. Hughes. New York: Golden Stair, 1932, pp.
  9–18

SHIPS, SEA AND AFRICA
  Crisis, Dec. 1923, pp. 69–71

SIMPLE AND DOGS
  BNH, 1945, pp. 100–103

SIMPLE AND ME
  Phylon, Winter 1945, pp. 349–352

SIMPLE AND THE BOMB SHELTER
  Saturday Review, June 16, 1962, p. 6

SIMPLE AND THE LADIES
  BNH, 1945, pp. 103–106

SIMPLE AND THE ROSENWALD FUND
  Phylon, Fall 1948, pp. 229–231

SIMPLE AND THE SECOND COMING
  Common Ground, Fall 1945, pp. 105–106

SIMPLE DISCUSSES COLLEGES AND COLOR
  Phylon, Winter 1949, pp. 399–400

SIMPLE ON BOP MUSIC
  BNF, 1958, pp. 608–609

SIMPLE ON COUNTRY LIFE
  BNF, 1958, pp. 617–618

SIMPLE ON GOSPEL SINGERS
  BNF, 1958, pp. 610–612

SIMPLE ON HOUSE CLEANING
  BNF, 1958, pp. 615–616

SIMPLE ON INDIAN BLOOD
  BNF, 1958, pp. 612–615

SIMPLE ON MILITARY INTEGRATION
  BNF, 1958, pp. 605–607

SIMPLE PINS ON MEDALS
  Negro Digest, April, 1945, pp. 53–54

SIMPLY HEAVENLY
  L. H. Reader, 1958, pp. 244–313
  Five Plays, 1963, pp. 113–181

SISTER JOHNSON'S STORY
  New Masses, June 1930, pp. 6–8
  Kalendar Delnik, New York, 1931, pp. 56–61

SLAVE ON THE BLOCK
  Scribner's Magazine, Sept. 1933, pp. 141–144
  Ways of White Folks, 1934, pp. 19–31
  Editor's Choice, ed. A. Dashiell. New York: Putnam, 1934, pp. 160–169
  30 Dnei, No. 8, 1934, pp. 63–65
  NC, 1941, pp. 90–96
  PWF, 1945, pp. 217–224

Moderne Amerikanske Noveller. Kobenhavn: Thaning and Appels, 1954, pp. 41–50
L. H. Reader, 1958, pp. 11–17

SLICE HIM DOWN
   Esquire, May 1936, pp. 44–45, 190
   Laughing, 1952, pp. 59–75
   Something in Common, 1963, pp. 80–93

SOLVING THE RACE PROBLEM, A STATE OR FEDERAL ISSUE
   Negro Digest, April 1944, pp. 37–38

SOME PRACTICAL OBSERVATIONS (A conversation between Mr. Hughes and the editor)
   Phylon, Winter, 1950, pp. 307–311

SOMETHING IN COMMON
   Laughing, 1952, pp. 9–14
   L. H. Reader, 1958, pp. 34–37
   Something in Common, 1963, pp. 232–236

SONGS CALLED THE BLUES
   Phylon, Summer 1941, pp. 143–145

SORROW FOR A MIDGET
   Literary Review of Fairleigh Dickinson University, Fall 1960, pp. 83–86
   Something in Common, 1963, pp. 143–146
   Negro Digest, Oct. 1961, p. 4

SOUL GONE HOME
   One Act Play Magazine, July 1937, pp. 195–200
   Contemporary One Act Plays, ed. W. Kozlenko. New York: Scribner, 1938, pp. 14–19
   Sadsa Encore, Spring 1949, pp. 33–35
   L. H. Reader, 1958, pp. 239–243
   Kansas Renaissance, ed. W. Kliewer and S. Solomon. [n.p.] Coronado, 1961, pp. 43–47
   Five Plays, 1963, pp. 37–42

SOUTHERN GENTLEMEN, WHITE PROSTITUTES, MILL OWNERS AND NEGROES
   Contempo, Dec. 1931, p. 1

SOVIET THEATER IN CENTRAL ASIA
   Asia, Oct. 1934, pp. 590–593

SPANISH BLOOD
   Metropolis, Dec. 29, 1934, pp. 21–24

Stag, Aug. 1937, pp. 9–11
Laughing, 1952, pp. 35–45
L. H. Reader, 1958, pp. 37–44
Something in Common, 1963, pp. 58–67

SPEAK WELL OF THE DEAD
Ebony, Oct. 1958, pp. 30–34

STORM (from Not Without Laughter)
Out of the Midwest, ed. J. Frederick. New York: McGraw Hill, 1944,
pp. 257–263

SUGAR BROWN *see* A GOOD JOB GONE

SWEET CHARIOTS *see* BRIGHT CHARIOTS

SYNAGOGUES ET CRAYONS, UN PORTRAIT D' ARTHUR
KOESTLER
L'Arche, Oct. 1957, pp. 30–31

TAIN'T SO
Fight Against War and Fascism, May 1937, pp. 21, 29
Laughing, 1952, pp. 77–82
L. H. Reader, 1958, pp. 51–54
Something in Common, 1963, pp. 101–105
Gehort Gelesen, June 1962, pp. 677–679

TAMARA KHANUM, SOVIET ASIA'S GREATEST DANCER
Theatre Arts, Nov. 1934, pp. 829–835

TAMBOURINES TO GLORY
Five Plays, 1963, pp. 183–258

THE TASK OF THE NEGRO WRITER AS AN ARTIST
Negro Digest, April, 1965, p. 65

TEN THOUSANDS BEDS
L. H. Reader, 1958, pp. 489–491

THANK YOU M'AM
L. H. Reader, 1959, pp. 77–80
Something in Common, 1963, pp. 1–4

THERE OUGHT TO BE A LAW
Treasury of American Political Humor, ed. L. Lewin. New York: Dial,
1964, p. 375

THOSE WHO HAVE NO TURKEY
Brownie's Book, Nov. 1921, pp. 324–326

TO NEGRO WRITERS
  American Writers Congress, ed. H. Hart. New York: International, 1935, pp. 139–141

TOO MUCH OF RACE
  Crisis, Sept. 1937, p. 272

TRAGEDY AT THE BATHS
  Esquire, Oct. 1935, pp. 80, 122
  Laughing, 1952, pp. 165–172
  L. H. Reader, 1958, pp. 62–66
  Something in Common, 1963, pp. 195–201

TRIBUTE TO W. E. B. DU BOIS
  Freedomways, Winter 1965, p. 11

TROUBLE WITH THE ANGELS
  New Theatre, July 1935, pp. 6–7
  Laughing, 1952, pp. 173–181
  Something in Common, 1963, pp. 201–207

THE TWENTIES: HARLEM AND ITS NEGRITUDE
  African Forum, Spring 1966, pp. 11–20

TWO AT THE BAR
  Negro Story, Aug./Sept. 1945, pp. 7–8

UNCLE SAM SIMPLE
  Saturday Review, Dec. 9, 1961, p. 6

UNCLE TOM'S CABIN *see* Introduction

UP TO THE CRATER OF AN OLD VOLCANO
  Brownie's Book, Dec. 1921, pp. 334–338

THE VIRGIN OF GUADULUPE
  Crisis, Dec. 1921, p. 77

WAGES OF SIN ARE NOT ALWAYS DEATH
  Negro Digest, Oct. 1951, pp. 3–6

WALT WHITMAN AND THE NEGRO
  Nocturne, Brooklyn College, Spring 1955, p. 9

WASHINGTON, OUR WONDERFUL SOCIETY
  Opportunity, Aug. 1927, pp. 226–227

WATER FRONT STREETS
  La Parola del Papolo, Oct./Nov. 1961, p. 45

WAY OF A NEGRO (from The Big Sea)
  Ost und West, Feb. 1949, pp. 16–26

WHAT SHALL WE DO ABOUT THE SOUTH?
Common Ground, Winter 1943, p. 3–6
PWF, 1945, pp. 451–456

WHAT THE NEGRO WANTS
Common Ground, Fall 1941, pp. 52–54
AANL, 1944, pp. 262–265

WHEN THE NEGRO WAS IN VOGUE
Town and Country, July 1940, pp. 49, 61–66
Empire City, ed. A. Klein. New York: Reinhart, 1955, pp. 265–269

WHEN I WORKED FOR DR. WOODSON
Negro History Bulletin, May 1950, p. 13

WHEN I WORKED FOR DR. WOODSON
Negro History Bulletin, October 1957, p. 17

WHITE SHADOWS IN A BLACK LAND, AN IMPRESSION OF HAITI
Crisis, May 1932, p. 157

WHITE FOLKS DO THE FUNNIEST THINGS
Common Ground, Spring 1944, pp. 42–46
Negro Digest, Feb. 1944, pp. 31–36
Modern Digest, 1944, pp. 24–28
BNH, 1945, pp. 91–100

WHITE GOLD IN SOVIET ASIA
New Masses, August 1934, pp. 14–15

WHO'S PASSING FOR WHO?
Negro Story, Dec./Jan. 1945–1946, pp. 35–38
Laughing, 1952, pp. 1–7
L. H. Reader, 1958, pp. 30–33
Something in Common, 1963, pp. 40–45

WHY, YOU RECKON?
Laughing, 1952, pp. 25–32
As I Pass, O Manhattan, ed. E. McCullogh. New York: Taylor, 1956,
  pp. 552–557
Something in Common, 1963, pp. 51–57

WRITER'S POSITION IN AMERICA
Mainstream, July 1957, pp. 46–48
L. H. Reader, 1958, pp. 483–485

WRITERS: BLACK AND WHITE
American Negro Writer and his Roots. New York: American Society
  of African Culture, 1960, pp. 41–45

THE YOUNG GLORY OF HIM
The Messenger, June 1927, pp. 177–178

Poems by Langston Hughes

ABE LINCOLN
Voices, May/Aug., 1960, p. 17

ACCEPTANCE
Beloit Poetry Journal Chapbook, 1957, p. 24
NP, 1957, p. 80
L. H. Reader, 1958, p. 129

ADDITION
Carmel Pine Cone, May 2, 1941, p. 7
Voices, May/Aug. 1953, p. 16

ADVERTISEMENT FOR OPENING OF THE WALDORF ASTORIA
New Masses, Jan. 1935, pp. 11–12
Nueva Culture (Valencia) Jan. 1936, p. 8

ADVICE
Scholastic, April 5, 1946, p. 19
*Montage,** 1951, p. 22
L. H. Reader, 1958, p. 100
Selected Poems, 1959, p. 237

AESTHETE IN HARLEM
Opportunity, June 1930, p. 182
*Dear L. Death,*** 1931, n. p.
BANV, 1931, p. 239 [Esthete in Harlem]
Wikor, Feb. 1955, p. 69
ANACD, 1960, p. 34 [Esthete in Harlem]

AFRAID
Weary Blues, 1926, p. 101
AS, 1929, p. 44
Nouvel Age, Dec., 1931, p. 1063
MPB, 1939, p. 144
Crisis, Nov. 1942, p. 21
United Asia, March 1955, p. 70

AFRICA
Long Island University Review, June 1952, p. 12
Crisis, March 1953, p. 167
Africa South, April/June 1957, p. 128

*Montage of a dream deferred.
**Dear lovely death.
178

ANGELS WINGS
  Fine Clothes, 1927, p. 52
  Selected Poems, 1959, p. 25

ANNE SPENCER'S TABLE
  Crisis, July 1930, p. 235

ANNOUNCEMENT
  *Shakespeare,** 1942, p. 115

APRIL RAIN SONG
  Brownies Book, April, 1921, p. 111
  Dream Keeper, 1932, p. 8
  Sung Under the Silver Umbrella, ed. D. Lathrop, New York: Macmillan, 1943, p. 147
  Pocketful of Rhymes, ed. K. Love, New York: Crowell, 1946
  AM, 1947, p. 167
  TiPo, 1952, p. 149
  FP, 1957, p. 74
  TiPoa, 1959, p. 326
  Instructor, March 1964, p. 117

ARDELLA
  Weary Blues, 1926, p. 64
  APNA, 1936, p. 36
  Selected Poems, 1959, p. 67

ARGUMENT
  New Masses, Dec. 1926, p. 10
  Montage, 1951, p. 62
  L. H. Reader, 1958, p. 119
  Selected Poems, 1959, p. 262

AS I GREW OLDER
  Weary Blues, 1926, pp. 55–56
  AS, 1929, pp. 107–108
  BANP, 1931, pp. 240–241
  Dream Keeper, 1932, pp. 74–75
  AM, 1947, p. 168
  Selected Poems, 1959, pp. 11–12
  La Procellaria, May/June 1961, p. 18

AS BEFITS A MAN
  Selected Poems, 1959, p. 46

ASK YOUR MAMA
  Ask Your Mama, 1961, pp. 61–65
  SOM, 1963, pp. 589–591

*Shakespeare in Harlem.

ASPIRATION
  Shakespeare, 1942, p. 33

AUNT SUE'S STORIES
  Crisis, July 1921, p. 121
  Weary Blues, 1926, p. 57
  AS, 1929, p. 88
  RFN, 1931, p. 18
  Dream Keeper, 1932, p. 65
  Selected Poems, 1959, p. 6
  La Procellaria, Sept./Oct. 1960, p. 3

AUTUMN THOUGHT
  Brownie's Book, Nov. 1921, p. 307
  Dream Keeper, 1932, p. 6

AWE
  Black Orpheus, May, 1959, p. 29

AZIKIWE IN JAIL
  LIU, 1954, p. 29

BABY
  Fine Clothes, 1927, p. 61
  Dream Keeper, 1932, p. 56
  Selected Poems, 1959, p. 193

BAD LUCK CARD
  Fine Clothes, 1927, p. 60
  AS, 1929, p. 154
  Selected Poems, 1959, p. 41

BAD MAN
  Fine Clothes, 1927, p. 21

BAD MORNING
  One Way Ticket, 1949, p. 48
  BNF, 1958, p. 557
  Selected Poems, 1959, p. 37

BAD WEATHER
  Wikor, Feb. 1955, p. 69

BALLAD OF BOOKER T.
  Common Sense Historical Review, May 1953, p. 17

BALLAD OF GIN MARY
  Fine Clothes, 1927, p. 35
  AS, 1929, p. 101
  International Literature, No. 5, 1934, p. 89

BALLAD OF LITTLE SALLIE
Opportunity, Dec. 1940, p. 364

BALLAD OF MARGIE POLITE
One Way Ticket, 1949, pp. 75–76

BALLAD OF MARY'S SON
L. H. Reader, 1958, pp. 127–128

BALLAD OF NEGRO HISTORY
Negro History Bulletin, Feb. 1952, p. 92

BALLAD OF NEGRO HISTORY
Negro History Bulletin, October 1967, p. 17

BALLAD OF OZIE POWELL
American Spectator, April 1936, p. 36
New Song, 1938, p. 17

BALLAD OF ROOSEVELT
New Republic, Nov. 14, 1934, p. 9
New Republic, Nov. 22, 1954, p. 64

BALLAD OF SAM SOLOMON
*Jim Crow,** 1943, p. 22

BALLAD OF THE FORTUNE TELLER
Shakespeare, 1942, pp. 89–90
Selected Poems, 1959, pp. 144–145

BALLAD OF THE GIRL WHOSE NAME IS MUD
Shakespeare, 1942, p. 91
Selected Poems, 1959, p. 149

BALLAD OF THE GYPSY
Shakespeare, 1942, pp. 93–94
Selected Poems, 1959, p. 124

BALLAD OF THE KILLER BOY
Shakespeare, 1942, pp. 87–88

BALLAD OF THE LANDLORD
Krasnaya, Nov. 4, 1933, p. 106
Opportunity, Dec. 1940, p. 364
Jim Crow, 1943, p. 20
Holiday, April 1949, p. 166
Montage, 1951, pp. 24–25
L. H. Reader, 1958, pp. 101–102
Selected Poems, 1959, pp. 238–239

BALLAD OF THE MAN WHO'S GONE
Shakespeare, 1942, pp. 97–98

*Jim Crow's last stand.

BLB, 1958, p. 22
Selected Poems, 1959, p. 198

BALLAD OF THE MISER
Opportunity, Dec. 1940, p. 363

BALLAD OF THE PAWNBROKER
Shakespeare, 1942, pp. 95–96

BALLAD OF THE SEVEN SONGS
Common Ground, Winter, 1959, pp. 21–27

BALLAD OF THE SINNER
Shakespeare, 1942, pp. 85–86

BALLAD OF THE SPANISH CIVIL GUARD
New Masses, March 1, 1938, p. 6

BALLAD OF THE TWO THIEVES
Shenandoah, Winter 1953, pp. 26–27

BALLADS OF LENIN
Pr. Lt., 1935, pp. 166–167
International Literature, No. 1, 1936, p. 27
New Song, 1938, p. 20
PoMeSp, 1939, p. 69

BAR
Selected Poems, 1959, p. 243
Montage, 1951, p. 31
L. H. Reader, 1958, p. 106

BAREFOOT BLUES
Masses and Mainstream, Feb. 1949, p. 53

BARREL HOUSE: INDUSTRIAL CITY
SePoSe, 1944, pp. 48–49

BARREN STONE
PoNe, 1949, pp. 380–381

BE-BOP BOYS
Montage, 1951, p. 36
Selected Poems, 1959, p. 246

BEAUMONT TO DETROIT
Common Ground, Winter 1943, p. 104

BEAUTY
Opportunity, July 1938, p. 203

BEALE STREET LOVE
  Palms, Nov. 1926, pp. 35–37
  Fine Clothes, 1927, p. 57
  Carmel Pine Cone, May 2, 1941, p. 10
  Fields of Wonder, 1947, p. 18
  Selected Poems, 1959, p. 78

BED TIME
  Shakespeare, 1942, p. 5

BEGGAR BOY
  Crisis, Sept. 1922, p. 219
  Weary Blues, 1926, p. 85
  Nouvel Age, Dec. 1931, p. 1064
  Dream Keeper, 1932, p. 23
  Southern Workman, April 1924, p. 179

BEING OLD
  Crisis, Oct. 1927, p. 265
  AMV, 28, 1928, p. 181

BEING WALKERS WITH THE DAWN *see* POEM

BIG BUDDY
  Negro Quarterly, Spring 1942, p. 38
  Jim Crow, 1943, p. 21

BIG CITY PRAYER
  Opportunity, Oct. 1940, p. 308

BIG SUR
  Carmel Pine Cone, July 18, 1941, p. 6
  Fields of Wonder, 1947, p. 5

BIG TIMER
  Negro Mother, 1931, pp. 12–15

BIRD IN ORBIT
  Ask Your Mama, 1961, pp. 69–74

BIRTH
  Christian Register, May 1947, p. 190
  Fields of Wonder, 1947, p. 9

BITTER RIVER
  Negro Quarterly, Fall 1942, pp. 249–251
  Jim Crow, 1943, pp. 11–13
  SePoSe, 1944, pp. 42–44

BLACK CLOWN
Negro Mother, 1931, pp. 8–11
Crisis, Feb. 1932, p. 52

BLACK DANCERS
Crisis, May 1933, p. 110

BLACK GAL
Fine Clothes, 1927, p. 66

BLACK MAN SPEAKS
Jim Crow, 1943, p. 5
SePoSe, 1944, p. 41

BLACK MARIA
Poetry, May, 1941, pp. 74–75
Shakespeare, 1942, pp. 121–122
Selected Poems, 1959, p. 118

BLACK PIERROT
Les Continents, July 1924
Weary Blues, 1926, p. 61
Nouvel Age, Dec. 1931, p. 1063
Dream Keeper, 1932, p. 39
Selected Poems, 1959, p. 66

BLACK SEED
Opportunity, Dec. 1930, p. 371

BLACK WORKERS
Crisis, April 1933, p. 80

BLESSED ASSURANCE
Konkret, Jan. 1962, pp. 20–21

BLIND
The Span, v. 2 no. 2, n. d., p. 6
Women's Society of World Service Bulletin 1964–1965, p. 62

BLUE BAYOU
Jim Crow, 1943, p. 10
One Way Ticket, 1949, pp. 53–54
Selected Poems, 1959, p. 170

BLUE MONDAY
Selected Poems, 1959, p. 130

"BLUES"
Nigger Heaven, by C. Van Vechten, New York: Knopf, 1926, pp. 34–35,
52, 137, 139

BLUES AT DAWN
  Montage, 1951, p. 61
  L. H. Reader, 1958, p. 119
  BNF, 1958, pp. 556–557
  Selected Poems, 1959, p. 261

BLUES FANTASY
  Weary Blues, 1926, pp. 37–38

BLUES IN STEREO
  Poetry, Aug. 1961, pp. 288–289
  Ask Your Mama, 1961, pp. 35–37
  SOM, 1963, pp. 587–588

BLUES ON A BOX
  Poetry, Feb. 1947, pp. 248–249
  One Way Ticket, 1949, p. 112

BOARDING HOUSE
  One Way Ticket, 1949, p. 119

BOOGIE: 1 A.M.
  Montage, 1951, p. 43
  L. H. Reader, 1958, p. 110
  Selected Poems, 1959, p. 250

BORDER LINE
  Fields of Wonder, 1947, p. 13
  Selected Poems, 1959, p. 81

BOUND NO'TH BLUES
  Opportunity, Oct. 1926, p. 315
  Fine Clothes, 1927, p. 87
  AS, 1929, p. 153
  Dream Keeper, 1932, p. 40
  International Literature, No. 5, 1933, p. 36
  ANP, 1963, p. 65
  Fontaine, June/July 1943, p. 196
  Selected Poems, 1959, p. 174

BOUQUET
  Colorado Review, Spring Summer, 1957, p. 76

BRAND NEW CLOTHES
  L. H. Reader, 1958, p. 152

BRASS SPITTOONS
  New Masses, Dec. 1926, p. 10
  Fine Clothes, 1927, pp. 28–29

CAFE: 3 A.M.
Montage, 1951, p. 32
L. H. Reader, 1958, p. 106
Selected Poems, 1959, p. 243

CALL OF ETHIOPIA
Opportunity, Sept. 1935, p. 276

CALL TO CREATION
Unrest, ed. J. Conroy, New York: Harrison, 1931, p. 52
Nouvel Age, Dec. 1931, p. 1062
New Masses, Feb. 1931, p. 4

CARIBBEAN SUNSET
Weary Blues, 1926, p. 76

CAROL OF THE BROWN KING
Crisis, Dec. 1958, p. 615

CAROLINA CABIN
Fields of Wonder, 1947, pp. 48–49

CASUAL
Hearse, 1958, n. p.

CASUALTY
Voices, Winter, 1950, p. 33
Montage, 1951, p. 59
L. H. Reader, 1958, p. 117
Selected Poems, 1959, p. 259

THE CAT AND THE SAXOPHONE
Weary Blues, 1926, p. 27

CATCH
Minnesota Quarterly, Spring 1950, p. 22
Selected Poems, 1959, p. 50

CHANT FOR MAY DAY
New Song, 1938, pp. 14–15

CHANT FOR TOM MOONEY
New Song, 1938, pp. 13–14

CHILDHOOD OF JIMMY
Crisis, May 1927, p. 84

CHILDREN'S RHYMES
Montage, 1951, pp. 5–6
L. H. Reader, 1958, p. 91
Selected Poems, 1959, pp. 223–224
SOM, 1963, pp. 596–597

CHIPPY
    Poetry Magazine: Australia, Dec. 1946, p. 9
    Fields of Wonder, 1947, p. 67

CHORD
    Montage, 1951, p. 64
    L. H. Reader, 1958, p. 120
    Selected Poems, 1959, p. 264

CHRIST IN ALABAMA
    Contempo, Dec. 1, 1931, p. 1
    Scottsboro Limited, 1932, p. 5
    Phylon, Fall 1947, p. 208

CHRISTIAN COUNTRY
    New Masses, Feb. 1931, p. 4

CHRISTMAS EVE
    American Christmas, ed. W. Schoo and R. Myers. Kansas City: Hallmark, 1965, p. 49

CHRISTMAS STORY, THE
    Catholic Interracialist, Jan. 1952, p. 4

CIRCLES
    Fields of Wonder, 1947, p. 20

CITY
    Wikor, Feb. 1955, p. 69
    FP, 1957, p. 244
    Opening Doors, April/June 1960, p. 7
    Instructor, March 1964, p. 28

CITY: SAN FRANCISCO
    GoSl, 1941, p. 133

CLOSING TIME
    Fine Clothes, 1927, p. 32

COLLEGE FORMAL: RENAISSANCE CASINO
    Negro Digest, June 1951, p. 56
    Montage, 1951, p. 41
    LIV, 1954, p. 25
    L. H. Reader, 1958, p. 109
    Selected Poems, 1959, pp. 248–249

COLOR
    Jim Crow, 1943, p. 7

COLORED SOLDIER
Negro Mother, 1931, pp. 1–3

COLUMBIA
International Literatura, No. 2, 1933, p. 54

COMMENT AGAINST A LAMP POST
Montage, 1951, p. 18
L. H. Reader, 1958, p. 98

COMMENT ON CURB
Montage, 1951, p. 74
IZ, 1958, p. 110
Selected Poems, 1959, p. 271

COMMENT ON STOOP
Montage, 1951, p. 7

COMMENT ON WAR
Crisis, June 1940, p. 190

COMMUNION
Fields of Wonder, 1947, p. 98

COMMUNIQUE
Free Lance, 1958, p. 3

CONSERVATORY STUDENT STRUGGLES WITH HIGHER
INSTRUMENTATION
See Julliard Student

CONSIDER ME
American Scholar, Winter 1951–52, pp. 100–101
Selected Poems, 1959, pp. 286–287

CONSUMPTIVE
Dear L. Death, 1931, n. p.
Crisis, Feb. 1933, p. 31

CONVENT
Opportunity, March 1938, p. 82
Fields of Wonder, 1947, p. 22

CORA
Fine Clothes, 1927, p. 58
Selected Poems, 1959, p. 146

CORNER MEETING
Montage, 1951, p. 25
L. H. Reader, 1958, pp. 102–103
Selected Poems, 1959, p. 240

COULD BE
One Way Ticket, 1949, p. 100
Selected Poems, 1959, p. 40

COUNTRY
L. H. Reader, 1958, p. 151

CRAP GAME
Fine Clothes, 1927, p. 34

CROON
Montage, 1951, p. 11
L. H. Reader, 1958, p. 94
Selected Poems, 1959, p. 228

CROSS
Crisis, December 1925, p. 66
Weary Blues, 1926, p. 52
Four, 1927, p. 26
Atlantis, Sept. 1929, p. 549
AS, 1929, p. 82
BLMA, 1930, pp. 272–273
LA, 1930, p. 541
LIV (4), 1930, p. 14
BANP, 1931, pp. 236–237
Crisis, Nov. 1931, p. 381
APNA, 1936, pp. 35–36
LaNeuva Democracia, Aug. 1938, p. 15
D Sp, 1941, p. 810
ThAD, 1944, p. 133
PoNe, 1949, p. 103
Negro Digest, June 1950, p. 14
APA, 1956, p. 221
Poetry as Experience, ed. N. Stageberg, New York: American Book
    Co., 1952, pp. 23–24
Phylon, Jan. 1958, p. 397
Selected Poetry, 1959, p. 158
ANP, 1963, p. 62
Intermarriage, ed. A. Gordon, Boston: Beacon, 1964, p. 263
FANP, 1965, p. 70

CROSSING
Shakespeare, 1942, pp. 69–70
Selected Poetry, 1959, p. 138

CROSSING JORDON
Poetry, May 1941, pp. 73–74
ECR, 1945, pp. 196–197

CROWING HEN BLUES
Poetry, Sept. 1943, pp. 313–314

CROWNS AND GARLANDS
Nation, January 16, 1967, p. 92

CUBES
New Masses, March 13, 1934, p. 22

CULTURAL EXCHANGE
Ask Your Mama, 1961, pp. 3–9

CURIOUS
One Way Ticket, 1949, p. 97

CYCLE
GoSl, 1941, p. 180
FP, 1957, pp. 216–217
Instructor, March, 1964, p. 28

DANCER
Montage, 1951, p. 21
L. H. Reader, 1958, pp. 99–100
Selected Poetry, 1959, p. 236

DANCERS
Fields of Wonder, 1947, p. 68

DANSE AFRICAINE
Crisis, Aug. 1922, p. 167
Southern Workman, April 1924, p. 180
Weary Blues, 1926, p. 105
Nouvel Age, Dec. 1931, p. 1062
Selected Poetry, 1959, p. 7
La Procellaria, Feb. 1961, p. 32

DARE
Voices, Winter 1949, p. 31

DARK YOUTH OF THE U.S.A.
Negro Mother, pp. 19–20
Common Sense Historical Review, Aug. 1953, p. 12

DAY
Opportunity, March 1927, p. 85

DAYBREAK
Shakespeare, 1942, p. 6

DAYBREAK IN ALABAMA
Unquote, June 1940, p. 3
Jim Crow, 1943, p. 25

DELINQUENT
Selected Poetry, 1959, p. 133

DEMAND
Dear L. Death, 1931, n. p.
Selected Poetry, 1959, p. 96

DEMOCRACY
Jim Crow, 1943, p. 6
One Way Ticket, 1949, pp. 87–88
Selected Poetry, 1959, p. 285

DEPARTURE
Free Lance, 1958, p. 2

DESERT
Fields of Wonder, 1947, p. 27
Negro Digest, Dec. 1950, p. 68
Selected Poetry, 1959, p. 93

DESIRE
Fields of Wonder, 1947, p. 55
Selected Poetry, 1959, p. 90

DIME
Montage, 1951, p. 62
L. H. Reader, 1958, p. 119
Selected Poetry, 1959, p. 262

DIMOUT IN HARLEM
Panorama, March 1943, p. 7
SePoSe, 1944, p. 50
Span, Dec. 1944/Jan. 1945, p. 14
Fields of Wonder, 1947, pp. 95–96

DISILLUSION
Crisis, Dec. 1925, p. 67
Weary Blues, 1926, p. 104
Nouvel Age, Dec. 1931, p. 1063
Phylon, 1952, p. 276

DIVE
Montage, 1951, p. 33
L. H. Reader, 1958, p. 106
Selected Poetry, 1959, p. 245

DIXIE SOUTH AFRICA
Free Lance, 1958, p. 3

DOORKNOBS
Outsider, Fall 1961, p. 30
Konkret, Jan. 1962, p. 30.

DO YOU RECKON?
Deer and Dachshund No. 6, n. d., n. p.

THE DOVE
Outcry, Summer 1962, p. 56

DOWN AND OUT
Opportunity, Oct. 1926, p. 314
Shakespeare, 1942, pp. 101–102
Selected Poems, 1959, p. 147

DOWN WHERE I AM
Voices, Winter 1950, p. 33

DRAFTEES
LIU, 1954, pp. 25–26

DRAMA FOR WINTER NIGHT
Workers Monthly, March 1925, p. 225

DREAM
Opportunity, Sept. 1933, p. 282
Fields of Wonder, 1947, pp. 56–57
Selected Poems, 1959, p. 97

DREAM BOOGIE
Montage, 1951, p. 3
L. H. Reader, 1958, pp. 89–90
Selected Poems, 1959, p. 221
SOM, 1963, p. 593

DREAM BOOGIE: VARIATION
Montage, 1951, p. 68
L. H. Reader, 1958, p. 124
Selected Poems, 1959, p. 268

DREAM DUST
Fields of Wonder, 1947, p. 79
Selected Poems, 1959, p. 75

DREAM KEEPER
Survey Graphic, March 1, 1925, p. 663
Weary Blues, June 1926, p. 94
Dream Keeper, 1932, p. 3

DREAM OF FREEDOM
Wayne State University Graduate Comment, July 1964, p. 108

DREAM VARIATION
  Current Opinion, Sept. 1924, p. 361
  New Negro, 1925, p. 143
  Survey Graphic, March 1, 1925, p. 663
  Weary Blues, 1926, p. 42
  CDC, 1927, p. 149
  FOUR, 1927, p. 27
  Opportunity, April 1927, p. 111
  Crisis, July 1928, p. 128
  RFN, 1931, p. 19
  Dream Keeper, 1932, p. 69
  PoNe, 1949, pp. 97–98
  APA, 1956, p. 221
  Selected Poems, 1959, p. 14
  ANP, 1963, p. 66
  Black Like Me, by J. H. Griffin. Boston: Houghton, 1961 as frontice

DREAMER
  Ebony and Topaz, ed. C. Johnson, New York: Opportunity, 1927, p. 36

DREAMS
  Dream Keeper, 1932, p. 7
  GoSl, 1941, p. 194
  BoChLi, 1950, p. 567
  AML, 1950, p. 55
  IHP, 1948, p. 375

DRESSED UP
  Palms, Nov. 1926, p. 37
  Fine Clothes, 1927, p. 65
  Dream Keeper, 1932, p. 31
  GoSl, 1941, p. 117

DRUM
  Dear L. Death, 1931, n. p.
  Poetry Quarterly, Spring, 1931, p. 12
  MoAmPox, 1936, p. 612
  PoMeSp, 1939, p. 34
  ECR, 1945, p. 195
  MaAnDe, 1952, p. 40
  Selected Poems, 1959, p. 87

DRUMS
  Liberator, Aug. 1964, p. 4

DRUNKARD
  Montage, 1951, p. 32
  L. H. Reader, 1958, p. 106
  Selected Poems, 1959, p. 244

DUSK
   Fields of Wonder, 1947, p. 108

DUST BOWL
   Poetry, May 1941, p. 72
   Fields of Wonder, 1947, p. 15

DYING BEAST
   Poetry, Oct. 1931, pp. 18–19

EARLY EVENING QUARREL
   Compass, April, 1941
   Living Age, June 1941, p. 382
   Shakespeare, 1942, pp. 113–114
   Selected Poems, 1959, p. 44

EARTH SONG
   New Negro, 1925, p. 142
   Survey Graphic, March 1, 1925, p. 663
   Fields of Wonder, 1947, p. 106
   ASA, 1932, p. 86

EASY BOOGIE
   Montage, 1951, p. 12
   L. H. Reader, 1958, p. 95

ELDERLY RACE LEADERS
   Den Gulden Winckel, Sept. 1937, p. 10

ELEVATOR BOY
   Fire, Nov. 1926, p. 20
   Fine Clothes, 1927, p. 38
   Selected Poems, 1959, p. 195

EMPTY HOUSE
   Buccaneer, May 1925

ENCOUNTER
   Voices, Jan./April 1962, p. 24

END
   Fields of Wonder, 1947, p. 28
   Selected Poems, 1959, p. 86

ENGLISH, THE
   Crisis, July 1930, p. 235

ENNUI
   Maryland Quarterly, 1944, pp. 74–75
   Selected Poems, 1959, p. 131

ENVOY TO AFRICA
  Crisis, April 1953, p. 252

EPILOGUE *see* I TOO

ESTHETE IN HARLEM *see* AESTHETE IN HARLEM

EVENIN' AIR BLUES
  Common Ground, Spring 1941, p. 57
  Shakespeare, 1942, pp. 38–39

EVENING SONG
  Montage, 1951, p. 64
  L. H. Reader, 1958, p. 120
  Selected Poems, 1959, p. 264

EVIL
  Shakespeare, 1942, p. 15
  Selected Poems, 1959, p. 45

EVIL MORNING
  Shakespeare, 1942, p. 118

EVIL WOMAN
  Fine Clothes, 1927, p. 62

EXITS
  Fields of Wonder, 1947, p. 65

EXPENDABLE
  Voices, Jan./April 1957, p. 10

FACT
  Montage, 1951, p. 64
  L. H. Reader, 1958, p. 120
  Selected Poems, 1959, p. 264

FAIRIES
  Brownie's Book, Jan. 1921, p. 32
  Dream Keeper, 1932, p. 5

FAITHFUL ONE
  Fields of Wonder, 1947, p. 85
  Poems in Process, ed. P. Bartlett, New York: Oxford, 1951, p. 103

FANTASY IN PURPLE
  Vanity Fair, Sept. 1925, p. 62
  Weary Blues, 1926, p. 46
  CDC, 1927, p. 148
  TBM, 1927
  BANP, 1931, p. 242
  Selected Poems, 1959, p. 103

FLIGHT
   Opportunity, June 1930, p. 182
   Dear L. Death, 1931, n. p.

FLORIDA ROAD WORKERS
   Dear L. Death, 1931, n. p.
   NANC, 1934, p. 427
   MoAmPox, 1936, p. 612
   GoSl, 1941, p. 33
   One Way Ticket, 1949, pp. 91–92

FOG
   Palms, Oct. 1926, p. 24

FOR AN INDIAN SCREEN
   Opportunity, March 1927, p. 85

FOR BILLIE HOLIDAY
   Eb R, 1948, p. 87
   One Way Ticket, 1949, pp. 47–48
   Selected Poems, 1959, p. 102

FOR DEAD MIMES
   Fields of Wonder, 1947, p. 37

FORTUNE TELLER BLUES
   Vanity Fair, May 1926, p. 70

FRAGMENTS
   Fields of Wonder, 1947, p. 26

FREE MAN
   Shakespeare, 1942, p. 31
   La Nueva Democracia, Feb. 1943, p. 23

FREEDOM
   Jim Crow, 1943, p. 7

FREEDOM SEEKERS
   Crisis, Oct, 1927, p. 265

FREEDOM TRAIN
   Los Angeles Welcome News, Dec. 1947/Feb. 1948, pp. 8–9
   New Republic, Sept. 1947, p. 27
   Our World, Oct. 1947, pp. 26–27
   Montage, 1951, pp. 45–50
   Selected Poems, 1959, pp. 276–278

FREEDOM'S PLOW
Century Club Bulletin, Nov. 1943, p. 21
New World, Aug. 1943, pp. 21–23
Opportunity, April, 1943, pp. 66–69
America (Mexico City), Oct. 1946, pp. 63–70
Kenyon College Magazine, March 1947, p. 3
L. H. Reader, 1958, pp. 131–135
Selected Poems, 1959, pp. 291–297

FROM SELMA
EbR, 1948, p. 88

FROM SPAIN TO ALABAMA
Volunteer for Liberty, Nov. 15, 1937, p. 3
Experiment, Summer 1949, p. 276

FULFILMENT
Fields of Wonder, 1947, pp. 43–44
Selected Poems, 1959, p. 63

FUNERAL
One Way Ticket, 1949, p. 120

GAL'S CRY FOR A DYING LOVER
Fine Clothes, 1927, p. 82
Saturday Review Literature, April 9, 1927, p. 712
AS, 1929, p. 155

GANGSTER
Crisis, Sept. 1941, p. 295

GARDEN
Dear L. Death, 1932, n. p.
Selected Poems, 1959, p. 82

GARMENT
GoSl, 1941, p. 175

GAUGE
Montage, 1951, p. 31
L. H. Reader, 1958, p. 106
Selected Poems, 1959, p. 243

GENIUS CHILD
Opportunity, Aug. 1937, p. 239
Fields of Wonder, 1947, p. 78
Selected Poems, 1959, p. 83

GEORGIA DUSK
Olivant Quarterly, 2nd Quarter, 1955, p. 135
Selected Poems, 1959, p. 279

GHOSTS
Liberator, July 1964, p. 21

GIFTS
Fields of Wonder, 1947, p. 19

GIRL
Fields of Wonder, 1947, pp. 35–36

GOD
Poetry, Oct. 1931, p. 19

GOD TO HUNGRY CHILD
Worker's Monthly, March 1925, p. 234

GONE BOY
Voices, Jan./April 1957, p. 9
Selected Poems, 1959, p. 109

GOOD BLUFFERS
Approach, Spring 1962, p. 4

GOOD MORNING
Montage, 1951, pp. 71–72
America the Land and its writers, ed. D. Scherman, New York: Dodd,
   1956, p. 76
L. H. Reader, 1958, p. 124
Selected Poems, 1959, p. 269
ANP, 1963, p. 68

GOOD MORNING REVOLUTION
Nueva Cultura, Jan. 1936, p. 8
New Masses, Sept. 1932, p. 5

GOOD MORNING STALINGRAD
Jim Crow, 1943, pp. 27–29
SePoSe, 1944, pp. 44–46

GOODBY CHRIST
Negro Worker, Nov./Dec. 1932, p. 32
NANC, 1934, p. 428
The Negro's God, by B. Mays, Boston: Chapman, 1938, pp. 238–239
Saturday Evening Post, Dec. 21, 1940, p. 34

GOSPEL CHA CHA
Ask Your Mama, 1961, pp. 49–52

GRADUATION
Common Ground, Autumn, 1945, pp. 86–87
One Way Ticket, 1949, pp. 127–128
Selected Poems, 1959, pp. 182–183

GRANDPA'S STORIES
L. H. Reader, 1958, p. 151

GRANT PARK
Messenger, Nov. 1924, p. 27

GRAVEYARD
Fields of Wonder, 1947, p. 21

GREEN MEMORY
Harlem Quarterly, Winter 1949–50, p. 9
Montage, 1951, p. 22
L. H. Reader, 1958, p. 100

GRIEF
Fields of Wonder, 1947, p. 69

GROCERY STORE
L. H. Reader, 1958, p. 153

GYPSY MAN
AMV, 1926, pp. 209–210
New Republic, April 14, 1926, p. 223
Fine Clothes, 1927, p. 22

GYPSY MELODIES
Carmel Pine Cone, July 18, 1941, p. 6
Fields of Wonder, 1947, p. 24
Selected Poems, 1959, p. 64

HAITI
New Republic, Sept. 25, 1961, p. 22

HARD DADDY
Fine Clothes, 1927, p. 86
BANP, 1931, p. 238
Selected Poems, 1959, p. 150

HARD LUCK
Poetry, Nov. 1926, p. 88
Opportunity, Oct. 1926, p. 315
Fine Clothes, 1927, p. 18
NPo, 1932, pp. 237–238

HARLEM
Montage, 1951, p. 71
L. H. Reader, 1958, p. 124
IZ, 1958, p. 108
A Raisin in the Sun, by L. Hansberry, New York: Random House, 1958, as Preface
Selected Poems, 1959, p. 268
Presence Africaine, June/Sept. 1960, p. 214
ANP, 1963, pp. 67–68
SOM, 1963, p. 600

HARLEM DANCE HALL
Fields of Wonder, 1947, p. 94

HARLEM NIGHT CLUB
AS, 1929, p. 99
Weary Blues, 1926, p. 32

HARLEM NIGHT SONG
Weary Blues, 1926, p. 62
AS, 1929, p. 102
Selected Poems, 1959, p. 61

HARLEM SWEETIES
Shakespeare, 1942, pp. 18–20
PoNe, 1949, pp. 101–102
Asp, 1956, pp. 770–771

HAVANNA DREAMS
Opportunity, June 1933, p. 181
GoSl, 1941, p. 135
Fields of Wonder, 1947, p. 34
PoNe, 1949, p. 100
Selected Poems, 1959, p. 49

HEART
Fields of Wonder, 1947, pp. 31–32

HEAVEN
GoSl, 1941, p. 144
Fields of Wonder, 1947, p. 3 and p. 115 (Reprise)
TiPo, 1952, p. 192
LIU, 1954, p. 24–25
Selected Poems, 1959, p. 55
TiPoa, 1959, p. 400
La Procellaria, July/Aug. 1963, p. 39

HELEN KELLER
  Double Blossoms, Helen Keller Anthology, ed. E. Porter, New York: Copeland Co., 1931, p. 95

HERO INTERNATIONAL BRIGADE
  Heart of Spain, ed. A. Bessie, New York: Abraham Lincoln Brigade, 1952, p. 326

HEY!
  Fine Clothes, 1927, p. 17

HEY! HEY!
  Fine Clothes, 1927, p. 89

HEY-HEY BLUES
  New Yorker, Nov. 25, 1939, p. 70
  Shakespeare, 1942, pp. 52–53

HIGH TO LOW
  Midwest Journal, Summer 1949, p. 26
  Montage, 1951, p. 43
  L. H. Reader, 1958, p. 111
  Selected Poems, 1959, pp. 250–251

HISTORY
  Opportunity, Nov. 1934, p. 339
  New Song, 1938, p. 19

HOMECOMING
  Experiment, Summer 1949, p. 276
  Selected Poems, 1959, p. 135

HOMESICK BLUES
  Literary Digest, July 3, 1926, p. 30
  CDC, 1927, pp. 147–148
  Fine Clothes, 1927, p. 24
  AS, 1929, p. 146
  MoAmPo, 1930, p. 794
  Dream Keeper, 1932, p. 36
  MoAmPox, 1936, p. 611
  WOK, 1959, p. 101
  PWD, 1960, pp. 272–273

HONEY BABE
  One Way Ticket, 1949, p. 40

HOPE "Sometimes when I'm lonely"
  Shakespeare, 1942, p. 16
  Selected Poems, 1959, p. 35

HOPE "He rose up on his dying bed"
  Montage, 1951, p. 68
  L. H. Reader, 1958, p. 123
  Selected Poems, 1959, p. 267

HOPE FOR HARLEM
  Our World, Aug. 1952, pp. 34–36

HORN OF PLENTY
  Ask Your Mama, 1961, pp. 41–46

HOUSE IN TAOS
  Palms, Nov. 1926, pp. 35–37
  CDC, 1927, p. 152
  Prize Poems, ed. C. Wagner, New York: Boni, 1930, p. 170
  PoWoSp, 1940, pp. 132–133
  Fields of Wonder, 1947, pp. 73–75
  LIU, 1954, pp. 30–32
  Selected Poems, 1959, pp. 94–95

HOUSE IN THE WORLD
  NANC, 1934, p. 427

HOW ABOUT IT DIXIE?
  Jim Crow, 1943, p. 9

HOW THIN A BLANKET
  Opportunity, Dec. 1939, p. 361
  Span, Oct./Dec. 1946

HURT
  Harlem, Nov. 1928, p. 38

I DREAM A WORLD
  Teamwork, Feb. 1945, p. 1
  ANP, 1963, pp. 71–72

I THOUGHT IT WAS TANGIERS I WANTED
  Opportunity, Dec. 1927, p. 368
  AMV28, 1928, pp. 180–181

I, TOO
  New Negro, 1925, p. 145
  Survey Graphic, March 1, 1925, p. 683
  Weary Blues, 1926, p. 109 [Epilogue]
  CDC, 1927, pp. 145–146
  FOUR, 1927, p. 29
  AS, 1929, p. 42
  ANL, 1929, pp. 210–211

Atlantis, Sept. 1929, p. 549
Nouvel Age, Dec. 1931, p. 1064
Dream Keeper, 1932, p. 76
ASA, 1932, p. 90
SIN, 1934, p. 18
NANC, 1934, p. 3
NPTP, 1935, p. 203
APNA, 1936, p. 35
El Mono Azul, Aug. 19, 1937, p. 1
La Nueva Democracia, Aug. 1938, p. 15
DSp, 1941, p. 811
Sustancia, July 1942
Antioch Review, Sept. 1942, p. 368
THI, 1942, p. 513
Democracy For All, ed. H. Mudgett, Minneapolis: University of Minnesota Press, 1945, p. 107
MPN, 1946, pp. 48–49
Pre P, 1946, p. 343
NPTPo, 1947, p. 245
PoNe, 1949, p. 97
VS, 1955, pp. 235–236
United Asia, March 1955, p. 106
CP, 1958, p. 89
Selected Poems, 1959, p. 275
The Broadcaster, May 1960, p. 120
ANP, 1963, p. 64
New South, Oct. 1961, back cover

IF-ING
Shakespeare, 1942, p. 32

IF YOU WOULD
Rong, Wrong, No. 2, P. 2 [n.d.]

IMAGINE
Chelsea Eight, Oct. 1960, p. 42

IN A TROUBLED KEY
Shakespeare, 1942, p. 49

IN EXPLANATION OF OUR TIMES
Olivant Quarterly, 2nd quarter, 1955, pp. 136–137
Africa South, April/June, 1957, p. 100
Selected Poems, 1959, pp. 281–283

IN TIME OF SILVER RAIN
Opportunity, June 1938, p. 176
GlSl, 1941, p. 108

Fields of Wonder, 1947, pp. 41–42
TiPo, 1952, p. 150
Selected Poems, 1959, p. 56
TiPoa, 1959, p. 327
Highlights, May 1965, p. 3

INTERNE AT PROVIDENT
One Way Ticket, 1949, pp. 134–136
Selected Poems, 1959, pp. 184–185

IRISH WAKE
Dream Keeper, 1932, p. 35

IS IT TRUE
Ask Your Mama, 1961, pp. 55–58

ISLAND "Wave of Sorrow"
Minnesota Quarterly, Spring 1950, p. 22 [Wave]
BLB, 1958, p. 23
IZ, 1958, p. 112
Selected Poems, 1959, p. 78

ISLAND "Between Two Rivers"
Montage, 1951, p. 75
L. H. Reader, 1958, p. 126
Selected Poems, 1959, p. 272
ANP, 1963, p. 70

IT'S ALL THE SAME
International Literature, No. 5, 1933, p. 36

JAIME
Fields of Wonder, 1947, p. 84

JAM SESSION
Montage, 1951, p. 35
L. H. Reader, 1958, p. 108
BNF, 1958, pp. 559–560
Selected Poems, 1959, p. 246

JAZZ BAND IN A PARISIAN CABARET *see* TO A NEGRO JAZZ
BAND IN A PARISIAN CABARET

JAZZONIA
Crisis, Aug. 1923, p. 162
New Negro, 1925, p. 226
Survey Graphic, March 1, 1925, p. 665
Weary Blues, 1926, p. 25
FOUR, 1927, p. 22
BANP, 1931, p. 236

JULIET
Fields of Wonder, 1947, p. 58–59
Selected Poems, 1959, p. 89

A JULLIARD STUDENT STRUGGLES WITH HIGHER INSTRU-
MENTATION
Swing Book, ed. L. Hampton, Chicago: Negro Story Press, 1946, p. 142
L. H. Reader, 1958, p. 130 [Conservatory student]

JUSTICE
New Song, 1938, p. 11
Scottsboro Limited, 1932, p. 1

KID IN THE PARK
Minnesota Quarterly, Spring 1950, p. 22 [Waif]
Selected Poems, 1959, p. 101

KID SLEEPY
Carmel Pine Cone, May 2, 1941, p. 10
Shakespeare, 1942, pp. 24–25
Selected Poems, 1959, p. 126

KIDS WHO DIE
New Song, 1938, pp. 18–19

KU KLUX
Shakespeare, 1942, pp. 81–82
Selected Poems, 1959, p. 163
La Procellaria, May/June 1962, p. 14

LABOR STORM
New Republc, July 30, 1946, p. 19

LADY IN CABARET
Harlem, Nov. 1928, p. 38

LADY'S BOOGIE
Montage, 1951, p. 44
L. H. Reader, 1958, p. 111
Selected Poems, 1959, p. 251

LAMENT, FOR DARK PEOPLES
Crisis, June 1924, p. 60
Weary Blues, 1926, p. 100
AS, 1929, p. 73
United Asia, March 1955, p. 76

LAMENT OF A VANQUISHED BEAU
Brownie's Book, Aug. 1921, p. 229

LAMENT OVER LOVE
  Vanity Fair, May 1926, p. 70
  Fine Clothes, 1927, p. 81
  Selected Poems, 1959, p. 153

LAST CALL
  NP, 1957, p. 79

LAST FEAST OF BELSHAZZAR
  Crisis, Aug. 1923, p. 162

LATE CORNER
  NP, 1957, p. 81

LATE LAST NIGHT
  One Way Ticket, 1949, p. 95
  Selected Poems, 1959, p. 36

LAUGHERS
  Fine Clothes, 1927, pp. 77–78

LENOX AVENUE: MIDNIGHT
  Weary Blues, 1926, p. 39
  AS, 1929, p. 48
  BLB, 1958, p. 23

LENIN
  New Masses, Jan. 22, 1946, p. 5

LET AMERICA BE AMERICA AGAIN
  Esquire, July 1936, p. 92
  New Song, 1938, pp. 9–11
  D. Sp, 1941, pp. 812–814
  NeCa, 1941, pp. 370–372
  Pocket Book of America, ed. P. Van Doren Stern, New York: Pocket
    Book, 1942, p. 319–322
  Br A, 1943, pp. 196–197
  Poetry of Freedom, ed. W. Benet, New York: Random, 1945, pp. 537–
    540
  NPTPo, 1947, pp. 321–322
  PoNe, 1949, pp. 106–108
  CP, 1958, pp. 102–104
  Poets of Today, ed. W. Lowenfels, New York: International, 1964, p.
    15

LETTER (Dear Mama)
  L. H. Reader, 1958, pp. 125–126
  BLB, 1958, p. 23

IZ, 1958, p. 112
Selected Poems, 1959, pp. 271–272
ANP, 1963, p. 70

LETTER (Dear Cassie)
Shakespeare, 1942, pp. 10–11
Montage, 1951, p. 75
L. H. Reader, 1958, pp. 125–126

LIARS
Opportunity, March 1925, p. 90

LIFE FACE TO FACE
American Review, Spring 1961, p. 10

LIFE IS FINE
One Way Ticket, 1949, pp. 38–39
Selected Poems, 1959, pp. 121–122
WOK, 1959, p. 103

LIKEWISE
Montage, 1951, p. 66
L. H. Reader, 1958, p. 122
Selected Poems, 1959, pp. 266–267

LINCOLN MONUMENT: WASHINGTON
Opportunity, March 1927, p. 85
Dream Keeper, 1932, p. 68

LINCOLN THEATRE
One Way Ticket, 1949, p. 46

LINCOLN UNIVERSITY, 1954
LIU, 1954, p. 24

LISTEN HERE BLUES
Fine Clothes, 1927, p. 85

LITANY
Selected Poems, 1959, p. 24

LITTLE CATS
Voices, Jan./April 1959, p. 16

LITTLE FRIGHTENED CHILD
Crisis, Oct. 1923, p. 28

LITTLE GRAY DREAMS
Opportunity, June 1924, p. 20

LITTLE GREEN TREE BLUES
  Tomorrow, July 1945, p. 15
  PoNe, 1949, pp. 99–100
  One Way Ticket, 1949, p. 111
  MS, 1949, p. 67–68
  Selected Poems, 1959, p. 137

LITTLE JULIE
  Olivant Quarterly, 2nd quarter, 1955, pp. 134–135

LITTLE LYRIC
  Shakespeare, 1942, p. 21
  Selected Poems, 1959, p. 127

LITTLE OLD LETTER BLUES
  The Old Line, April 1943, p. 20

LITTLE SONG
  Fields of Wonder, 1947, p. 82
  Opportunity, July 1948, p. 99
  L. H. Reader, 1958, p. 155

LITTLE SONG ON HOUSING TO PUT IN YOUR PIPE AND SMOKE
  Phylon, June 1955, p. 148

LIVE AND LET LIVE
  Montage, 1951, p. 31
  L. H. Reader, 1958, p. 105
  Selected Poems, 1959, p. 242

LONESOME CORNER
  Tomorrow, July 1945, p. 60
  One Way Ticket, 1949, p. 99

LONESOME PLACE
  Opportunity, Oct. 1926, p. 314

LONG VIEW
  Harpers, April 1965, p. 186

LONG TRIP
  Weary Blues, p. 73
  Dream Keeper, 1932, p. 18
  Selected Poems, 1959, p. 52

LOVE
  Shakespeare, 1942, p. 124
  Selected Poems, 1959, p. 69

LOVE AGAIN BLUES
  Poetry, April 1940, p. 21
  Shakespeare, 1942, pp. 103–104

LOVE SONG FOR LUCINDA
  Opportunity, May 1926, p. 164

LOVER'S RETURN
  The Carolina Magazine, May 1928, p. 21
  Poetry, Oct. 1931, p. 16
  Shakespeare, 1942, pp. 119–120
  Selected Poems, 1959, p. 112

LOW TO HIGH
  Midwest Journal, Summer 1949, p. 25
  Montage, 1951, p. 42
  L. H. Reader, 1958, p. 110
  Selected Poems, 1959, p. 249

LUCK
  Fields of Wonder, 1947, p. 64
  Selected Poems, 1959, p. 99

LULLABY
  Crisis, March 1926, p. 221
  Dream Keeper, 1932, pp. 57–58

LUMUMBA'S GRAVE
  Magisterio, Nov. 1961, p. 66

LUNCH IN A JIM CROW CAR
  Selected Poems, 1959, p. 280

LYNCHING SONG
  New Song, 1938, p. 30
  One Way Ticket, 1949, p. 58

MA LORD
  Crisis, June 1927, p. 123
  Dream Keeper, 1932, p. 55
  GoSl, 1941, p. 64
  Catholic Interracialist, Oct. 1951, p. 7
  BNF, 1958, p. 556

MA MAN
  Fine Clothes, 1927, p. 88

MADAM AND HER MADAM
  Common Ground, Winter 1943, pp. 89–90
  Negro Story, Oct./Nov. 1944, p. 55
  One Way Ticket, 1949, pp. 5–6
  Selected Poems, 1959, p. 202

MADAM AND HER MIGHT HAVE BEEN
   CR, 1944, pp. 434–435
   One Way Ticket, 1949, pp. 24–25
   Selected Poems, 1959, pp. 215–216

MADAM AND THE ARMY
   Common Ground, Winter 1943, p. 89
   Negro Today, Oct./Nov. 1944, p. 55

MADAM AND THE CENSUS MAN
   One Way Ticket, 1949, pp. 26–27
   Selected Poems, 1959, pp. 217–218

MADAM AND THE CHARITY CHILD
   Poetry, Sept. 1943, pp. 311–312
   Negro Story, March/April, 1945, p. 47
   One Way Ticket, 1949, pp. 16–17
   Selected Poems, 1959, p. 210

MADAME AND THE FORTUNE TELLER
   One Way Ticket, 1949, pp. 18–19
   Selected Poems, 1959, p. 211

MADAM AND THE MINISTER
   CR, 1944, pp. 433–434
   One Way Ticket, 1949, pp. 22–23
   Selected Poems, 1959, pp. 213–214

MADAM AND THE INSURANCE MAN
   Negro Story, March/April, 1945, p. 47

MADAM AND THE MOVIES
   Common Ground, Winter 1943, p. 90
   Negro Story, Oct./Nov. 1944, p. 55

MADAM AND THE NEWSBOY
   Negro Story, Dec./Jan. 1944–45, p. 50

MADAM AND THE NUMBER WRITER
   Contemporary Poetry, 1943, p. 6
   Negro Story, March/April 1945, p. 47
   One Way Ticket, 1949, pp. 11–12
   Selected Poems, 1959, pp. 206–207

MADAM AND THE PHONE BILL
   One Way Ticket, 1949, pp. 13–15
   Selected Poems, 1959, pp. 208–209

MADAM AND THE RENT MAN
  Poetry, Sept. 1943, pp. 312–313
  Negro Story, Dec./Jan. 1944–45, p. 50
  One Way Ticket, 1949, pp. 9–10
  Selected Poems, 1959, pp. 204–205

MADAM AND THE WRONG VISITOR
  CR, 1944, pp. 435–436
  One Way Ticket, 1949, pp. 20–21
  Selected Poems, 1959, p. 212

MADAM'S CALLING CARDS
  Poetry, Sept. 1943, p. 310
  Negro Story, Dec./Jan. 1944–45, p. 50
  One Way Ticket, 1949, pp. 7–8
  Selected Poems, 1959, p. 203

MADAM'S PAST HISTORY
  Common Ground, Winter 1943, p. 88
  Negro Story, Oct./Nov. 1944, p. 54
  One Way Ticket, 1949, pp. 3–4
  Selected Poems, 1959, p. 201

MAGNOLIA FLOWERS
  Fine Clothes, 1927, p. 70
  Selected Poems, 1959, p. 159

MAMA AND DAUGHTER
  One Way Ticket, 1949, pp. 31–32
  Selected Poems, 1959, p. 132

MAMMY
  FOUR, 1927, p. 28
  Fine Clothes, 1927, p. 76

MAN
  Fields of Wonder, 1947, p. 60

MAN INTO MEN
  One Way Ticket, 1949, p. 85

MARCH MOON
  Weary Blues, 1926, p. 47
  Selected Poetry, 1959, p. 60

MAZIE DIES ALONE
  Harlem, Nov. 1928, p. 38

MAYBE
  Selected Poems, 1959, p. 111

ME AND MY SONG
Jim Crow, 1943, p. 26

ME AND THE MULE
Shakespeare, 1942, p. 29
Negro Quarterly, Spring 1942, p. 37
Selected Poems, 1959, p. 125

MEAN OLD YESTERDAY
Olivant Quarterly, 2nd quarter, 1955, p. 134

MELLOW
Montage, 1951, p. 30
L. H. Reader, 1958, p. 104
Selected Poems, 1959, p. 242

MEMO TO NON-WHITE PEOPLE
Africa South, April/June 1957, p. 99

MEMORIES OF CHRISTMAS
Circuit, Dec. 1946, pp. 2–3

MERRY CHRISTMAS
New Masses, Dec. 1930, p. 4

MERRY-GO-ROUND
Common Ground, Spring 1942, p. 27
Shakespeare, 1942, p. 80
BrA, 1943, p. 196
ThAO, 1944, p. 136
PoNe, 1949, p. 104
Mayfair, Aug. 1958, p. 26
BLB, 1958, p. 20
FANP, 1965, p. 73
La Procellaria, May/June 1961, p. 24
Selected Poems, 1959, p. 194

MEXICAN MARKET WOMAN
Crisis, March 1922, p. 210
Weary Blues, 1926, p. 91
Dream Keeper, 1932, p. 22
Gaily we parade, ed. J. Brewton, New York: Macmillan, 1944, p. 17
TiPo, 1952, p. 13
Selected Poems, 1959, p. 65
TiPoa, 1959, p. 30

MIDNIGHT CHIPPIE'S LAMENT
Shakespeare, 1942, pp. 105–106

MIDNIGHT DANCER
  Selected Poems, 1959, p. 129

MIDNIGHT RAFFLE
  One Way Ticket, 1949, p. 107
  Selected Poems, 1959, p. 107

MIDWINTER BLUES
  New Republic, April 14, 1926, p. 223
  FOUR, 1927, p. 23
  AMV, 1926, pp. 208–209
  Fine Clothes, 1927, p. 84
  Selected Poems, 1959, p. 151

MIGRANT
  One Way Ticket, 1949, pp. 125–126
  Selected Poems, 1959, pp. 178–179

MIGRATION
  Fields of Wonder, 1947, pp. 99–100

MINNIE SINGS HER BLUES
  Fine Clothes, 1927, p. 64
  Messenger, May 1926, p. 132

MINSTREL MAN
  Crisis, Dec. 1925, pp. 66–67
  New Negro, 1925, p. 144
  FOUR, 1927, p. 25
  Dream Keeper, 1932, p. 38
  SIN, 1934, p. 18
  NeCa, 1941, p. 370
  Negro in American Culture, by M. Butcher, New York: Knopf, 1956,
    pp. 132–133
  America, March 5, 1960, p. 678

MISERY
  Opportunity, Oct. 1926, p. 315
  Fine Clothes, 1927, p. 19
  Selected Poetry, 1959, p. 143

MISS BLUES CHILD
  Olivant Quarterly, 2nd quarter, 1955, p. 135
  Selected Poems, 1959, p. 113

MISSISSIPPI
  New Republic, Aug. 21, 1961, p. 23

MISSISSIPPI LEVEE
  Shakespeare, 1942, pp. 46–47

MISTER SANDMAN
  Brownie's Book, Aug. 1921, p. 244

MOAN
  Fine Clothes, 1927, p. 51

MONA
  Opportunity, June 1927, p. 161
  AMV 27, 1927, pp. 159–160

MONOTONY
  Crisis, May 1923, p. 35

MONROE'S BLUES
  One Way Ticket, 1949, p. 108
  Selected Poems, 1959, p. 116

MONTMARTRE
  Fields of Wonder, 1947, p. 25
  Sinn und Form, No. 3, 1949, p. 116

MONTMARTRE BEGGAR WOMAN
  Crisis, Nov. 1927, p. 303

MOON *see* A HOUSE IN TAOS

MOONLIGHT IN VALENCIA
  SePoSe, 1944, p. 51

MOONLIGHT NIGHT: CARMEL
  Carmel Pine Cone, June 15, 1934, p. 8
  Opportunity, July 1934, p. 217
  Den Gulden Winckel, Sept. 1937, p. 10
  Fields of Wonder, 1947, p. 6
  Selected Poems, 1959, p. 54

MORNING AFTER
  Shakespeare, 1942, p. 44
  Selected Poems, 1959, p. 43

MOTHER TO SON
  Crisis, Dec. 1922, p. 87
  Weary Blues, 1926, p. 107
  FOUR, 1927, p. 26
  CDC, 1927, pp. 151–152
  LIU (4), 1930, p. 15
  RFN, 1931, p. 19
  Bookman: London, Oct. 1931, p. 17
  Father, ed. M. Doud, New York: Dutton, 1931, pp. 103–104
  Dream Keeper, 1932, p. 73

SIN, 1934, p. 18
I Hear America Singing, ed. R. Barnes, Chicago: Winston, 1937, p. 211
National Education Association Journal, Dec. 1940, p. 258
Story of Verse for Children, ed. M. Huber, New York: Macmillan, 1940, p. 162
GoSl, 1941, p. 170
PoNe, 1949, p. 105
MS, 1949, pp. 69–70
AML, 1950, pp. 57–58
IHP, 1948, p. 295
BoChLi, 1950, p. 567
LIU, 1954, p. 32
Asp, 1956, p. 773
BLB, 1958, p. 19
CP, 1958, p. 99
Willie Mae, by E. Kytle, New York: Knopf, 1958, as Preface
Selected Poems, 1959, p. 187
ANP, 1963, p. 67
La Procellaria, July/Aug. 1963, p. 39

MOTHERLAND
   Jim Crow, 1943, p. 15
   Fields of Wonder, 1947, p. 97

MOTTO
   Montage, 1951, p. 19
   L. H. Reader, 1958, p. 98
   BNE, 1958, p. 558
   Selected Poems, 1959, p. 234

MOVIES
   Montage, 1951, p. 15
   L. H. Reader, 1958, p. 96
   Selected Poems, 1959, p. 230

MULATTO
   Saturday Review Literature, Jan. 29, 1927, p. 547
   Fine Clothes, 1927, pp. 71–72
   ANL, 1929, pp. 211–213
   APNA, 1936, pp. 41–43
   NPTPo, 1947, pp. 249–250
   Selected Poems, 1959, pp. 160–161
   La Parola, Aug./Sept. 1962, p. 34

MY BELOVED
   Crisis, March 1924, p. 202

MY LOVER
   Crisis, May 1922, p. 32

MY MAN
   AMV, 1926, p. 210
   New Republic, April 14, 1926, p. 223
   New Republic, Nov. 22, 1954, p. 64

MY PEOPLE
   Crisis, June 1922, p. 72
   Weary Blues, 1926, p. 58 [Poem]
   CDC, 1927, p. 150
   AS, 1929, p. 23
   RFN, 1931, p. 17
   Dream Keeper, 1932, p. 67
   NPT Po, 1947, p. 246
   Selected Poetry, 1959, p. 13

MYSTERY
   Montage, 1951, pp. 55–56
   L. H. Reader, 1958, pp. 114–115
   Selected Poems, 1959, pp. 255–256

NAACP
   Crisis, June 1941, p. 201

NATCHA
   Weary Blues, 1926, p. 79
   Selected Poems, 1959, p. 72

NAZIS
   Jim Crow, 1943, p. 8
   Span, Dec. 1944/Jan. 1945, p. 14

NECESSITY
   Montage, 1951, p. 8
   L. H. Reader, 1958, pp. 92–93
   Selected Poems, 1959, p. 226

NEGRO
   Crisis, Jan. 1922, p. 113
   Current Opinion, March 1922, p. 397
   NPTP, 1923, pp. 200–201
   Les Continents, July, 1924
   Weary Blues, 1926, p. 19 [Proem]
   PJV, 1929, pp. 27–28
   AS, 1929, p. 15
   Kalendar Delnik, 1931, p. 57
   Dream Keeper, 1932, p. 72

CDC, 1927, pp. 149–150
Atlantis, Sept. 1929, p. 549
AS, 1929, p. 21
LIV (4), 1930, p. 13
BEMA, 1930, p. 273
Dream Keeper, 1932, p. 71
NPTP, 1935, pp. 201–202
APNA, 1936, pp. 36–37
Crisis, June 1941, p. 187
GoSl, 1941, p. 52
NeCa, 1941, p. 367
Carmel Pine Cone, May 2, 1941, p. 10
THAD, 1944, pp. 118–119
Scholastic, Feb. 12, 1945, p. 15
NPTPo, 1947, p. 243
Story of the Negro, by A. Bontemps, New York: Knopf, 1948 as Preface
Das Lot, 1948, p. 50
MS, 1949, pp. 71–72
PoNe, 1949, pp. 105–106
Hochland, February 1952, p. 14
LIV, 1954, p. 33
APA, 1956, p. 222
America, America, America, ed. K. Giniger, New York: Watts, 1957,
   p. 180
CP, 1958, p. 90
BLB, 1958, p. 21
L. H. Reader, 1958, p. 88
Selected Poems, 1959, p. 4
ANACD, 1960, p. 30
TSD, 1960, p. 107
De Kim Litterair pamflet No. 3, p. 3, n. d.
ANP, 1963, pp. 63–64
American Review, Spring 1961, p. 9
FANP, 1965, pp. 71–72

NEIGHBOR
   Montage, 1951, p. 63
   L. H. Reader, 1958, pp. 119–120
   Selected Poems, 1959, p. 263

NEON SIGNS
   Montage, 1951, p. 17
   L. H. Reader, 1958, p. 97

NEW CABARET GIRL
   Fine Clothes, 1927, p. 31
   AS, 1929, p. 100

NEW FLOWERS
L. H. Reader, 1958, p. 150

NEW GIRL
New Masses, Dec. 1926, p. 10

NEW MOON
Crisis, March 1922, p. 210
Fields of Wonder, 1947, p. 8

NEW SONG
Crisis, March 1933, p. 59
Opportunity, Jan. 1933, p. 23
New Song, 1938, pp. 24–25

NEW YORK
Phylon, Spring 1950, pp. 14–15

NEW YORKERS
Montage, 1951, pp. 11–12
L. H. Reader, 1958, pp. 94–95
Selected Poems, 1959, pp. 228–229

NIGHT: FOUR SONGS
Fields of Wonder, 1947, p. 14
Sinn und Form, No. 3, 1949, p. 115
Selected Poems, 1959, p. 98

NIGHT AND MORN
Dream Keeper, 1932, p. 47
AML, 1950, p. 56

NIGHT FUNERAL IN HARLEM
Montage, 1951, pp. 59–61
L. H. Reader, 1958, pp. 117–118
Selected Poems, 1959, pp. 259–261
SOM, 1963, pp. 598–599

NIGHT SONG
Fields of Wonder, 1947, pp. 45–46

NIGHTMARE BOOGIE
Montage, 1951, p. 58
L. H. Reader, 1958, p. 116
Selected Poems, 1959, p. 258

NO REGRET
Saturday Review of Literature, Jan. 26, 1952, p. 22

NOT A MOVIE
Montage, 1951, p. 16
L. H. Reader, 1958, pp. 96–97
Selected Poems, 1959, p. 231

NOT ELSE BUT
Voices, Jan./April 1959, p. 15

NOT FOR PUBLICATION
Crisis, March 1953, p. 167
Black Orpheus, May, 1959, p. 28

NOT OFTEN
L. H. Reader, 1958, p. 153

NOT WHAT WAS
Massachusetts Review, Winter 1965, p. 305

NOTE ON COMMERCIAL ART
Crisis, Feb. 1944, p. 58

NOTE ON COMMERCIAL THEATRE
Crisis, March, 1940, p. 79
Jim Crow, 1943, p. 24
One Way Ticket, 1949, pp. 81–82
Selected Poems, 1959, p. 190
American Negro Written and His Roots. New York: American Society
of African Culture, 1960, p. 43

NOTE ON MUSIC
Opportunity, April, 1937, p. 104

NUDE YOUNG DANCERS
New Negro, 1925, p. 227
Weary Blues, 1926, p. 33
FOUR, 1927, p. 22

NUMBER
South and West, Summer 1962, p. 9

NUMBERED
Hearse, 1958, n. p.

NUMBERS
Montage, 1951, p. 18
L. H. Reader, 1958, pp. 97–98
Selected Poems, 1959, p. 233

OCTOBER 16
> *Opportunity*, Oct. 1931, p. 299
> *Jim Crow*, 1943, p. 14
> *One Way Ticket*, 1949, pp. 89–90
> *Selected Poems*, 1959, p. 10
> *La Procellaria*, Sept./Oct. 1961, p. 42

ODE TO DINAH
> *Ask Your Mama*, 1961, pp. 25–32

OLD DOG QUEENIE
> *L. H. Reader*, 1958, p. 155

OLD SAILOR
> *Fields of Wonder*, 1947, p. 76–77

OLD WALT
> *Beloit Poetry Journal Chapbook*, Vol. 5, p. 10
> *The Pilot*, Dec. 26, 1954
> *Selected Poems*, 1959, p. 100

ON A CHRISTMAS NIGHT
> *Crisis*, Dec. 1958, p. 616

ON A PALLET OF STRAW
> *Crisis*, Dec. 1958, p. 614

ON THE MAKING OF POEMS
> *Wikor*, Feb. 1955, p. 69

ONE
> *Carmel Pine Cone*, July 18, 1941, p. 6
> *Fields of Wonder*, 1947, p. 17
> *Selected Poems*, 1959, p. 92

ONE WAY TICKET
> *One Way Ticket*, 1949, pp. 61–62
> *Selected Poems*, 1959, p. 177

ONLY WOMAN BLUES
> *Shakespeare*, 1942, pp. 50–51

125TH STREET: HARLEM
> *Voices*, Winter 1951, p. 32
> *Montage*, 1951, p. 33
> *L. H. Reader*, 1958, p. 106
> *Selected Poems*, 1959, p. 244

OPEN LETTER TO THE SOUTH
  International Literature, No. 1, 1933, p. 85
  New Song, 1938, pp. 27–28

OPPRESSION
  Fields of Wonder, 1947, p. 112
  LIU, 1954, pp. 28–29
OUR LAND
  Opportunity, May 1924, p. 142
  Survey 6, March 1, 1925, p. 678
  New Negro, 1925, p. 144
  Weary Blues, 1926, p. 99
  FOUR, 1927, p. 29
  AS, 1929, p. 45
  Bookman: London, Oct. 1931, p. 17

OUR SPRING
  International Literature, No. 5, 1933, p. 35

OUT OF WORK
  Poetry, April 1940, p. 20
  Shakespeare, 1942, pp. 40–41

Ph. D.
  Opportunity, Aug. 1932, p. 249

PAIR IN ONE
  Approach, Spring 1962, p. 5

PARADE
  Montage, 1951, pp. 4–5
  L. H. Reader, 1958, p. 90
  Selected Poems, 1959, pp. 222–223
  SOM, 1963, pp. 594–595

PARK BENCH
  Worker's Monthly, April 1925, p. 261
  Pr. Lt., 1935, p. 168
  New Song, 1938, p. 12
  Phylon, Fall 1947, pp. 206–207

PARISIAN BEGGAR WOMAN
  Dream Keeper, 1932, p. 24

PASSING
  Phylon, Spring 1950, pp. 14–15
  L. H. Reader, 1958, p. 116
  Selected Poems, 1959, pp. 257–258

PASSING LOVE
  Opportunity, March 1927, p. 85
  Dream Keeper, 1932, p. 42
  Tiempo Vivo, July/Dec. 1948

PASTORAL
  L. H. Reader, 1958, p. 129

PAY DAY
  Shakespeare, 1942, pp. 8–9

PEACE
  Opportunity, July 1948, p. 99

PEACE CONFERENCE IN AN AMERICAN TOWN
  Common Ground, Winter, 1946, p. 25

PENNSYLVANIA STATION
  Approach, Spring 1962, p. 4
  ANP, 1963, p. 71
  Progressive Architecture, March 1964, p. 14

PERSONAL
  Crisis, Oct. 1933, p. 238
  Fields of Wonder, 1947, p. 83
  PoNe, 1949, p. 100
  Selected Poems, 1959, p. 88
  ANP, 1963, p. 66

PICTURES TO THE WALL
  Palms, Oct. 1926, p. 24

PIERROT
  Weary Blues, 1926, pp. 67–68

PIGGY BACK
  L. H. Reader, 1958, p. 151

PLAINT
  Voices, Sept./Dec. 1955, p. 17

PO' BOY BLUES
  Poetry, Nov. 1926, p. 89
  Fine Clothes, 1927, p. 23
  Anthologie de la nouvelle poésie Américaine, ed. E. Jolas, 1928, pp.
    108–109
  BANP, 1931, p. 237–238
  Dream Keeper, 1932, p. 44
  Sustancia, July 1942
  NPTPo, 1947, pp. 247–248

POEM: NIGHT IS BEAUTIFUL — *see* MY PEOPLE

POEM "I am waiting for my mother"
Crisis, Aug. 1924, p. 173

POEM "Being walkers with the dawn and morning"
New Negro, 1925, p. 142
Survey Graphic, March 1925, p. 663
PJU, 1929, p. 238
LIU (4), 1930, p. 13 (as "Being Walkers with the Dawn")
Dream Keeper, 1932, p. 63 (as "Walkers with the Dawn")

POEM "I loved my friend"
Crisis, May 1925, p. 11
Weary Blues, 1926, p. 95
Dream Keeper, 1932, p. 12
AM, 1947, p. 167

POEM "We have tomorrow" — *see* YOUTH

POEM "I am a Negro" — *see* NEGRO

POEM "For the portrait of an African boy after the manner of Gauguin"
Weary Blues, 1926, p. 102
AS, 1929, p. 80
MPN, 1946, pp. 52–53

POEM FOR AN INTELLECTUAL ON THE WAY UP
Contemporary Poetry, Autumn 1944, p. 11

POEM TO A DEAD SOLDIER
Worker's Monthly, April 1925, p. 261

POEM: TO THE BLACK BELOVED
Weary Blues, 1926, p. 65
TL, 1935
United Asia, March 1955, p. 119

POEME D'AUTOMNE
Weary Blues, 1926, p. 45

POET TO BIGOT
Phylon, June 1953, p. 206
LIU, 1954, pp. 29–30
L. H. Reader, 1958, p. 129

POET TO PATRON
American Mercury, June 1939, p. 147
Unquote, June 1940, p. 3

POOR ROVER
L. H. Reader, 1958, p. 153

PORT TOWN
Weary Blues, 1926, p. 74
APNA, 1936, p. 37
Selected Poems, 1959, p. 71

PORTER
Fine Clothes, 1927, p. 39
AS, 1929, p. 60
Selected Poems, 1959, p. 169

POPPY FLOWER
Crisis, Feb. 1925, p. 167
Fields of Wonder, 1947, p. 23

PRAYER "Gather Up"
Contemperaneos, Sept./Oct. 1931, p. 158
Fields of Wonder, 1947, p. 70

PRAYER "I ask you this"
Buccaneer, May 1925, p. 20
CDC, 1927, p. 146
Fine Clothes, 1927, p. 48
Dream Keeper, 1932, p. 53
Sociology and Social Research, Sept. 1936, p. 51
Selected Poems, 1959, p. 18

PRAYER "Oh God of dust"
Voices, Sept./Dec. 1955, p. 18

PRAYER MEETING
Crisis, Aug. 1923, p. 162
Fine Clothes, 1927, p. 46
Dream Keeper, 1932, p. 59
Selected Poems, 1959, p. 27

PREFERENCE
Montage, 1951, p. 8
L. H. Reader, 1958, p. 92
Selected Poems, 1959, p. 225

PRELUDE TO OUR AGE: A NEGRO HISTORY POEM
N. Y. Public Library, Branch Library Book News, Oct. 1960, pp. 105–110
Crisis, Feb. 1951, pp. 87–90

PRESENT
Shakespeare, 1942, p. 30

PRIDE
Opportunity, Dec. 1930, p. 371
New Song, 1938, p. 16

PRIZE FIGHTER
Fine Clothes, 1927, p. 35
AS, 1929, p. 59

PROBLEMS
L. H. Reader, 1958, p. 152

PROEM *see* NEGRO

PROJECTION
Montage, 1951, p. 26
L. H. Reader, 1958, p. 103
Selected Poems, 1959, p. 240

PROJECTION OF A DAY
New Masses, Jan. 1, 1946, p. 11

PUBLIC DIGNITARIES
Unquote, June 1940, p. 4

PUZZLED
One Way Ticket, 1949, pp. 71–72
Literary America, ed. D. Scherman, New York: Dodd 1952, p. 156
Selected Poems, 1959, p. 191

QUESTION
Crisis, March 1922, p. 210
SePoSe, 1944, p. 49
Montage, 1951, p. 9
L. H. Reader, 1958, p. 93

QUICK AND THE DEAD
Poetry, Oct. 1931, p. 19

QUIET GIRL
Dream Keeper, 1932, p. 11

RAID
One Way Ticket, 1949, p. 110

RAILROAD AVENUE
Fire, Nov. 1926, p. 21
Fine Clothes, 1927, p. 27
Selected Poems, 1959, p. 186

RAIN from A HOUSE IN TAOS
ThAO, 1944, pp. 132–133

READER'S WRITER
Mark Twain Journal, Summer 1962, p. 19

REASONS WHY
Dream Keeper, 1932, p. 32

RED CLAY BLUES by Richard Wright and Langston Hughes
New Masses, Aug. 1, 1939, p. 14

RED CROSS
Jim Crow, 1943, p. 8

RED ROSES
Poetry, Nov. 1926, p. 90

RED SILK STOCKINGS
Fine Clothes, 1927, p. 73

REFUGEE
Carmel Pine Cone, July 18, 1941, p. 6

REFUGEE IN AMERICA
Saturday Evening Post, Feb. 6, 1943, p. 64
American Decade, ed. E. Bishop, Cummington, Mass.: Cummington, Press, 1943, p. 48
Poets Speak, New York: New York Public Library, 1943, p. 15
Fields of Wonder, 1947, p. 105
United Asia, Dec. 1954, p. 288
Selected Poems, 1959, p. 290
WOK, 1959, [There are words like freedom] p. 102

RELIEF
Harlem Quarterly, Winter 1949, 1950, p. 10
Montage, 1951, p. 21
L. H. Reader, 1958, p. 101
Selected Poems, 1959, p. 238

REMEMBRANCE
Fields of Wonder, 1947, p. 33

REPRISE *see* HEAVEN

REQUEST
Montage, 1951, p. 50
L. H. Reader, 1958, p. 113
Selected Poems, 1959, p. 254

REQUEST FOR REQUIEMS
One Way Ticket, 1949, p. 115
BNF, 1958, pp. 557–558

REQUEST TO GENIUS
Poetry Quarterly, Spring 1931, p. 12

RESTRICTIVE COVENANTS
One Way Ticket, 1949, p. 64

REVERIE ON THE HARLEM RIVER
Shakespeare, 1942, p. 123
Sustancia, July 1942
La Nueva Democracia, Feb. 1943, p. 23
Selected Poems, 1959, p. 42

REVOLUTION
Harpers, July 1935, p. 135
New Masses, Feb. 1934, p. 28

RIDE, RED, RIDE
Ask Your Mama, 1961, p. 13–15
La Procellaria, Dec. 1961, p. 29

RING, THE
Crisis, April 1926, p. 284

RISING WATERS
Worker's Monthly, April 1925, p. 267

ROAR CHINA
Volunteer for Liberty, Sept. 6, 1937, p. 3
New Masses, Feb. 22, 1938, p. 20
AnMaVe, 1942, pp. 223–225

ROLAND HAYES BEATEN
One Way Ticket, 1949, p. 86
Selected Poems, 1959, p. 167
The Day they changed Their minds. New York: National Association
for the Advancement of colored People, 1960, p. 1

ROOM
Voices, May/Aug. 1953, p. 17

RUBY BROWN
Crisis, Aug. 1926, p. 181
Fine Clothes, 1927, p. 30
AS, 1929, pp. 62–63
Selected Poems, 1959, p. 166

A RUINED GAL
Fine Clothes, 1927, p. 63
Port C, 1927, p. 203

S-SSS-SS-SH!
One Way Ticket, 1949, pp. 33–34
Selected Poems, 1959, p. 134

SAILING DATE
Fields of Wonder, 1947, pp. 86–87

SAILOR
Poetry, Oct. 1931, p. 18
Literary Digest, Nov. 21, 1931, p. 26
Dear L. Death, 1931, n. p.
Dream Keeper, 1932, p. 20
GoSl, 1941, p. 102

SALUTE TO SOVIET ARMIES
New Masses, Feb. 1944, p. 10

SAME IN BLUES
Montage, 1951, pp. 72–73
L. H. Reader, 1958, pp. 124–125
Selected Poems, 1959, pp. 270–271
SOM, 1963, pp. 601–602
ANP, 1963, pp. 69–70

SATURDAY NIGHT
New Masses, Dec. 1926, p. 10
Fine Clothes, 1927, p. 41
MoAmPo, 1930, pp. 795–796
MoAmPox, 1936, p. 612

SCOTTSBORO
Opportunity, Dec. 1931, p. 379
Scottsboro limited, 1932, p. 3

SEARCH
Opportunity, July 1937, p. 207

SEA CALM
Weary Blues, 1926, p. 75
Dream Keeper, 1932, p. 19
Selected Poems, 1959, p. 74

SEA CHARM
Survey Graphic, March 1, 1925, p. 663
Weary Blues, 1926, p. 80
Dream Keeper, 1932, p. 27
RFN, 1931, p. 17

SEASCAPE
Weary Blues, 1926, p. 78
Dream Keeper, 1932, p. 21
Bridled with rainbows, ed. S. Brewton, New York: Macmillan, 1949,
p. 14
Selected Poems, 1959, p. 53

SEASHORE THROUGH DARK GLASSES
Poetry, Feb. 1947, p. 248
One Way Ticket, 1949, p. 45
Selected Poems, 1959, p. 192

SECOND GENERATION: NEW YORK
Common Ground, Spring 1949, p. 47

SEVEN MOMENTS OF LOVE
Esquire, May 1940, pp. 60–61
Girls from Esquire. New York: Random House, 1952, pp. 256–260

SHADES OF PIGMEAT
Ask Your Mama, 1961, pp. 19–21

SHADOWS
Crisis, Aug. 1923, p. 162

SHAKESPEARE IN HARLEM
Shakespeare, 1942, p. 111

SHALL THE GOOD GO DOWN?
Span, Vol. 2, No. 2, 1943, p. 7

SHAME ON YOU
Phylon, Spring 1950, pp. 14–15
Montage, 1951, p. 50
L. H. Reader, 1958, p. 113
Selected Poems, 1959, pp. 254–255

SHARE CROPPERS
PrLt, 1935, p. 167
Shakespeare, 1942, p. 77
Selected Poems, 1959, p. 165

SHEARING TIME
L. H. Reader, 1958, p. 151

SHEPHERD'S SONG AT CHRISTMAS
Crisis, Dec. 1958, p. 615
L. H. Reader, 1958, pp. 155–156

SHOUT
>   *Fine Clothes*, 1927, p. 49
>   *Selected Poems*, 1959, p. 19

SHOW FARE PLEASE
>   *Free Lance*, No. 2, 1961, p. 5
>   *Ask Your Mama*, 1961, pp. 81–83

SICK ROOM
>   *Weary Blues*, 1926, p. 88

SILENCE
>   *Carmel Pine Cone*, July 18, 1941, p. 6
>   *Fields of Wonder*, 1947, p. 47

SILHOUETTE
>   *Anthology of Revolutionary Poetry*, ed. M. Graham, New York: Active
>   Press, 1929, p. 208–209
>   *Den Gulden Winckel*, Sept. 1937, p. 10
>   *SePoSe*, 1944, pp. 49–50
>   *One Way Ticket*, 1949, p. 56
>   *Selected Poems*, 1959, p. 171

SINNER
>   *Fine Clothes*, 1927, p. 53
>   *Dream Keeper*, 1932, p. 52
>   *Selected Poems*, 1959, p. 23

SISTER
>   *Montage*, 1951, p. 7
>   *L. H. Reader*, 1958, pp. 91–92
>   *Selected Poems*, 1959, pp. 224–225

SISTER JOHNSON MARCHES
>   *The Fight Against War and Fascism*, May 1937, p. 11
>   *New Song*, 1938, p. 26

SITUATION
>   *Montage*, 1951, p. 20
>   *L. H. Reader*, 1958, p. 99
>   *Selected Poems*, 1959, p. 235

SIX BITS BLUES
>   *Opportunity*, Feb. 1939, p. 54
>   *Shakespeare*, 1942, p. 37

SLAVE SONG
>   *Voices*, Winter 1949, p. 31

SLEEP
Fields of Wonder, 1947, p. 51

SLIVER
Montage, 1951, p. 67
L. H. Reader, 1958, p. 123
Selected Poems, 1959, p. 267

SLIVER OF SERMON
Montage, 1951, p. 56
L. H. Reader, 1958, p. 115
Selected Poems, 1959, p. 257

SMALL MEMORY
Renaissance, No. 3, 1964, p. 7

SNAIL
Carmel Pine Cone, July 18, 1941, p. 6
GoSl, 1941, p. 149
Fields of Wonder, 1947, p. 4
TiPo, 1952, p. 59
FP, 1957, p. 140
Selected Poems, 1959, p. 59
TiPoa, 1959, p. 105
Instructor, March 1964, p. 116

SNAKE
Poetry Quarterly, Spring 1931, p. 12
Fields of Wonder, 1947, p. 7

SNOB
Shakespeare, 1942, p. 27

SO?
Colorado Review, Spring/Summer 1957, p. 76
Black Orpheus, May 1959, p. 29

SO LONG
Selected Poems, 1959, pp. 251–252

SOLEDAD
Weary Blues, 1926, p. 89
Opportunity, Dec. 1925, p. 378

SONG
Survey Graphic, March 1, 1925, p. 663
New Negro, 1925, p. 143
FOUR, 1927, p. 27
Bookman, Feb. 1927, p. 729
Dream Keeper, 1932, p. 41

SONG AND DREAMS
  AM, 1947, p. 167

SONG FOR A BANJO DANCE
  Crisis, Oct. 1922, p. 267
  Southern Workman, April 1924, p. 180
  Weary Blues, 1926, p. 36
  Dream Keeper, 1932, pp. 45–46

SONG FOR A DARK GIRL
  Crisis, May 1927, p. 94
  Saturday Review of Literature, April 9, 1927, p. 712
  CDC, 1927, p. 147
  Fine Clothes, 1927, p. 75
  FOUR, 1927, p. 28
  ANL, 1929, p. 211
  AS, 1929, p. 72
  Nouvel Age, Dec. 1931, p. 1064
  Bookman: London, Oct. 1931, p. 17
  Krasnaya Nov, No. 4, 1933, p. 106
  APNA, 1936, p. 38
  NeCa, 1941, pp. 369–370
  ECR, 1945, p. 199
  MPN, 1946, pp. 50–51
  NPTPo, 1947, pp. 250–251
  MS, 1949, pp. 73–74
  PoNe, 1949, pp. 103–104
  DeTsjerne, Jan./Feb. 1950, p. 42
  CP, 1958, p. 97
  Selected Poems, 1959, p. 172
  PWD, 1960, p. 250
  TSD, 1960, p. 49

SONG FOR A SUICIDE
  Crisis, May 1924, p. 23

SONG OF SPAIN
  International Literature, No. 5, 1937, p. 3
  New Song, 1938, pp. 21–23
  Deux Poemes, printed by Nancy Cunard and Pablo Neruda [1937],
    n. p.

SONG TO A NEGRO WASH WOMAN
  Crisis, Jan. 1925, p. 115
  GoSl, 1941, pp. 41–42
  NeCa, 1941, pp. 373–374
  NIA, 1964, pp. 117–118

SONGS
Fields of Wonder, 1947, p. 50

SONGS FOR OUR NATION OF NATIONS
L. H. Reader, 1958, p. 155
Common Ground, Spring 1947, pp. 31–33

SONGS TO THE DARK VIRGIN
Weary Blues, 1926, p. 63
Palms, Jan. 1926, p. 14

SOUTH, THE
Crisis, June 1922, p. 72
Weary Blues, 1926, p. 54
Selected Poems, 1959, p. 173

SOUTHERN MAMMY SONGS
Poetry, May 1941, pp. 72–73
Shakespeare, 1942, pp. 75–76
Selected Poems, 1959, p. 162
Million, ed. J. Singer, Glasgow, Scotland: W. McClellan, N.D., p. 14

SOUTHERN NEGRO SPEAKS
Opportunity, Oct. 1941, p. 308

SPEAK WELL OF THE DEAD
Ebony, Oct. 1958, pp. 31–34

SPIRITUALS
Home Quarterly and Guide to Personal and Family Devotion, July/
    Aug. 1944, p. 5 [Song]
Fields of Wonder, 1947, pp. 113–114
Selected Poems, 1959, p. 28

SPORT
FOUR, 1927, p. 24
Fine Clothes, 1927, p. 40

SPRING FOR LOVERS
Crisis, July 1930, p. 235

STALINGRAD: 1942
War Poems of the United Nations, ed. J. Davidman, New York: Dial
    Press, 1943, pp. 321–324

STARS
Fields of Wonder, 1947, p. 101
Selected Poems, 1959, p. 188

STATEMENT
  Shakespeare, 1942, p. 28

STILL HERE
  Jim Crow, 1943, p. 19

STILL LOVE
  One Way Ticket, 1949, p. 49
  Selected Poems, 1959, p. 123

STONY LONESOME *see* DEATH CHANT

STRANGE HURT SHE KNEW
  AMV, 1926, p. 208
  Fields of Wonder, 1947, pp. 80–81
  Selected Poems, 1959, p. 84

STRANGER IN TOWN
  One Way Ticket, 1949, p. 41

STREET SONG
  Montage, 1951, p. 33
  L. H. Reader, 1958, p. 106
  Selected Poems, 1959, p. 244

SUBWAY FACE
  Crisis, Dec. 1924, p. 71

SUBWAY RUSH HOUR
  Montage, 1951, p. 65
  L. H. Reader, 1958, p. 121
  Selected Poems, 1959, p. 265

SUICIDE
  Poetry, Nov. 1926, p. 91
  Fine Clothes, 1927, p. 20
  NPTPo, 1947, p. 247

SUICIDE'S NOTE
  Vanity Fair, Sept. 1925, p. 62
  Weary Blues, 1926, p. 87
  CDC, 1927, p. 151
  Caroline Magazine, May 1927, p. 46
  AS, 1929, p. 147
  Contemporaneos, Sept./Oct. 1931, p. 159
  LDP, 1944
  Selected Poems, 1959, p. 85

SUMMER EVENING
 Poetry Quarterly: (London), Winter, 1947, p. 232
 One Way Ticket, 1949, pp. 123–124
 American Sampler, ed. F. Rosenberger, Iowa City: Prairie Press, 1951,
  p. 27
 Selected Poems, 1959, pp. 180–181

SUMMER NIGHT
 Crisis, Dec. 1925, p. 66
 Weary Blues, 1926, p. 103

SUN *see* A HOUSE IN TAOS

SUN SONG
 FOUR, 1927, p. 28
 Fine Clothes, 1927, p. 69
 AS, 1929, p. 49
 Dream Keeper, 1932, p. 70
 Selected Poems, 1959, p. 5
 La Procellaria, March/April 1961

SUNDAY
 Shakespeare, 1942, p. 7

SUNDAY BY THE COMBINATION
 Montage, 1951, p. 58
 L. H. Reader, 1958, p. 116
 Selected Poems, 1959, p. 259

SUNDAY MORNING PROPHECY
 New Yorker, June 20, 1942, p. 18
 One Way Ticket, 1949, pp. 35–37
 Selected Poems, 1959, pp. 21–22

SUNSET IN DIXIE
 Crisis, Sept. 1941, p. 277

SUNSET CONEY ISLAND
 New Masses, Feb. 1928, p. 13

SUPPER TIME
 Shakespeare, 1942, p. 4

SYLVESTER'S DYING BED
 Poetry, Oct. 1931, pp. 17–18
 Literary Digest, Nov. 21, 1931, p. 26
 Shakespeare, 1942, pp. 67–68
 Selected Poems, 1959, p. 38

TAG
Montage, 1951, p. 36
Selected Poems, 1959, p. 247

TAMBOURINES
Selected Poems, 1959, p. 29

TAPESTRY
Crisis, July 1927, p. 158

TEACHER
Opportunity, May 1926, p. 167

TELL ME
Montage, 1951, p. 16
L. H. Reader, 1958, p. 96
Selected Poems, 1959, p. 231

TERMINAL
Opportunity, Feb. 1932, p. 52

TESTAMENT
NP, 1957, p. 80
L. H. Reader, 1958, p. 130

TESTIMONIAL
Montage, 1951, p. 57
L. H. Reader, 1958, p. 115
Selected Poems, 1959, p. 257

THANKSGIVING TIME
Brownie's Book, Nov. 1921, p. 328

THEME FOR ENGLISH B
Common Ground, Spring 1949, pp. 89–90
Montage, 1951, pp. 39–40
Current Thinking and Writing, ed. J. Bachelor and others. New York:
    Appleton, 1951, p. 2
L. H. Reader, 1958, pp. 108–109
Selected Poems, 1959, pp. 247–248

THERE
Fields of Wonder, 1947, p. 88

THERE ARE WORDS LIKE FREEDOM *see* REFUGEE IN AMERICA

THERE'S ALWAYS WEATHER
L. H. Reader, 1958, p. 149

THIRD DEGREE
One Way Ticket, 1949, p. 130
Selected Poems, 1959, p. 197

THORN
Voices, Sept. 1955, p. 17

THREE POEMS ABOUT LYNCHING
Opportunity, June 1936, p. 170

TIRED
New Masses, Feb. 1931, p. 4

TO ARTINA
Selected Poems, 1959, p. 62

TO A BLACK DANCER IN "THE LITTLE SAVOY"
Weary Blues, 1926, p. 35

TO A DEAD FRIEND
Crisis, May 1922, p. 21

TO A LITTLE LOVER-LASS, DEAD
Weary Blues, 1926, p. 31

TO A NEGRO JAZZ BAND IN A PARISIAN CABARET
Crisis, Dec. 1925, p. 67
Fine Clothes, 1927, p. 74
BANP, 1931, pp. 239–240
MoAmPox, 1936, p. 612 [Jazz Band in a Parisian Cabaret]

TO BE SOMEBODY
Phylon, Winter 1950, p. 311
Selected Poems, 1959, p. 189

TO BEAUTY
Crisis, Oct. 1926, p. 317

TO CAPTAIN MULZAC
Jim Crow, 1943, pp. 16–18

TO CERTAIN BROTHERS
Worker's Monthly, July 1925, p. 406

TO CERTAIN NEGRO LEADERS
NANC, 1934, p. 427
Den Gulden Winckel, Sept. 1937, p. 10
New Masses, Feb. 1931, p. 4

TO MIDNIGHT NAN AT LEROY'S
Vanity Fair, Sept. 1925, p. 62
Weary Blues, 1926, p. 30
Opportunity, Jan. 1926, p. 22
Cornelian, ed. H. Acton, London: Chatto and Windus, 1928, p. 76
Carolina Magazine, May 1928, p. 18
LA, 1930, p. 540
NeCa, 1941, pp. 368–369

TO THE BLACK BELOVED
Crisis, Dec. 1925, p. 67

TO THE DARK MERCEDES OF "EL PALACIO DE AMOR"
Weary Blues, 1926, p. 90

TO THE LITTLE FORT OF SAN LAZARO
New Masses, May, 1931, p. 11

TO THE RED ARMY
Soviet Russia Today, July 1944, p. 20

TODAY
Opportunity, Oct. 1937, p. 310
Fields of Wonder, 1947, p. 111

TOMORROW
AS, 1929, p. 139
Crisis, Nov. 1947, p. 331
Montage, 1951, p. 30
L. H. Reader, 1958, p. 104
Selected Poems, 1959, p. 242
Comprendre, 1960, p. 260
Lincoln University Bulletin, Spring 1961, p. 16

TOMORROW'S SEED
Heart of Spain, ed. A. Bessie, New York: Abraham Lincoln Brigade, 1952, p. 325

TOO BLUE
Contemporary Poetry, Autumn, 1943, p. 5
One Way Ticket, 1949, p. 102

TOWER
Crisis, July 1930, p. 235
Dear L. Death, 1931, n. p.
Wikor, Feb. 1955, p. 69

TOWN OF SCOTTSBORO
Scottsboro Limited, 1932, p. 7

UNION
New Song, 1938, p. 31
APNA, 1936, p. 41

UP-BEAT
Montage, 1951, p. 35
L. H. Reader, 1958, p. 107
Selected Poems, 1959, p. 245

US COLORED
Free Lance, 1st half of 1955, p. 4

VAGABONDS
Opportunity, Dec. 1941, p. 367
Fields of Wonder, 1947, p. 63
Selected Poems, 1959, p. 91

VARI-COLORED SONG
Phylon, Winter 1952, p. 42

VISITORS TO THE BLACK BELT
Opportunity, Jan. 1940, p. 13
Jim Crow, 1943, p. 19
One Way Ticket, 1949, pp. 65–66

WAIF IN THE PARK *see* KID IN THE PARK

WAKE
Shakespeare, 1942, p. 65
New Yorker, June 10, 1944, p. 65
BNF, 1958, p. 557
Selected Poems, 1959, p. 39

WALKERS WITH THE DAWN *see* POEM

WALLS
Palms, Nov. 1926, p. 37
Fields of Wonder, 1947, p. 66

WARNING
Montage, 1951, p. 11
L. H. Reader, 1958, p. 94
Selected Poems, 1959, p. 228

WARNING: AUGMENTED
Montage, 1951, p. 34
L. H. Reader, 1958, p. 107
Selected Poems, 1959, p. 245

WATER-FRONT STREETS
Weary Blues, 1926, p. 71
Dream Keeper, 1932, p. 17
Krasnaya Nov, No. 4, 1933, p. 106
Selected Poems, 1959, p. 51

WAVE *see* ISLAND

WAYS
Buccaneer, May, 1925, p. 21

WEARY BLUES
Opportunity, May 1925, p. 143
Survey, June 1, 1925, p. 301
Forum, Aug. 1925, p. 238–239
Weary Blues, 1926, pp. 23–24
FOUR, 1927, p. 21
ANL, 1929, pp. 213–214
Dream Keeper, 1932, pp. 34–35
NeCa, 1941, pp. 366–368
THI, 1924, pp. 512–513
AM, 1947, p. 169
PoNe, 1949, pp. 98–99
Opportunity, Jan. 1949, p. 8
AML, 1950, pp. 56–57
Asp, 1956, pp. 773–774
Untune the Sky, ed. H. Plotz, New York: Crowell, 1957, p. 47
CP, 1958, pp. 95–96
L. H. Reader, 1958, pp. 87–88
BLB, 1958, p. 18
Selected Poems, 1959, pp. 33–34

WEST TEXAS
Shakespeare, 1942, pp. 78–79
Selected Poems, 1959, p. 164

WHAT?
Selected Poems, 1959, p. 108

WHAT? SO SOON!
Montage, 1951, p. 18
L. H. Reader, 1958, p. 98
Selected Poems, 1959, pp. 233–234

WHEN SUE WEARS RED
Crisis, Feb. 1923, p. 174
Weary Blues, 1926, p. 66
Dream Keeper, 1932, p. 43

GoSl, 1941, p. 111
BLB, 1958, p. 21
Selected Poems, 1959, p. 68

WHEN THE ARMIES PASSED
Fields of Wonder, 1947, pp. 109–110

WHERE? WHEN? WHICH?
Colorado Review, Winter 1956/1957, p. 34
NP, 1957, p. 81

WHITE FELTS IN FALL
One Way Ticket, 1949, p. 109

WHITE MAN
New Masses, Dec. 1936, p. 34

WHITE ONES
Opportunity, March 1924, p. 68
Weary Blues, 1926, p. 106
LDP, 1944, p. 80

WHITE SHADOWS
Contempo, Sept. 15, 1931, p. 1

WHO BUT THE LORD?
Poetry, Feb. 1947, p. 249
One Way Ticket, 1949, pp. 73–74
Selected Poems, 1959, p. 196

WIDE RIVER
Dream Keeper, 1932, p. 37

WIDOW WOMAN
Shakespeare, 1942, pp. 107–108
Selected Poems, 1959, p. 139

WIND *see* A HOUSE IN TAOS

WINE–O
Montage, 1951, p. 22
L. H. Reader, 1958, p. 101
Selected Poems, 1959, p. 237

WINTER MOON
Crisis, Aug. 1923, p. 162
Weary Blues, 1926, p. 44
Dream Keeper, 1932, p. 4
LDP, 1944, p. 84
Selected Poems, 1959, p. 58

WINTER SWEETNESS
 Brownie's Book, Jan. 1921, p. 27
 Dream Keeper, 1932, p. 10
 GoSl, 1941, p. 182

WISDOM
 Saturday Evening Post, Jan. 30, 1943, p. 74
 Fields of Wonder, 1947, p. 107
 TiPo, 1952, p. 194
 TiPoa, 1959, p. 401

WISDOM AND WAR
 EbR, 1948, p. 88

WISE MEN
 Messenger, June 1927, p. 11

WITHOUT BENEFIT OF DECLARATION
 Free Lance, 1st half of 1955, p. 3
 ANP, 1963, p. 72

WONDER
 Montage, 1951, p. 12
 L. H. Reader, 1958, p. 95
 Selected Poems, 1959, p. 229

WORKIN' MAN
 Fine Clothes, 1927, p. 59

WORLD WAR II
 Harlem Quarterly, Winter 1949/1950, p. 9
 Montage, 1951, p. 51
 L. H. Reader, 1958, p. 114
 Selected Poems, 1959, p. 255

YEAR ROUND
 L. H. Reader, 1958, p. 150

YESTERDAY AND TODAY
 Poetry, Feb. 1947, p. 250
 One Way Ticket, 1949, p. 101

YOUNG BRIDE
 Crisis, Oct. 1925, p. 278
 Weary Blues, 1926, p. 93

YOUNG GAL'S BLUES
 FOUR, 1927, p. 24
 Fine Clothes, 1927, p. 83
 NeCa, 1941, p. 369

BNF, 1958, p. 555
Selected Poems, 1959, p. 148

YOUNG NEGRO GIRL
Carmel Pine Cone, July 18, 1941, p. 6
Shakespeare, 1942, p. 17

YOUNG PROSTITUTE
Crisis, Aug. 1923, p. 162
Weary Blues, 1926, p. 34

YOUNG SAILOR
Weary Blues, 1926, p. 77
Palms, Jan. 1926, p. 9
Selected Poems, 1959, p. 73

YOUNG SINGER
Crisis, Aug. 1923, p. 162
Weary Blues, 1926, p. 28

YOUTH
Crisis, Aug. 1924, p. 163
Survey Graphic, March 1925, p. 663
New Negro, 1925, p. 142
Weary Blues, 1926, p. 108 [Poem]
FOUR, 1927, p. 30
Caroline Magazine, May 1927, p. 48
LIU (4), 1930, p. 30
RFN, 1931, p. 17
Dream Keeper, 1932, p. 77
In A Minor Key, by I. Reid, Washington, D.C.: American Council on
    Education, 1940, as Preface
GOSI, 1941, p. 9
We Have Tomorrow, by A. Bontemps, Boston: Houghton, 1945, as
    Preface
LIU, 1954, pp. 33–34

Works about Langston Hughes

Including selected reviews of his major works

GENERAL

Adams, Russell. *Great Negroes Past and Present.* Chicago: Afro-Am Publishing Company, 1964, p. 127.

Bardolph, Richard. *The Negro Vanguard.* New York: Random House, 1959, pp. 202–219, scattered references.

Becker, Mary. *Progressivnay Negritynskay Literatura USA.* Leningrad: Sovetskii Pisatelo, 1957, pp. 156–187, 193–196, 209–219.

Brown, Deming. *Soviet Attitudes Toward American Writing.* Princeton: Princeton University Press, 1962, pp. 13, 126–128.

Burroughs, Margaret. "Langston Hughes Lives!" *Negro Digest,* XVI (September, 1967), pp. 59–60.

Butcher, Margaret. *The Negro in American Culture.* New York: Alfred A. Knopf, 1956, pp. 132–133, 175–176.

Cuban, Larry. *The Negro in America.* Chicago: Scott, Foresman, 1964, pp. 109–110.

Current Biography. New York: H. W. Wilson, 1940, pp. 410–412.

Davis, Arthur. "The Tragic Mulatto Theme in Six Works of Langston Hughes," *Phylon,* XVI (Winter, 1955), pp. 195–204.

Dickinson, Donald. "Langston Hughes and the Brownie's Book," *Negro History Bulletin* XXXI (December, 1968), pp. 8–10.

Emanuel, James. *Langston Hughes.* New York: Twayne, 1967.

Embree, Edwin, "Langston Hughes: Shakespeare in Harlem," in *Thirteen Against the Odds.* New York: Viking, 1944, pp. 117–138.

Evans, Mari. "I remember Langston," *Negro Digest* XVI (September, 1967), p. 36.

Fields, Julia. "The Green of Langston's Ivy," *Negro Digest* XVI (September, 1967), pp. 58–59.

Gayle, Addison. "Langston Hughes, A Simple Commentary," *Negro Digest* XVI (September, 1967), pp. 53–57.

Filatova, Lydia. "Langston Hughes: American Writer," *International Literature,* No. 1 (1933), pp. 103–105.

Jahn, Janheinz. Die Neoafrikanische Literatur, Gesamtbibliographie. Dusseldorf: Diedericks Verlag, 1965, pp. 268–275.

Johnson, James W. *Black Manhattan.* New York: Alfred A. Knopf, 1930, pp. 131–132.

Kamp, Stella. "Langston Hughes Speaks to Young Writers," *Opportunity* XXIV (April, 1946), p. 73.

Kunitz, Stanley and Haycraft, Howard. *Twentieth Century Authors.* New York: H. W. Wilson, 1942, pp. 683–684.

———. *Twentieth Century Authors,* first supplement. New York: H. W. Wilson, 1955, p. 467.

"Lengston Khyuz," *Internatsionalnava Literatura.* No. 11 (1937), pp. 213–214.

Matheus, John. "Langston Hughes as Translator," *CLA Journal* XI (June, 1968), pp. 319–330.

Mayfield, Julian. "Langston," *Negro Digest* XVI (September, 1967), pp. 34–35.

Meltzer, Milton. *Langston Hughes.* New York: Crowell, 1968.

Meltzer, Milton. "Hughes, Twain, Child and Sanger: Four who Locked Horns with the Censors," *Wilson Library Bulletin* XLIV (November, 1969), pp. 278–280.

O'Daniel, Therman. "Lincoln's Man of Letters," *Lincoln University Bulletin,* Langston Hughes Issue, LXVII (July, 1964), pp. 9–12.

———. "A Langston Hughes Bibliography," *CLA Journal* VII (Spring, 1951), pp. 12–13.

———. "A Selected Classified Bibliography," *CLA Journal* XI (June, 1968), pp. 349–366.

Ovington, Mary White. *Portraits in Color.* New York: Viking, 1927, pp. 194–204.

Patterson, Lindsay. "Langston Hughes An Inspirer of Young Writers," *Freedomways,* VIII (Spring, 1968), pp. 179–181.

Patterson, Louise. "With Langston Hughes in the USSR," *Freedomways* VIII (Spring, 1968), pp. 152–158.

Piquion, Rene. *Langston Hughes, un Chant Nouveau.* Port-au-Prince, Haiti: Imprimerie de L'Etat, 1940.

Presley, James. "The American Dream of Langston Hughes," *Southwest Review* XLVIII (Autumn, 1963), pp. 380–386.

Rollins, Charlemae. *Black Troubadour: Langston Hughes.* Chicago: Rand McNally, 1970.

Staples, Elizabeth. "Langston Hughes, Malevolent Force," *American Mercury,* CXXXVIII (January, 1959), pp. 46–50.

Vsesoyuznaya Gosudarstvennaya Biblioteka Inostrannoi Literatury. *Lengston Khyuz Bibliograficheskii Ukazatel.* Moskva: Izdatelstvo "Kniga," 1964, 90p.

Wagner, Jean. "Langston Hughes," *Informations and Documents,* (January 15, 1961), pp. 30–35.

Wertz, I. J. "Langston Hughes: Profile," *Negro History Bulletin*, March, 1964, pp. 146–147.

POETRY

Brawley, Benjamin. *The Negro Genius*. New York: Dodd, Mead, 1937, pp. 246–251.

Carmen, Y. "Langston Hughes, Poet of the People," *International Literature*, 1939, No. 1, pp. 192–194.

Combecher, Hans "Zu einem Gedicht von Langston Hughes: Minstrel Man," *Die Neueren Sprachen* XV (1966) pp. 284–287.

Davis, Arthur. "The Harlem of Langston Hughes' Poetry," *Phylon*, XIII (Winter, 1952), pp. 276–283.

———. "Langston Hughes: Cool Poet," *CLA Journal* XI (June, 1968), pp. 280–296.

Hentoff, Nat. "Langston Hughes, He Found Poetry in the Blues," *Mayfair*, (August, 1958), pp. 26–27.

Holmes, Eugene. "Langston Hughes: Philosopher Poet," *Freedomways* VIII (Spring, 1968), pp. 144–151.

Hudson, Theodore. "Langston Hughes' Last Volume of Verse," *CLA Journal* XI (June, 1968), pp. 345–348.

Isaacs, Harold. "Five Writers and Their African Ancestors," *Phylon*, XXI (Fall, 1960), pp. 247–254.

Jacobs, Leland. "Langston Hughes," *Instructor*, March 1964, p. 28.

Kerlin, Robert. "A Pair of Youthful Poets," *Southern Workman*, (April, 1924), pp. 178–181.

Kramer, Aaron. "Robert Burns and Langston Hughes," *Freedomways* VIII (Spring, 1968), pp. 159–166.

Lundkvist, Arthur. *Atlantvind*. Stockholm: Bonniers Forlag, 1932, pp. 110–115.

MacLeod, Norman. "The Poetry and Argument of Langston Hughes," *Crisis*, XXXVIII (November, 1938), pp. 358–359.

Parker, John. "Tomorrow in the Writing of Langston Hughes," *College English*, X (May, 1949), pp. 438–441.

Quinot, Raymond. *Langston Hughes*. Bruxelles: Editions CELF, 1964. 82p.

Redding, Saunders. *To Make a Poet Black*. Chapel Hill: University of North Carolina Press, 1939, pp. 113–117.

Rollins, Charlemae. *Famous American Negro Poets*. New York: Dodd, Mead, 1965, pp. 69–74.

Schoell, F. L. "Un Poete Negre," *Revue Politique et Litteraire*, LXVII (July 20, 1929), pp. 436–438.

Wagner, Jean. "Langston Hughes," in *Les Poetes Negres des Etats-Unis.* Paris: Librairie Istra, 1963, pp. 423–533.

Reviews—Poetry

THE WEARY BLUES—Reviews

Cullen, Countee. *Opportunity*, February, 1926, pp. 73–74.

Fauset, Jessie. *The Crisis*, March 1926, p. 239.

Heyward, DuBose. *New York Herald Tribune Books*, August 1, 1926, p. 4.

Locke, Alain. *Palms*, No. 1, 1926, pp. 25–26.

New York Times, March 21, 1926, p. 6, 16.

Sargeant, E. S. *New Republic*, May 12, 1926, pp. 371–372.

FINE CLOTHES TO THE JEW—Reviews

The Crisis, March, 1927, p. 20.

Deutsch, Babette. *Bookman*, April, 1927, p. 221.

Fearing, Kenneth. *New Masses*, Sept. 1927, p. 29.

Gorman, Harry S. *New York Times*, March 27, 1927, p. 2.

Heyward, DuBose. *New York Herald Tribune Books*, February 20, 1927, p. 5.

Larkin, Margaret. *Opportunity*, March, 1927, pp. 84–85.

Locke, Alain. *Saturday Review of Literature*, April 9, 1927, p. 112.

Niles, Abbe. *New Republic*, June 8, 1927, p. 77.

Potamkin, Harry. *Nation*, April 13, 1927, p. 403.

DREAM KEEPER—Reviews

Benet, William Rose. *Saturday Review of Literature*, November 12, 1932, p. 241.

Eaton, A. T. *New York Times*, July 17, 1932, p. 13.

SHAKESPEARE IN HARLEM—Reviews

Colum, M. M. *New York Times*, March 22, 1942, p. 9.

Dodson, Owen. *Phylon*, Fall, 1942, pp. 337–338.

Hays, H. H. *Poetry*, July, 1942, pp. 223–224.

Kreymborg, Alfred. *Saturday Review of Literature*, April 25, 1942, p. 9.

Nation, August 8, 1942, p. 119.

Walton, E. L. *New Masses*, June 1942, p. 23.

FIELDS OF WONDER—Reviews

Bontemps, Arna. *Saturday Review of Literature*, March 22, 1947, p. 13.

Creekmore, Hubert. *New York Times*, May 4, 1947, p. 10.

Jackson, Wallace. *Phylon*, Summer, 1947, pp. 199–200.

Lechlitner, Ruth. *New York Herald Tribune Books*, August 31, 1947, p. 4.

ONE WAY TICKET—Reviews

Chandler, G. Lewis. *Phylon*, Summer, 1949, pp. 189–190.

Daiches, David. *New York Herald Tribune Books*, January 9, 1949, p. 4.

Humphries, Rolfe. *Nation*, January 15, 1949, p. 80.

Redding, Saunders. *Saturday Review of Literature*, January 22, 1949, p. 24.

Webster, H. C. *Poetry*, February, 1950, pp. 300–302.

MONTAGE ON A DREAM DEFERRED—Reviews

Deutsch, Babette. *New York Times*, May 6, 1951, p. 23.

Humphries, Rolfe. *Nation*, March 17, 1951, p. 256.

Parker, John. *Phylon*, Summer, 1951, pp. 195–197.

Redding, Saunders. *New York Herald Tribune Books*, March 11, 1951, p. 5.

SELECTED POEMS OF LANGSTON HUGHES—Reviews

Baldwin, James. *New York Times*, March 29, 1959, p. 6.

Cardona-Hine, A. *Mainstream*, July 1959, pp. 55–56.

Parker, John. *Phylon*, Summer, 1959, pp. 196–197.

Winslow, H. F. *Crisis*, Oct. 1959, pp. 512–513.

ASK YOUR MAMA—Reviews

Blesh, Rudi. *New York Herald Tribune Books*, November 26, 1961, p. 4.

Fitts, Dudley. *New York Times Book Review*, October 29, 1961, p. 16.

PANTHER AND THE LASH—Reviews

Katz, Bill. *Library Journal*, June 1, 1967, p. 2163.

Kinnamon, Kenneth. *Nation*, December 4, 1967, p. 599.

Liberman, Lawrence. *Poetry*, August 1968, p. 339.

Whitman, A. *New York Times*, June 1, 1968, p. 25.

DON'T TURN YOUR BACK

Sutherland, Z. *Saturday Review*, May 9, 1970, p. 47.

PROSE AND DRAMA

Barton, Rebecca, *Witnesses for Freedom*. New York: Harper, 1948, pp. 206–220.

Bone, Robert. *The Negro Novel in America*. New Haven: Yale University Press, 1958, pp. 75–77.

Carey, Julian. "Jesse B. Semple Revisited and Revised," *Phylon* XXXI (Summer, 1971), pp. 158–163.

Clarke, John. "Langston Hughes and Jesse B. Semple," *Freedomways* VIII (Spring, 1968), pp. 167–169.

Emanuel, James. "Langston Hughes's First Short Story: Mary Winosky," *Phylon*, XXII (Fall, 1961), pp. 267–272.

———. The Short Stories of Langston Hughes. Unpublished Ph.D. dissertation, Columbia University, 1962.

———. "Bodies in the Moonlight," *Readers and Writers* I (November/ January, 1968), pp. 38–39, 42.

———. "The Short Fiction of Langston Hughes," *Freedomways* VIII (Spring, 1968), pp. 170–178.

Davis, Arthur. "Jesse B. Semple: Negro American." *Phylon*, XV (Spring, 1954), pp. 21–28.

Gloster, Hugh. *Negro Voices in American Fiction.* Chapel Hill: University of North Carolina Press, 1948, pp. 184–187, 219–222.

Jackson, Blyden. "A Word About Simple," *CLA Journal*, XI (June, 1968), pp. 310–318.

———. "The Negro's Image of the Universe as Reflected in His Fiction," *CLA Journal* IV (September, 1960), pp. 22–31.

Jones, Harry. "A Danish Tribute to Langston Hughes," *CLA Journal* XI (June, 1968), pp. 331–334.

King, Woodie. "Remembering Langston Hughes, a Poet of the Black Theatre," *Negro Digest* XVIII, pp. 27–32, 95–96.

Nichols, Lewis. "Langston Hughes Describes the Genesis of his 'Tambourines to Glory,'" *New York Times*, October 27, 1963, sect. 2. p. 3.

Rogge, Heinz von. "Die Figur des Simple im Werke von Langston Hughes," *Die Neuren Sprachen*, Heft 12, 1955, pp. 555–566.

Spencer, T. J. and Rivers, Clarence. "Langston Hughes: His Style and Optimism," *Drama Critique*, VII (Spring, 1964), pp. 99–102.

Turner, Darwin. "Langston Hughes as a Playwright," *CLA Journal* XI (June, 1968), pp. 297–309.

Turpin, Waters. "Four Short Fiction Writers of the Harlem Renaissance," *CLA Journal* XI (September, 1967), pp. 59–72.

Reviews—Prose and Drama

NOT WITHOUT LAUGHTER—Reviews

Brown, Sterling. *Opportunity*, September, 1930, pp. 279–280.

Carmon, W. *New Masses*, October, 1930, pp. 17–18.

Chamberlain, John. *Bookman*, February, 1930, p. 611.

Calverton, V. F. *Nation*, August 6, 1930, p. 157.

The Crisis, September, 1930, p. 321.

Ross, Mary. *New York Herald Tribune Books*, July 27, 1930, p. 5.

Saturday Review of Literature, August 23, 1930, p. 69.

THE WAYS OF WHITE FOLKS—Reviews

Anderson, Sherwood. *Nation*, July 11, 1934, p. 49.
Brickell, Herschel. *North American*, September, 1934, p. 286.
Gannett, Lewis. *New York Herald Tribune Books*, June 27, 1934, p. 15.
Gruening, Martha. *New Republic*, September 5, 1934, p. 108.
Holmes, E. C. *Opportunity*, September, 1934, pp. 283–284.
Locke, Alain. *Survey Graphic*, November, 1934, p. 565.
Loggins, Vernon. *Saturday Review of Literature*, July 14, 1934, p. 805.
Streator, George. *Crisis*, July, 1934, p. 216.

THE BIG SEA—Reviews

Embree, Edwin. *Survey Graphic*, February, 1941, p. 96.
Herod, Henrietta. *Phylon*, Spring, 1941, pp. 94–96.
Lewis, Theophilus. *The Crisis*, December, 1940, pp. 393–394.
Rugoff, Milton. *New York Herald Tribune Books*, August 25, 1940, p. 5.
Villard, Oswald. *Saturday Review of Literature*, August 31, 1940, p. 12.
Woods, Katherine. *New York Times*, August 25, 1940, p. 5.
Wright, Richard. *New Republic*, October 28, 1940, pp. 600–601.

SIMPLE SPEAKS HIS MIND—Reviews

Chandler, G. Lewis. *Phylon*, Spring, 1951, pp. 94–95.
Pfaff, William. *Commonweal*, May 26, 1950, p. 181.
Redding, Saunders. *New York Herald Tribune*, June 11, 1950, p. 13.
Smith, William. *New Republic*, September 4, 1950, p. 20.
Smythe, Hugh. *The Crisis*, June, 1950, pp. 377–378.
Van Vechten, Carl. *New York Times*, May 7, 1950, p. 10.

FIRST BOOK OF NEGROES—Reviews

Bechtel, L. S. *New York Herald Tribune*, November 16, 1952, p. 32.
Brooks, Hallie. *Phylon*, Fall, 1953, pp. 343–344.

LAUGHING TO KEEP FROM CRYING—Reviews

Bontemps, Arna. *Saturday Review*, April 5, 1952, p. 17.
Cooperman, Stanley. *New Republic*, May 5, 1952, p. 21.
Hedden, William T. *New York Herald Tribune*, March 30, 1952, p. 6.
Meier, August. *The Crisis*, June, 1952, pp. 398–399.
Moon, Bucklin. *New York Times*, March 23, 1952, p. 4.
Parker, John. *Phylon*, Fall, 1952, pp. 257–258.

SIMPLE TAKES A WIFE—Reviews

Berry, A. *Masses and Mainstream*, September, 1953, pp. 55–58.
Bontemps, Arna. *New York Herald Tribune*, June 14, 1953, p. 12.
Van Vechten, Carl. *New York Times*, May 31, 1953, p. 5.

FAMOUS AMERICAN NEGROES—Reviews

New York Times, May 2, 1954, p. 26.
Smythe, Mabel. *The Crisis*, January, 1955, p. 58.

FIRST BOOK OF JAZZ—Reviews

Ball, John. *Midwest Journal*, Summer, 1955, pp. 195–196.
Bechtel, L. S. *New York Herald Tribune*, February 27, 1955, p. 10.
Horn Book, June, 1955, p. 195.
Parker, John. *Phylon*, Fall, 1955, pp. 318–319.
Saturday Review, May 14, 1955, pp. 55–56.

THE SWEET FLYPAPER OF LIFE—Reviews

Field, Rose. *New York Herald Tribune*, December 18, 1955, p. 3.
Hatch, Robert. *Nation*, December 17, 1955, p. 538.
Milstein, Gilbert. *New York Times*, November 27, 1955, p. 5.
Parker, John. *Christian Century*, August 1, 1956, p. 905.

PICTORIAL HISTORY OF THE NEGRO IN AMERICA—Reviews

Aptheker, H. *Mainstream*, February, 1957, pp. 62–63.
Ivy, James. *The Crisis*, February, 1957, p. 123.
Redding, Saunders. *New York Herald Tribune*, November 18, 1956, p. 7.

I WONDER AS I WANDER—Reviews

Ford, Nick Aaron. *Phylon*, Spring, 1957, pp. 88–89.
Jackson, Luther. *The Crisis*, February, 1957, pp. 119–120.
Ottley, Roi. *Saturday Review*, November 17, 1956, p. 35.
Redding, Saunders. *New York Herald Tribune*, December 23, 1956, p. 6.

SIMPLE STAKES A CLAIM—Reviews

Bondsky, P. *Mainstream*, January, 1958, pp. 53–55.
Jackson, Luther. *The Crisis*, November, 1957, pp. 576–577.
Milstein, Gilbert. *New York Times*, September 29, 1957, p. 41.
Parker, John. *Phylon*, Winter, 1957, pp. 435–436.

TAMBOURINES TO GLORY—Reviews

Bontemps, Arna. *New York Herald Tribune*, December 7, 1958, p. 4.
Gehman, Richard. *Saturday Review*, November 22, 1958, pp. 19–20.
Ivy, James. *The Crisis*, January, 1959, p. 59.
Milstein, Gilbert. *New York Times*, November 23, 1958, p. 51.

Parker, John. *Phylon*, Spring, 1959, pp. 100–101.
Waterhouse, Keith. *New Statesman*, September, 1959, p. 366.

FIGHT FOR FREEDOM—Reviews
Dilliard, Irving. *Saturday Review*, September 29, 1962, pp. 32–33.
Kihss, Peter. *New York Times Book Review*, September 2, 1962, p. 12.

SIMPLE'S UNCLE SAM—Reviews
Campbell, Francis. *Library Journal*, November 1, 1965, p. 4806.
Poore, Charles. *New York Times*, November 11, 1965, p. 45.

BLACK MISERY
Adams, Phoebe. *Atlantic*, August 1969, p. 103.
Graves, E. *Commonweal*, November 21, 1969, p. 259.
Sutherland, Z. *Saturday Review*, August 16, 1969, p. 27.

References

BOOKS

Aaron, Daniel. *Writers on the Left.* New York: Harcourt, Brace, 1961.

American Negro Writer and His Roots. Selected Papers from the First Conference of Negro Writers. New York: American Society of African Culture, 1960.

Angoff, Allen. *American Writing Today.* New York: New York University Press, 1957.

Baldwin, James. *Another Country.* New York: Dial Press, 1960.

————. *The Fire Next Time.* New York: Dial Press, 1963.

Bardolph, Richard. *The Negro Vanguard.* New York: Random House, 1961.

Bone, Robert A. *The Negro Novel in America.* New Haven: Yale University Press, 1958.

Bontemps, Arna. (ed.) *American Negro Poetry.* New York: Hill and Wang, 1963.

The Borzoi, A sort of a record of 10 years of publishing. New York: Alfred A. Knopf, 1925.

Brawley, Benjamin. *The Negro Genius.* New York: Dodd, Mead, 1937.

Brown, Deming. *Soviet Attitudes Toward American Writing.* Princeton: Princeton University Press, 1962.

Brown, Glenora and Brown, Deming. *A Guide to Soviet Russian Translations of American Literature.* New York: King's Crown Press Columbia University, 1954.

Brown, Sterling. (ed.) *The Negro Caravan.* New York: Dryden Press, 1941.

Butcher, Margaret. *The Negro in American Culture.* New York: Alfred A. Knopf, 1956.

Canby, Henry S. *Walt Whitman.* Boston: Houghton, 1943.

Calverton, V. F. (ed.) *Anthology of American Negro Literature.* New York: Modern Library, 1929.

Cargill, Oscar. *Intellectual America.* New York: Macmillan, 1941.

Cullen, Countee. *Caroling Dusk.* New York: Harper, 1927.

Embree, Edwin. *13 Against the Odds.* New York: Viking, 1944.

Franklin, John Hope. *From Slavery to Freedom.* 2nd ed. New York: Alfred A. Knopf, 1956.

Frazer, E. Franklin. *Black Bourgeoisie.* Glencoe, Illinois: Free Press, 1957.

Gable, Mary. (ed.) *Many Colored Fleece.* New York: Sheed and Ward, 1950.

Gloster, Hugh. *Negro Voices in American Fiction.* Chapel Hill: University of North Carolina Press, 1948.

Gregory, Horace and Zaturenska, Marya. *A History of American Poetry. 1900–1940.* New York: Harcourt, 1942.

Hicks, Granville. (ed.) *Proletarian Literature in the United States.* New York: International Publishers, 1935.

Hill, Herbert. (ed.) *Soon One Morning.* New York: Alfred A. Knopf, 1963.

Hoffman, Frederick. *The Twenties.* new, revised ed. New York: Collier Books, 1962.

Hoffman, Frederick, *et al. The Little Magazine.* 2nd ed. Princeton: Princeton University Press, 1947.

Hughes, Langston. *The Big Sea.* New York: Alfred A. Knopf, 1940.

――――. *Fight for Freedom.* New York: Norton, 1962.

――――. *I Wonder as I Wander.* New York: Rinehart, 1956.

Johnson, James W. (ed.) *The Book of American Negro Poetry.* 2nd ed., New York: Harcourt, Brace, 1931.

――――. *Along This Way.* New York: Viking, 1933.

Kerlin, Robert. *Negro Poets and Their Poems.* Washington: Associated Press, 1923.

Kreymborg, Alfred. *Our Singing Strength.* New York: Coward-McCann, 1929.

Lewisohn, Ludwig. *Expression in America.* New York: Harper, 1932.

Locke, Alain. "Negro Poets of the United States," in *Anthology of Magazine Verse for 1926.* Boston: Brimmer, 1926.

――――. (ed.) *The New Negro.* New York: Boni, 1925.

――――. "The Poetry of Negro Life," introduction to *Four Negro Poets.* New York: Simon and Schuster, 1927.

Logan, Rayford. *The Negro in the United States.* Princeton: Van Nostrand, 1957.

――――. (ed.) *What the Negro Wants.* Chapel Hill: University of North Carolina Press, 1944.

Loggins, Vernon. *Negro Author and his Development in America.* New York: Columbia University Press, 1931.

Lueders, Edward. *Carl Van Vechten.* New York: Twayne, 1964.

Lueders, Edward. *Carl Van Vechten and the Twenties.* Albuquerque: University of New Mexico Press, 1955.

Monroe, Harriet and Henderson, Alice. (eds.) *The New Poetry*. 2nd ed., New York: Macmillan, 1923.

Myrdal, Gunnar., *et al. An American Dilemma*. New York: Harper, 1944.

Negro Yearbook, 1931–32, 1937–38, 1947. Tuskegee: Tuskegee Institute, 1932, 1938, 1947.

The New Negro Thirty Years Afterward, papers contributed to the sixteenth annual spring conference of the Division of Social Sciences. ed. by Rayford Logan. Washington: Howard University Press, 1955.

Quinot, Raymond. *Langston Hughes*. Bruxelles: Editions CELF, 1964.

Record, Wilson. *The Negro and the Communist Party*. Chapel Hill: University of North Carolina Press, 1951.

Redding, Saunders. *Lonesome Road*. New York: Doubleday, 1958.

———. *To Make a Poet Black*. Chapel Hill: University of North Carolina Press, 1939.

Rose, Arnold. *The Negro's Moral*. Minneapolis: University of Minnesota Press, 1949.

Smalley, Webster. (ed.) *Five Plays by Langston Hughes*. Bloomington: Indiana University Press, 1963.

Spiller, Robert. (ed.) *A Time of Harvest*. New York: Hill and Wang, 1962.

———. *et al.*, eds. *Literary History of the United States*, revised ed. New York: Macmillan, 1953.

Untermeyer, Louis. (ed.) *Modern American Poetry, Modern British Poetry*. New York: Harcourt, Brace, 1936.

Wagner, Jean. *Les Poetes Negres des Etats-Unis*. Paris: Librairie Istra, 1963.

White, N. I. and Jackson, W. C. (eds.) *An Anthology of Verse by American Negroes*. Chapel Hill: University of North Carolina Press, 1924.

White, Walter. "Negro Literature," in *American Writers on American Literature*, ed. John Macy. New York: Liveright, 1931.

Whitman, Walt. *Representative Selections*, ed. Floyd Stovall. New York: American Book Company, 1934.

Wright, Righard. "The Literature of the Negro in the United States," in *White Man Listen*. New York: Doubleday, 1957.

PERIODICALS

Baldwin, James. "Everybody's Protest Novel," *Partisan Review*, XVI (June, 1949), 578–585.

Bland, Edward. "Racial Bias and Negro Poetry," *Poetry*, LXIII (March, 1944), 328–333.

Bontemps, Arna. "The Harlem Renaissance," *Saturday Review of Literature*, XXX (March 22, 1947), 12–13.

Brown, Sterling. "The Blues," *Phylon*, XIII (Fall, 1952), 286–292.

———. "The Negro Author and his Publisher," *The Quarterly Review Of Higher Education Among Negroes*, IX (July, 1941), 140–146.

The Brownie's Book. (New York: National Association for the Advancement of Colored People), 1920–1921.

Chamberlain, John. "The Negro as a Writer," *Bookman*, LXX (February, 1930), 603–611.

Cowley, Malcolm. "They All Waited for Lefty," *Saturday Review*, XLVIII (June 6, 1964), 17–19.

The Crisis. (New York: National Association for the Advancement of Colored People), 1910-date.

Cullen, Countee. "The Negro Sings his Soul," *Survey Graphic*, VII (September, 1925), 583–584.

Davis, Allison. "Our Negro Intellectuals," *The Crisis*, XXXV (August, 1928), 268–269, 284–286.

Davis, Arthur. "The Harlem of Langston Hughes' Poetry," *Phylon*, XIII (Winter, 1952), 276–283.

———. "Jessie B. Semple: Negro American," *Phylon*, XV (Spring, 1954), 21–28.

———. "The Tragic Mulatto Theme in Six Works of Langston Hughes," *Phylon*, XVI (Winter, 1955), 195–204.

DuBois, W. E. B. "The Crisis," *The Crisis*, I (November, 1910), 10–11.

———. "The Crisis and the NAACP," *The Crisis*, XI (November, 1915), 26.

———. "The Future," *The Crisis*, XI (November, 1915), 28.

———. "Returning Soldiers," *The Crisis*, XVII (May, 1919), 14.

———. "The Younger Literary Movement," *The Crisis*, XXVII (February, 1924), 161–163.

Echeruo, M. J. C. "American Negro Poetry," *Phylon*, XXV (Spring, 1963), 62–68.

Ellison, Ralph. "Harlem is Nowhere," *Harpers*, CCXXIV (August, 1964), 53–57.

Gibson, Richard. "A No to Nothing," *Kenyon Review*, XIII (Spring, 1951), 252–255.

Glicksberg, Charles. "Negro Poets and the American Tradition," *Antioch Review*, VI (Winter, 1946), 243–253.

Hughes, Langston. "The Negro Artist and the Racial Mountain," *Nation*, CXXII (June 23, 1926), 692–694.

———. "Harlem Literati of the Twenties," *Saturday Review of Literature*, XXII (June 22, 1940), 13–14.

————. "Problems of the Negro Writer," *Saturday Review*, XLIV (April 20, 1963), 19–20.

————. "My Adventures as a Social Poet," *Phylon*, VIII (Fall, 1947), 205–212.

————. "Some Practical Observations: A Colloquy," *Phylon*, XI (Winter, 1950), 307–311.

Isaacs, Harold. "Five Modern Writers and Their African Ancestors," *Phylon*, XXI (Fall, 1960), 243–265.

Johnson, Charles S. "The Negro Enters Literature," *Carolina Magazine*, (May, 1927), 44–48.

————. "Jazz, Poetry and Blues," *Carolina Magazine*, (May, 1928), 16–20.

————. "The Rise of the Negro Magazine," *Journal of Negro History*, XIII (January, 1928), 7–21.

Johnson, James W. "The Dilemma of the Negro Author," *American Mercury*, XV (December, 1928), 477–481.

————. "The Making of Harlem," *Survey Graphic*, VII (March, 1925), 635–639.

————. "Race Prejudice and the Negro Artist," *Harpers*, CLVII (November, 1928), 769–776.

Kerlin, Robert. "A Pair of Youthful Poets," *Southern Workman*, (April, 1924), 178–181.

Knopf, Alfred A. "Reminiscences of Hergesheimer, Van Vechten and Mencken," *Yale University Library Gazette*, XXIV (April, 1950), 150–157.

Locke, Alain. "Enter the New Negro," *Survey Graphic*, VI (March, 1925), 631–634.

————. "The Negro's Contribution to American Art and Literature," *Annals of the American Academy of Political and Social Science*, CXL (November, 1928), 234–247.

————, "Youth Speaks," *Survey Graphic*, VI (March, 1925), 659–660.

MacLeod, Norman. "The Poetry and Argument of Langston Hughes," *The Crisis*, XXXVIII (November, 1938), 358–359.

Opportunity. (New York: National Urban League), 1923–1949.

Parker, John. "Tomorrow in the Writing of Langston Hughes," *College English*, X (May, 1949), 438–441.

Redding, Saunders. "The Negro Author: His Publisher, His Public and His Purse," *Publisher's Weekly*, CXLVII (March 24, 1945), 1284–1288.

————. "American Negro Literature," *American Scholar*, XVIII (April, 1949), 137–148.

Reedy, Sidney. "The Negro Magazine: A Critical Study of its Educational Significance," *Journal of Negro Education* (October, 1934), 598–604.

Rexroth, Kenneth. "Jazz Poetry," *Nation*, CLXXXVI (March 29, 1958), 282–283.

Rogge, Heinz von. "Die Figur des Simple im Werke von Langston Hughes," *Die Neueren Sprachen*, Heft 12, 1955, 555–566.

Schuyler, George. "The Van Vechten Revolution," *Phylon*, XI (Winter, 1950), 362–368.

Spingarn, Amy. "Amy Spingarn Prizes," *The Crisis*, XXX (September, 1924), 199.

Taussig, Charlotte. "The New Negro as Revealed in His Poetry," *Opportunity*, V (April, 1927), 108–111.

Thurman, Wallace. "Negro Poets and Their Poetry," *Bookman*, LXVII (July, 1928), 555–561.

Van Doren, Carl. "Negro Renaissance," *Century*, CXI (March, 1926), 635–637.

Wright, Richard. "Blueprint for Negro Writing," *The New Challenge*, I (Fall, 1937), 53–65.

UNPUBLISHED MATERIAL

Britt, D. D. "The Image of the White Man in the Fiction of Langston Hughes, Richard Wright, James Baldwin and Ralph Ellison," Unpublished PhD dissertation, Emory University, 1968.

Brooks, Hallie. "A Description of Negro Newsstand Magazines and an Analysis of the Contents of a Selected Number of Negro Magazines." Unpublished Master's thesis, Department of Library Science, University of Chicago, 1946.

Emanuel, James A. "The Short Stories of Langston Hughes." Unpublished Ph.D. dissertation, Department of English, Columbia University, 1962.

LETTERS

Hughes, Langston. A collection of 110 letters exchanged between Langston Hughes and members of the Alfred A. Knopf Company from 1925–1958. Yale University Library.

———. A collection of 170 letters exchanged between Langston Hughes and his agent, Maxim Lieber, from 1937–1955. Yale University Library.

————. A collection of 50 letters and postcards from Langston Hughes to Donald Dickinson, 1956–1965. In possession of Donald Dickinson.

Bontemps, Arna. Letter to Donald Dickinson dated April 4, 1963.

Bynner, Witter. Letter to Donald Dickinson dated March 29, 1963.

Van Vechten, Carl. Letter to Donald Dickinson dated July 3, 1961.

Index

(All entries preceded by *bib* refer to the page in Part II, *Bibliography* on which the main entry for that title will be found.)